THE SPECTACULAR FEW

ALTERNATIVE CRIMINOLOGY SERIES

General Editor: Jeff Ferrell

*Pissing on Demand: Workplace Drug
Testing and the Rise of the Detox Industry*
Ken Tunnell

*Empire of Scrounge: Inside the Urban
Underground of Dumpster Diving,
Trash Picking, and Street Scavenging*
Jeff Ferrell

*Prison, Inc.: A Convict Exposes
Life inside a Private Prison*
K. C. Carceral, edited by Thomas J. Bernard

*The Terrorist Identity: Explaining
the Terrorist Threat*
Michael P. Arena and Bruce A. Arrigo

*Terrorism as Crime: From Oklahoma
City to Al-Qaeda and Beyond*
Mark S. Hamm

*Our Bodies, Our Crimes: The Policing
of Women's Reproduction in America*
Jeanne Flavin

*Graffiti Lives: Beyond the Tag in
New York's Urban Underground*
Gregory J. Snyder

*Crimes of Dissent: Civil
Disobedience, Criminal Justice,
and the Politics of Conscience*
Jarret S. Lovell

*The Culture of Punishment:
Prison, Society, and Spectacle*
Michelle Brown

*Who You Claim: Performing Gang
Identity in School and on the Streets*
Robert Garot

*5 Grams: Crack Cocaine, Rap
Music, and the War on Drugs*
Dimitri A. Bogazianos

*Judging Addicts: Drug Courts and
Coercion in the Justice System*
Rebecca Tiger

*Courting Kids: Inside an
Experimental Youth Court*
Carla J. Barrett

*The Spectacular Few: Prisoner Radicalization
and the Evolving Terrorist Threat*
Mark S. Hamm

The Spectacular Few

*Prisoner Radicalization and the
Evolving Terrorist Threat*

Mark S. Hamm

NEW YORK UNIVERSITY PRESS
New York and London

NEW YORK UNIVERSITY PRESS
New York and London
www.nyupress.org

References to Internet websites (URLs) were accurate at the time of writing. Neither the author nor New York University Press is responsible for URLs that may have expired or changed since the manuscript was prepared.

LIBRARY OF CONGRESS CATALOGING-IN-PUBLICATION DATA
Hamm, Mark S.
The spectacular few : prisoner radicalization and the evolving terrorist threat / Mark S. Hamm.
p. cm.
Includes bibliographical references and index.
ISBN 978-0-8147-2544-3 (cl : alk. paper) — ISBN 978-0-8147-2396-8 (pb : alk. paper) —
ISBN 978-0-8147-2407-1 (e-book) — ISBN 978-0-8147-4437-6 (e-book)
1. Terrorists—Recruiting—United States. 2. Muslim prisoners—United States. 3.
Prisoners—United States. 4. Radicalism—Religious aspects—Islam. 5. Terrorism—
Religious aspects—Islam. 6. Terrorism—United States. I. Title.
HV6432.H3654 2013
363.325'110973—dc23   2012038066

New York University Press books are printed on acid-free paper, and their binding materials are chosen for strength and durability. We strive to use environmentally responsible suppliers and materials to the greatest extent possible in publishing our books.

Manufactured in the United States of America
c 10 9 8 7 6 5 4 3 2 1

p 10 9 8 7 6 5 4 3 2 1

In memory of John Irwin, penologist extraordinaire

CONTENTS

As I began this book, the United States confronted its most important terrorist threat since 9/11—the attempted suicide bombing of a U.S. jetliner bound
for Detroit on Christmas Day, 2009. "This was a serious reminder of the dangers that we face and the nature of those who threaten our homeland," said
President Barack Obama in his first comments on the attempt to kill three
hundred passengers aboard the Northwest Airlines flight from Amsterdam.
"This was not a failure to collect intelligence," explained the president after
conferring with his top counterterrorism officials. "It was a failure to integrate and understand the intelligence we already had."[1]

The intelligence lapses that had allowed twenty-three-year-old Umar
Farouk Abdulmutallab to board the Amsterdam-to-Detroit flight, carrying undetected explosives and a syringe in his underwear, included a CIA
report indicating that the wealthy young Nigerian had recently met with
al-Qaeda-affiliated rebels in Yemen known to be planning an attack on the
United States.[2] Following his arrest, Abdulmutallab told FBI agents that he
was trained in Yemen by members of Al-Qaeda in the Arabian Peninsula
(AQAP) who had equipped him with the explosive device and showed him
how to conceal it. AQAP instantly released a statement claiming responsibility for the operation, calling Abdulmutallab a "hero" and a "martyr" who
had successfully outwitted American intelligence.[3] Within the body of intelligence that U.S. analysts failed to "integrate and understand" was the uncom-
fortable fact that AQAP's commander—a thirty-six-year-old Saudi named
Said Ali al-Shihri—was a former detainee at the U.S. military garrison in
Guantanamo Bay, Cuba. Intelligence also included a statement from Shihri's
family who attributed his extremism to the five years he had spent in detention at Guantanamo.[4] In effect, the Christmas Day plot was orchestrated by a
former inmate radicalized in a U.S.-operated prison.

Apart from these intelligence lapses, the Christmas Day plot should have
come as no surprise to U.S. intelligence. Five months earlier, in July 2009,
following the discovery of several highly publicized terrorist plots originat-
ing from U.S. prisons, Attorney General Eric Holder told reporters, "The
American people would be surprised at the depth of the [terrorist] threat,"

adding that "the whole notion of radicalization is something that didn't loom as large a few months ago . . . as it does now. And that's the shifting nature of threats that keep you up at night."⁵ This threat had been worrying intelligence officials for years.

Responding to what the FBI termed a "fully operational" terrorist plot to attack U.S. army recruiting centers, Israeli government facilities, and Jewish synagogues in Los Angeles on the symbolic date of September 11, 2005—instigated by a fringe group of Sunni Muslims at California's New Folsom Prison called Jam'iyyat Ul-Islam Is-Saheeh (The Assembly of Authentic Islam, or JIS)—FBI Director Robert Mueller warned that "prisons are . . . fertile ground for extremists. Inmates may be drawn to an extreme form of Islam because it may help justify their violent tendencies."⁶ The JIS plot, too, should not have come as a complete surprise to the FBI. After all, it is well known that Folsom Prison has a long and storied radical history—one that inspired California's "convict revolutionaries" of the 1960s.⁷

In 2007, the Department of Homeland Security responded to the JIS threat by forming a special unit to combat the danger posed by extremists in American prisons.⁸ Congress then deliberated (but did not pass for bipartisan reasons) the Violent Radicalization and Homegrown Terrorism Prevention Act, calling for the formation of a national commission to study the mitigation of "violent radicalization" and "ideologically based violence in prison." Testifying in support of the act was Charles Allen, Chief Intelligence Officer for DHS and a legendary figure in the counterterrorism community. As a CIA warnings officer in 1990, Allen predicted Saddam Hussein's invasion of Kuwait; at DHS in 2007, Allen warned of the recruitment potential of jihadist websites; in 2008 he issued the first warning on the American-born Muslim cleric Anwar al-Awlaki (1971–2011), who would go on to incite a U.S. Army psychiatrist, Major Nidal Hasan, to kill thirteen soldiers at Fort Hood, Texas, in November 2009 (a month before the Christmas Day plot). Now Allen advised Congress that radicalization in U.S. prisons was becoming increasingly common due to an interrelated set of factors: namely, the nature of prison environments, coupled with the social marginalization of inmates, cultivates a strong desire for bonding, group identity, and spiritual guidance. Allen warned Congress that these factors may be exploited by prisoners in pursuit of terrorist goals.⁹

Shortly after the Christmas Day plot, the U.S. Senate Foreign Relations Committee released a report indicating that the underwear bomber represented the vanguard of an evolving terrorist threat. According to the report, thirty-six Americans who had converted to Islam while incarcerated in the United States had recently traveled to Yemen, ostensibly to study Arabic, and had "dropped off the radar." Some of them, it is believed, had joined AQAP. The report advised that these Americans may pose a special danger because they can travel abroad on U.S. passports, return home with "clean skin," and operate undetected inside American cities and towns. The report said that these radicalized ex-prisoners from America may have joined forces with a group consisting of some two dozen al-Qaeda fighters who had escaped from a Yemen prison in 2000, and some thirty of Saudi Arabia's most-wanted terrorism suspects, eleven of whom are former Guantanamo detainees. The threat of al-Qaeda and its nearby Somali affiliate, al-Shabaab (Arabic for "the youth"), is also increasing. Most worrisome is that al-Shabaab has recruited a number of Somali Americans from Minneapolis, Minnesota, who may be planning suicide attacks inside the United States. The report concluded that "the Christmas Day plot was a nearly catastrophic illustration of a significant new threat from a network previously regarded as a regional danger, rather than an international one."[10]

Weeks later, Saudi Arabian security forces arrested more than a hundred militants as they were planning attacks against the country's vast southern oil fields. All of them were affiliated with AQAP.[11] The intelligence warning on former Guantanamo detainees continued into the next year. According to a 2010 report by the Director of U.S. National Intelligence, 25 percent of released Guantanamo detainees are suspected of terrorist or insurgent activity after their discharge. Because their time at Guantanamo is seen as a badge of honor in the international jihadist community, detainees who leave the camp are treated like "rock stars" and are often elevated to leadership roles in al-Qaeda.[12] Much the same can be said of their protégés.

On January 24, 2010, no less a figure than Osama bin Laden emerged from hiding to proclaim: "The message delivered to you through the plane of the heroic warrior Umar Farouk Abdulmutallab was a confirmation of the previous messages sent by the heroes of September 11."[13] Although the Nigerian's bombing attempt was a tactical failure, for bin Laden it was a strategic victory inasmuch as it created widespread fear in the West and proved that al-Qaeda was not on the ropes as many thought. In a March audio message to jihadist Internet forums, Anwar al-Awlaki applauded Abdulmutallab's attempted bombing as a "defensive" action against U.S. aggression against Muslims, citing the abuse of detainees at Guantanamo as its primary catalyst.[14] In October, AQAP attempted to blow up another U.S.-bound jetliner, this time concealing explosives inside a computer printer. Once again, the plot was linked to a former Guantanamo detainee.[15] And the beat went on. Several months later, an intelligence source told me that the underwear bomber had emerged as a prayer leader among Muslim prisoners on his cellblock at the Federal

Penitentiary in Milan, Michigan. In October 2011 Abdulmutallab pleaded guilty to terrorism charges and in February 2012 he was brought before a federal court in Detroit for sentencing. Before he was given four consecutive life sentences, Abdulmutallab shouted "Allahu Akbar" (God is Great), adding that Muslims were "proud to kill in the name of God, and that is what God told us to do in the Koran."[16]

* * *

The killing of Osama bin Laden by U.S. forces during a May 2011 raid in Pakistan represents a turning point for the United States in its struggle to defeat al-Qaeda. Yet as President Obama clearly acknowledged in his subsequent *National Strategy for Counterterrorism*, America still faces an important threat from "al-Qaeda's affiliates, and its adherents."[17] The prisoner radicalization problem is intricately tied to this attempt by al-Qaeda associates to inspire individuals within the United States to conduct attacks on their own, without direct assistance from al-Qaeda Central. And not just in the United States. Great Britain, France, Spain, and Israel all have reasons for concern.

As this book will show, Islam is now sweeping across Western prisons, bringing with it both unprecedented security challenges and exceptional possibilities for progressive reform. It is no accident that the prisoner radicalization movement is taking place against the backdrop of a widespread economic meltdown. Protests, strikes, and civil unrest often rise during periods of economic turmoil as affected groups take to the streets *and* to the prison yards.[18] In 2010, a year before the Occupy movement began, a flood of reports appeared on riots and disturbances in severely overcrowded and mismanaged state prisons across America. That August, guards at Folsom Prison tried to break up a major riot and opened fire on two hundred inmates, sending five convicts to the hospital with gunshot wounds.[19] As the Golden State teetered on the brink of economic ruin, commentators began referring to California as a "failed state," a term characteristically reserved for places like Yemen, Afghanistan, and Somalia—places that generate Islamic terrorists by the thousands. The empirical basis for this book is a two-year study I conducted for the U.S. Department of Justice, focusing on trends in prisoner radicalization in U.S. correctional institutions, including both Folsom Prison and New Folsom Prison, where I interviewed a number of prisoners who had undergone conversions to Islam during their incarceration, including members of JIS. In no uncertain terms, the research shows that these are failed prisons. And within that failure is the greater story of how America is creating terrorists within its own borders.

The financial crisis and prisoner radicalization are attributable to what criminologists call *crimes of omission,* wherein the omission of policies addressing criminality—represented here by the failures of financial regulators and prison officials to do their jobs—is at the root of "the injury, the suffering and the victimization of many."[20] There is a deeply human corollary at work in these crimes. In both cases, the criminals tend to surprise you. For years, tens of thousands of trusting investors believed that the Wall Street tycoon Bernard Madoff could defy the markets. Year after year financial statements revealed that Madoff's investors were making money. Few wondered if it was somehow possible that all their wealth and status would vanish in a puff of smoke on a single day.[21] But it did. In one fell swoop, everything was gone. Year after year passes without a terrorist attack against America. We are lulled into a sense of well-being. And then, suddenly, CNN reports breaking news about a plane in trouble over the Atlantic.

1

The Invisible History of Prisoner Radicalization

Although prisoner radicalization is currently a matter of grave concern, it is actually a very old issue with consequences that can be astonishingly different in their outcomes. Prisoner radicalization is best described as a double-edged sword, capable of producing both positive and negative results. Some prison radicals have achieved great heights of public service as presidents and prime ministers, Nobel Peace Prize winners, and leaders of national liberation movements. Others have committed unspeakable acts of terrorism and genocide. Time spent in prison cuts both ways.

A study of four historic individuals—Winston Churchill, Mahatma Gandhi, Nelson Mandela, and Adolf Hitler—shows that prisoner radicalization is tempered and shaped by the prevailing political events of the times in which it occurs. Not only do these cases offer insights into the political motivations for radicalization but they also provide a framework for understanding how radicalization emerges from personal strategies used by prisoners to cope with various conditions of their confinement—some deplorable and some not. We begin by turning back the clock to more than a hundred years ago, in Pretoria, South Africa.

＊ ＊ ＊

After failing to win election to the British Parliament in 1899, twenty-five-year-old Winston Churchill sought to jump-start his career by going to South Africa to cover the Second Boer War as a journalist. While traveling with a scouting expedition in hostile territory, Churchill was fired upon and captured by a Boer commander, Louis Botha (who later became South Africa's first prime minister). Churchill was taken to a POW camp in Pretoria and housed in a dormitory with some sixty other POWs. "We had so much liberty within our bounds, and were so free from observation during the greater part of the day and night," wrote Churchill in his autobiography of the period, "that we could pursue our aim unceasingly."[1] Churchill actually had two aims: manipulating the guards and planning his escape.

The escape plan required information about the prison and surrounding areas, leading the POWs to devise what Churchill called "a scheme of desperate and magnificent audacity."[2] The information would come from British soldiers imprisoned in a barbed-wire encampment at the Pretoria racetrack, some two miles away from the POW camp. The channel of communication between the soldiers and the POWs became the black servants who were assigned to white guards inside the camps. Because the servants were treated ruthlessly by the racist South African guards, they frequently requested transfers between camps. As servants left the POW camp they were replaced by servants from the racetrack camp who brought with them information related to details of Boer security. Churchill gathered this information over a four-week period and used it to plan his brilliant getaway—thereby violating unprincipled penal law for what he saw as a greater good. Essentially, Churchill turned the apartheid prison system on its head by exploiting its own internal weaknesses.

When the opportunity presented itself to go over the wall, Churchill took it. He wore a civilian suit, in which he carried £75 in his pocket and several slabs of chocolate. Churchill had no water or compass, and he spoke neither Dutch nor any black language. But he did know basic astronomy. Following the stars Churchill made his way to a railroad spur where he hopped a moving freight train headed for the South African border. Hoping to switch trains along the line, Churchill missed a connection and found himself stranded, so he set off on foot for hours through swamps and high grass, leaving him drenched and exhausted. At this point, Churchill wrote, "I prayed long and earnestly for help and guidance."[3] His prayers were answered in the form of a British miner with the coincidental name of John Howard (coincidental because another man named John Howard [1726-1790] was the first English prison reformer).

By now police were searching for the escaped convict as wanted posters appeared along the lines, reading "CHURCHILL dead or alive, 25 pound REWARD."[4] At great risk to himself, Howard fed Churchill and hid him in a mining tunnel. Churchill waited in the tunnel for four days—sipping whiskey, fighting off a pack of white rats, and reading Robert Louis Stevenson's Kidnapped—until Howard arranged for Churchill to be stowed away beneath some cotton bales aboard a freight train to British-controlled Durban, South Africa. "I reached Durban to find myself a popular hero," wrote Churchill. "I was received as if I had won a great victory. The harbor was decorated with flags. Bands and crowds thronged the quays."[5] Churchill's daring prison escape made him a national hero in Britain, ushering in his remarkable career as a public figure.[6]

In 1910, Churchill was appointed Home Secretary and placed in charge of all British prisons, whereupon he implemented reforms that have proven to be exceptionally resilient over time. Churchill condemned punishment in favor of rehabilitation and advocated an early form of "just desserts" sentencing—that the prison time must fit the crime. Churchill met with discharged convicts—those who had "paid their dues in the hard coinage of punishment," as he called them—and discussed their futures, representing one of the earliest experiments with after-care. Churchill also introduced legislation designed to bring the prisoner's plight to a wider public. "The mood and temper of the public in regard to the treatment of crime and criminals," he advised the House of Commons in an oft-quoted line from a July 20, 1910, address, "is one of the most unfailing tests of the civilization of any country."[7] British penologists generally agree that Churchill's reforms were grounded in his personal experience as a prisoner.[8] "I certainly hated every minute of my captivity more than I have ever hated any other period in my whole life," Churchill wrote as dark clouds gathered over Europe in 1939. "Luckily it was very short."[9]

* * *

By any definition of the term, Mahatma Gandhi and Nelson Mandela were prison radicals of the first order. Like Churchill, Gandhi and Mandela were two of the great moral and political leaders of the 20th century. Yet, unlike Churchill, who managed by his own cunning to escape from prison in short order, Gandhi and Mandela would define their careers by the ways in which they endured the misery of prison.

Gandhi was imprisoned for his nonviolent civil disobedience campaigns against British rule (what Gandhi called *satyagraha*, or "asking for truth") numerous times, both in South Africa in 1919 and in his native India between 1922 and 1944.[10] Highly influenced by Gandhi's satyagraha was the African National Congress (ANC), the organization through which Nelson Mandela launched an armed struggle against the intransigent apartheid government of South Africa. In 1964, after living as a fugitive for several years, Mandela was captured and convicted of sabotage and treason. At the age of forty-seven, Mandela was sentenced to life in prison and was incarcerated with other black political prisoners at the former leper colony on Robben Island near Cape Town where he would spend the next eighteen years.

Gandhi and Mandela both served time under austere conditions. Fearing their influence on other prisoners, officials often segregated Gandhi and Mandela from the general prisoner populations, even sometimes in solitary confinement. Both lost loved ones and experienced painful separations from their children while in prison; both of their wives were imprisoned at various times (Gandhi's wife, Kasturba, would die in captivity); and both were assaulted by common criminals. Yet they differed dramatically in how they adapted to these conditions of confinement.

Gandhi was that rare human who actually saw spectacular advantages in prison life. "Prison never held any terrors for him," wrote one of Gandhi's biographers, Robert Payne. "He was accustomed to them; sometimes he wooed [prisons] like a bride."[11] Gandhi's cell at the Yeravda Jail in Poona, where he ultimately served some ten years, was nothing more than a concrete box with no electricity and a cow-dung floor. Nevertheless, Gandhi was a model prisoner who accepted his confinement as part of the satyagraha struggle, because the struggle was useless unless it involved suffering. Prison tested Gandhi's mettle and offered him unlimited time to read, write, meditate, and organize. Gandhi was a voracious reader in prison and was granted unlimited access to reading material. He claimed that reading rescued his mind from wandering off "like a monkey" and dwelling on unpleasant thoughts.[12] Already spiritually inclined, Gandhi immersed himself in the Bible, Plato's *Dialogues*, Francis Bacon's *Essays*, the *Gita Govinda*, the erotic hymn on the loves of Krishna, and the *Bhagavad Gita*, whose affirmation of righteous war Gandhi reinterpreted as a parable of nonviolence. Gandhi believed that all of the ancient religions conveyed the same essential realities, and he reasoned that love, truth, and nonviolence were synonymous. Of special concern to him was Islam. Though a devout Hindu, Gandhi regularly read the Koran and poured through such works of Islamic literature as Washington Irving's *The Lives of Mahomet and His Successors* and Amir Ali's *Short History of the Saracens*. Gandhi studied Urdu and wrote a sermon on the necessity of fusing together the Hindi and Urdu languages, thus bridging the gap between Hindus and Muslims.[13] Gandhi was also a prodigious writer, sometimes penning as many as forty letters a day, and for a while he edited his own broadside from prison.[14] During his time at the Yeravda Jail in 1923, Gandhi handwrote thirty chapters of his first autobiography, *Satyagraha in South Africa*.[15]

Gandhi's ambitious program of reading, writing, and organizing represented a defining characteristic of prisoner radicalization: these activities were undertaken in an effort to influence civil affairs beyond prison walls, in collaboration with political and religious militants. More than simply projecting his ideals of inclusivity and nonviolence to British rulers and the Indian public, Gandhi's prison activism embodied the dynamic of satyagraha. First and foremost, this involved breaking discriminatory laws through nonviolent collective action, thereby forcing the British to punish protestors with brutal physical beatings and imprisonment. Metaphorically,

Gandhi brought a prayer to a gunfight. He believed that the suffering of pro-testors would touch the hearts of the oppressors, thus revealing to them their own humanity. Once exposed to the injustice of their rule, the British would have no choice but to leave India.

Gandhi's greatest moment, among many great moments, had everything to do with the political potential that prison offered him. This moment began on the morning of March 12, 1930, when Gandhi led his epic Salt March to the sea in protest against the British monopoly on salt. The 240-mile walking journey attracted a crowd of some fifty thousand followers. Salt from the sea, Gandhi proclaimed as he knelt in his white robe by the shore at Dandi and scooped a pinch of salt in his fingertips, was the birthright of every person— not just the British government. The Salt March led to the widespread non-cooperation movement in India and the subsequent imprisonment of some one hundred thousand Gandhi sympathizers, including an unprecedented number of women (as a household necessity, salt was of special interest to women).[16] On May 5, Gandhi was arrested himself and taken to the Yeravda Jail where he was sentenced without trial to an indeterminate term as an enemy of the state, pushing India to the brink of anarchy. In prison, Gandhi reached the pinnacle of his power. Across the country, British-owned shops and mills were forced to close, scores of government officials resigned, and daily routines of society ground to a halt as a result of the boycott. For the moment, Gandhi's civil disobedience campaign effectively strained imperial control by denying the British both the labor and capital that made it pos-sible for them to hold India together.[17] With this, the potential of satyagraha became realized by the Indian masses. More than a humble religious trans-formation achieved through suffering, satyagraha became a practical method for protestors to overcome their adversaries and drive the British out.

Gandhi was released in January 1931, and he spent much of that year in London trying to negotiate terms of Indian independence but to no avail. Fearing a resumption of Gandhi's massive noncooperation campaign, upon his return to the Port of Bombay on January 4, 1932, the British Viceroy ordered Gandhi's arrest for sedition. Once again he disappeared behind the walls of the Yeravda Jail.

There, on September 20, 1932, Gandhi announced a "fast unto death" in protest against the voting status of Hindu Untouchables. Gandhi's prime objection was a voting statute that further separated Untouchables from the Hindu fold along cultural lines. Gandhi had gone on eight previous fasts—surrounded by family, doctors, and friends—but this was his first one in custody and it was likely to be more dangerous. This was of par-ticular concern to Her Majesty's Government. By this time Gandhi was the symbol of Indian independence and an international hero renowned for his marches, boycotts, and arrests. British authorities were loath to allow Gandhi to die in their custody because Britain's international reputation would have suffered as a result.

And Gandhi, at sixty-three years old, came into the throes of great suffering, all of it self-inflicted. Lying on a cot in the shade of a mango tree on the dusty prison yard, Gandhi took only water and salt for six days. He shriveled to 107 pounds, his blood pressure soared, his lungs and kidneys became infected, and he could no longer walk and had to be carried on a stretcher to the toilet. "What I want, and what I am living for, and what I should delight in dying for," Gandhi said in a press interview, "is the eradication of untouchability root and branch."[18] Millions of Indians fasted in support of Gandhi and prayers were sung throughout the country.

Gandhi's prison fast was a phenomenal success. On September 25, British Prime Minister Ramsey MacDonald announced that his government would make arrangements for the election of the Depressed Classes. Across India, Hindus opened their temple doors to the Untouchables and allowed them to use common water wells. "The Untouchables were no longer untouchable," wrote Payne. "Gandhi's fast had electrified the country."[19]

Gandhi soon grew dissatisfied with the progress of his anti-untouchable campaign, however, and announced that he would undertake another fast unto death. At noon, on May 8, 1933, Gandhi was again on his cot beneath the mango tree at the Yeravda Jail. This time, within a matter of hours the government issued Gandhi a pardon and set him free.[20] Thus was set in motion a cat-and-mouse game between Gandhi and the government in which Gandhi would be imprisoned time and again at the Yeravda Jail, where he would undergo a fast. Each time his condition deteriorated rapidly and authorities would release him, thus depriving Gandhi of his main organizing platform. "Where else," he asked, "could a Satyagrahi die more honorably than in prison?"[21]

Gandhi's fasting had a profound effect on the British. "Facts have shown that Saint Gandhi's hunger pain is mightier than the sword," wrote the editors of *Time* magazine on March 13, 1939. "Native riflemen have not got a fraction of the concessions from Britain that Saint Gandhi's torturing fasts have."[22] By the mid-1940s Gandhi was able to unify the diverse elements of the Indian independence movement, forcing concessions from the British that led to Indian independence in 1947. The following year, Gandhi was assassinated by a Hindu nationalist. In a 1949 tribute to Gandhi, Albert Einstein famously wrote, "Generations to come, it may be, will scarce believe that such a one as this ever in flesh and blood walked upon this earth."[23] Gandhi's spectacle of human suffering was his most potent weapon against the British.

* * *

"We did not accept suffering," recalled Nelson Mandela. "We reacted against it."[24] Mandela's weapon would be collective resistance against the inevitability of imprisonment as part of the struggle against South African apartheid. "I was as uncooperative on my first day of prison as I possibly could be," Mandela recalled. "I refused to wear the prison shorts and I refused to eat the prison food. They gave me long trousers, and food that was somewhat more palatable, but at a heavy price. I was placed in solitary confinement where I discovered that human company was infinitely more valuable than any material advantage."[25]

Mandela was incarcerated in what sociologists call a total institution, where every facet of his social and intellectual life was monitored by prison censors. More than any other South African institution at the time, Robben Island exemplified apartheid's grand design of total thought control over blacks. Prisoners were segregated by race, with black prisoners receiving fewer rations and privileges than whites. Black political prisoners were assigned to D-group, the lowest classification. They were housed with hardened criminals—including murderers and rapists—who were tasked by Robben Island officials to act as provocateurs and informants against the political prisoners. Hidden listening devices were planted in their cells, and rule violators were punished by the denial of food, lashes with a whip, and even extended prison sentences.[26] The political prisoners were sentenced to hard labor (breaking rocks in a limestone quarry) and required to follow a strict rule of silence, which prohibited them from speaking to one another. The silence policy lasted until all prisoners defied the rule and authorities were no longer able to enforce it.

At Robben Island, Mandela was locked up in a cramped and perpetually damp six-foot-square cell with a straw mat on a stone floor, threadbare blankets, and a "slop bucket" for a toilet.[27] This cruel confinement, the hard labor, the small prison-issued shorts meant to psychologically reduce him to childhood, the thought control, the informers, and the casual brutality were all intended to teach Mandela that he was less than human. "Nelson Mandela had many teachers in his life," wrote his biographer Richard Stengel, "but the greatest of them all was prison. Prison taught him self-control, discipline, and focus . . . and it taught him how to be a full human being."[28] As with Gandhi, Mandela would survive through a personal campaign of reading, writing, and organizing.

Mandela was part of a study group, known informally as Mandela University, yet the censors prohibited the group members from reading books on politics and military history, fearing—as Gandhi had aptly demonstrated—that an intellectual prisoner is likely to be a radical prisoner. Common news sources, such as *Time, The Guardian*, and BBC radio were also off-limits. "Newspapers were more valuable to political prisoners than gold or diamonds," wrote Mandela, "more hungered for than food or tobacco; they were the most precious contraband on Robben Island."[29] Mandela did have limited access to formal education, however, and he undertook a correspondence course through the University of London, eventually earning a Bachelor of Laws degree. Mandela spent much of his cell time reading law books and books about gardening, though his study group was once permitted to read Tolstoy's *War and Peace*, which would have an immense influence on Mandela in years to come.

Mandela was allowed to write and receive only one letter every six months, restricted to immediate family members. His incoming mail was delayed for long periods and heavily redacted by censors who often used razor blades to slash entire paragraphs. Mandela was able to skirt the severe restrictions on communication, however, by relying on a sophisticated transmission system created by ANC prisoners at Robben Island. Due to this ingenious prisoner communication system, Mandela would eventually come to embody and symbolize the injustices of South African apartheid.[30]

In this system, ANC prisoners bribed guards for newspapers, which were then mined for relevant political information that was summarized and smuggled to other prisoners. Messages were passed between Robben Island prisoners, and then to ANC members throughout South Africa, via short notes scribbled on toilet paper (what today are called "kites" in U.S. prisons or "stiffs" in British prisons), concealed in plastic and hidden in the bottom of food buckets, inside dirty dishes, or within toilet seats. Other notes were written with milk, which would dry and become invisible on white paper but would then reappear when sprayed with the disinfectant prisoners used to keep their cells clean.[31] The system was also used to create Mandela's crowning literary achievement, his autobiography, *Long Walk to Freedom*.

He began the work in late 1975, shortly after his fifty-seventh birthday. The memoir was intended not only to tell Mandela's personal story but also to introduce Mandela to the outside world as the spokesman for a new South Africa. Mandela adopted a routine where he would stay up through the night writing in near total darkness, save the moonlight shining into his cell, producing ten to fifteen pages each night without the benefit of references or access to what he had written on previous nights. Each day, these pages were secretly passed to an ANC prisoner who edited the writing. That prisoner would then pass the pages to another prisoner who transferred the writing into what Mandela called "microscopic shorthand, reducing ten pages of foolscap to a single small piece of paper."[32] Once this was accomplished, the pages were passed to yet another prisoner who buried them with other pages in the prison's vegetable garden. In 1976, five hundred coded pages were taken from the garden and smuggled out of Robben Island by the released ANC prisoner Mac Maharaj, who delivered the manuscript to comrades in London where it stayed for nearly twenty years.

By the mid-1970s, violence between the South African police and anti-apartheid activists had reached disastrous proportions. On June 16, 1976, some six hundred students were killed at Soweto in protests against the use of Afrikaans curriculum and poor educational conditions. Reflecting the breadth of his knowledge about the international Black Liberation movement, from his cell at Robben Island Mandela wrote that the Soweto massacre would lead South African children "to discover their political idols and to model their own lives on those of past heroes . . . the American Black Muslims, Muhammad Ali, himself a Black Muslim, and the Black Panther movement."[33] When Steve Biko, leader of the student protest movement, was killed in police custody the following year, violent uprisings spread across the townships. Tens of thousands of young black males were arrested and detained without trial. Some were tortured and others were killed outright.

As the government expanded bed space at Robben Island to accommodate the sudden influx of new political prisoners, Mandela became widely known as the most significant black leader in South Africa. So great was his reputation that in 1981 he was nominated for the position of chancellor of the University of London.[34] Accordingly, Mandela was offered freedom if he would curtail his activism in support of the outlawed ANC. Mandela refused the offer. In an effort to isolate him from the younger prisoners, in March 1982 authorities transferred Mandela and other senior ANC leaders to Cape Town's Poolsoor Prison. By the mid-1980s, international pressure had mounted on the South African government to release Mandela, thus giving rise to the popular slogan *Free Nelson Mandela!* By this time sanctions against the apartheid regime had crippled the nation's economy. Finally recognizing that the apartheid system was untenable, in 1988 authorities transferred Mandela yet again, this time to a house on the grounds of Victor Verster Prison, where representatives of President P. W. Botha's government began secret talks with him. All the while, Mandela continued his contact with the ANC through the secret communication system, by now including the transfer of information via computer disks.[35]

On February 11, 1990, after twenty-seven years in captivity, Nelson Mandela was released from prison to worldwide media acclamation. The newly appointed president F. W. de Klerk then lifted the ban on the ANC and abolished apartheid in the prison system. In 1993, Mandela and de Klerk received the Nobel Peace Prize, and in 1994 black South Africans were allowed to vote for the first time. The ANC won a majority of seats in the national assembly and Mandela was elected as the first black president of South Africa. His first steps were to appoint a racially mixed government of national unity and to introduce policies aimed at reducing long entrenched social and economic inequalities, including reforms in education, health care, welfare, and social services. Later that year, Mandela's prison memoir—*Long Walk to Freedom*—was published to global renown. Robben Island was subsequently converted to a museum and World Heritage Site, which now receives tens of thousands of visitors from around South Africa and the world. Symbolizing the importance of prisoner resistance to the nation's history, today a replica of Mandela's cell hangs in the South African parliament. And along with Mandela's rise to the status of a global icon, prisoner resistance movements have flourished around the world. But the secret history of prisoner radicalization also has a dark side. Alas, it is a double-edged sword.

* * *

On November 9, 1923, following Germany's decision to resume its payments of World War I reparations to Britain and France, Adolf Hitler's Nazi Party launched the famous Munich Beer Hall *putsch*—the party's first attempt at seizing the German government by force. The uprising was instantly crushed; after two days in hiding, Hitler was arrested and held for trial in an old fortress prison at Landsberg, a picturesque village some forty miles west of Munich. There Hitler became despondent and threatened to kill himself.[36] Some historians claim that the suicide threat was the result of a two-week hunger strike undertaken by Hitler, but that is hard to verify and even harder to imagine. When the putsch trial began on February 24, 1924, Hitler was barely known outside the state of Bavaria. By the time the trial ended on April 1—during which time Hitler was given a media platform for his views—he had captured the national limelight.

As a result of the trial, the Nazi Party was banned and Hitler was sentenced to five years for high treason. He was escorted back to Landsberg and taken to a wing of the prison set aside for political prisoners. Known as the *Festung* ("the Fort" in English), the area was more spacious than other sections of the prison and featured large windows opening onto a lilac garden.[37] Hitler was treated like royalty there, due to the fact that the prison superintendent, Otto Leybold, and many of the guards were Nazi sympathizers: some guards greeted him with "Heil Hitler."[38] Hitler was permitted to wear his own clothes (he is typically photographed in a suit and tie), furnish his own cell, receive gifts and visitors, and keep a private staff including a personal servant and a chauffeur. Hitler was allowed to take daily walks through the village and permitted to dine in a social room with some forty fellow Nazis, also convicted in the putsch trial, where smoking and drinking were permitted. Hitler sat at the head of a table with a swastika banner above him. When he turned thirty-five on April 20, Hitler's cell and two adjoining rooms overflowed with birthday gifts and flowers. No restrictions were placed on his correspondence, which allowed him to develop personal relationships with future leaders of the German Reich—one of whom was a 1921 Ph.D. graduate in philology from Heidelberg University named Joseph Goebbels, the future Minister of Propaganda and Enlightenment and creator of the *Kristallnacht,* the Night of Broken Glass (November 9, 1938), when Nazi gangs attacked Jews and their property across Germany and Austria.[39]

Hitler was allowed unrestricted reading privileges—he would remark that Landsberg prison was his "university paid for by the state"—but historians agree that Hitler's choice of reading material was confined to a narrow range of books that only reinforced his existing worldview. In addition to pseudo-scientific pamphlets on racial mysticism, these included works by Nietzsche, Marx, Bismarck, and, most importantly, Houston Stewart Chamberlain's *The Foundations of the Nineteenth Century* (1899), detailing the historical antecedents of Aryan superiority.[40]

A surviving 1924 photograph of Hitler's cell shows a sunlit room with two barred windows, one of which is open to the breeze, a cot with a white blanket, a bedside lamp, and a polished writing desk. A bouquet of flowers sits on the desk and above it is an unidentifiable painting. The room is neatly kept and void of books or any other reading material.[41] It was here that Hitler received a steady flow of friends, journalists, and members of the banned Nazi Party. Historians claim that Hitler received visitors for up to six hours a day and that he met with some five hundred visitors during his first three months at Landsberg.[42] It was also here that Hitler gathered his entourage of fellow Fort prisoners who would confirm upon him the status of the divinely appointed Fuhrer. "Filled with this consciousness," wrote the German historian Joachim Fest about the Fuhrer cult at Landsberg, "Hitler managed to impress this image of himself upon his fellow prisoners. From this time on, the sense of mission never left him. It froze his features in that mask which no smile, no altruistic gesture, no moment of spontaneity ever softened."[43] What are we to make of the conversations that took place in this cell?

It is certain that Hitler was concerned with his own future and that of the Nazi Party. Ian Kershaw, one of the world's leading experts on Nazi Germany, describes Hitler's conversations with the Fort prisoners in these terms: "As usual, they were subjected at length to 'the chief's' monologues—on 'the social question,' 'racial questions,' the meaning of political revolution, how to gain control of the state, the architectural shape of the future."[44] Had Alfred Rosenberg been involved in these discussions—and there is every reason to believe so given that Hitler had placed the chairmanship of the Nazi Party in Rosenberg's hands during his incarceration—then conversations were likely to have turned to the Nazi occult.[45]

Both Rosenberg and Heinrich Himmler, the future leader of the SA (the Gestapo), were pagan enthusiasts who would later champion a German policy making the summer solstice, June 21, a Nazi holiday. Himmler's paganism also involved a bizarre theory holding that the original Aryans emerged from beneath a global ice shield.[46] In this way, paganism was used to advance the cause of anti-Semitism. By linking the nature of the human soul to the nature of land, the Nazis were able to define the Jews as desert people: because of the barrenness of the desert landscape, the Jews were conceived as a spiritually barren people, devoid of profundity and creativity.[47] In the words of one historian, this "pagan earthiness freed [the Nazis] of any of the claims of conscience and the aspirations of the ideal."[48] As the Nazi's chief racial theorist, Alfred Rosenberg grafted onto this paganism a "religion of the blood" based upon what he called positive Christianity, which advanced the idea that Jesus belonged to a Nordic enclave in ancient Galilee who struggled against Judaism.[49] According to the British author Anthony Read, it was in Landsberg that Rosenberg introduced Hitler to the *Protocols of the Elders of Zion*, a famously anti-Semitic book of fiction about Jewish plans for world domination.[50]

Despite his special accommodations and unrestricted visitation privileges, Hitler remained moody and depressed.[51] He was advised by his business manager, the fellow Fort prisoner Max Amman, to put his energies into writing an autobiography that would capitalize on the celebrity Hitler had achieved during the trial. Hitler had never mastered the art of writing and was opposed to the idea, but he agreed to do so after Amman suggested that he might dictate his thoughts to a ghostwriter. Superintendent Leybold agreed that Hitler's chauffeur could live in the prison and carry out this task; however, the chauffeur was a poor writer as well, so the assignment fell to another Fort prisoner, a thirty-year-old named Rudolf Hess, a former political science student at the University of Munich who was serving a seven-month sentence for his role in the putsch. It was Hess, during their days at Landsberg, who gave Hitler the title of Fuhrer.[52] Hess attempted to turn Hitler's spoken ideas into written words, but given Hitler's proclivity to use language as a form of invective and assault, the result was abrasive, monotonous, and wildly egocentric.

The project continued apace, however, resulting in fifteen narrative chapters covering a mixture of autobiography, political ideas, and an explanation of the techniques of propaganda. Hitler held forth on subjects as diverse as the legalisms of National Socialism, the twin evils of communism and Judaism (a concept originated by Alfred Rosenberg), the "science of German conquest," the destruction of Germany's parliamentary system, interracial marriage, the cultivation of roses, syphilis, and boxing. But his main thesis was about "the Jewish peril" and he spoke of a Zionist conspiracy to gain world dominance. Hitler described the process by which he came to believe that Germans should expand eastward, liquidate the Jews, and turn the Slavs into slave labor, thus predicting both the stages of Germany's political emergence on the world scene and Hitler's policy to annihilate European Jewry ("the Final Solution").[53] The two-volume work was originally titled *My Four Years of Struggle against Lies, Stupidity, and Cowardice*. When Amman saw the title, he reduced it to simply *My Struggle*, or *Mein Kampf*.[54]

On December 20, 1924, Adolf Hitler was released from Landsberg after serving nine months of his five-year term. He had put on weight in prison and appeared flabby in photographs, leading Hitler to adopt a vegetarian and alcohol-free lifestyle.[55] Hitler's friend Kurt Ludecke would write, "Landsberg had done him a world of good. Gone from his manner was the nervous intensity which formerly had been his most unpleasant characteristic."[56] Hitler would later attribute his self-confidence and optimism to his time in Landsberg because it was there that Hitler refined his strategy to gain power and elevated his self-belief through the Fuhrer cult established by Rudolph Hess and the Fort entourage. So substantial was Landsberg Prison to Nazi mythology that by 1934 the village was christened "the city of youth" in honor of the Hitler Youth groups who staged loyalty marches to the prison where they were given tours of the "Hitler Cell"—marketed by local tourism officials as "the birthplace of the ideas of National Socialism."[57] (Nazi war criminals were later hung at Landsberg Prison.) Volumes 1 and 2 of *Mein Kampf* were published in 1925 and 1926, respectively. By the time Hitler came to power in 1933, *Mein Kampf* had achieved enormous popularity in Germany, eventually selling more than ten million copies before the end of World War II, making Hitler a wealthy man. The book was given free to every newlywed couple in Germany and every soldier fighting on the front lines during the war.[58]

Due to its racist content and its inspiration for the horrors that the Nazi conquest inflicted on Europe, *Mein Kampf* is considered the most morally autistic book of all time. Disparagements of *Mein Kampf* came from opponents of Nazism and allies alike. The Italian Fascist dictator Benito Mussolini called the thing "a boring tome that I have never been able to read."[59] Churchill argued that no book ever deserved more scrutiny. Of *Mein Kampf*, he wrote, "Here was the new Koran of faith and war: turgid, verbose, shapeless, but pregnant with its message."[60] The British historian Hugh Trevor-Roper summarized the book with this evocative image: "Imposing indeed in its granite harshness and yet infinitely squalid with miscellaneous cumber—like some huge barbarian monolith, the expression of giant strength and savage genius, surrounded by a festering heap of refuse—old tins and dead vermin, ashes and eggshells and ordure—the intellectual *detritus* of centuries."[61] During the 1942 bombing campaign on Liverpool, Hitler explained to a gathering of Nazi elites that *Mein Kampf* would never have been written had he not been sent to prison.[62]

* * *

The themes informing these narratives of radicalization—cunning, suffering, collective resistance, and nihilism—continue to echo within prisoner subcultures to this day, as do the strategies that turned these tropes into action: a spirit of self-help supported by kinship networks, clandestine communication systems, obscure religions, and, most important of all, charismatic leadership—what Max Weber described as "a certain quality of an individual personality, by virtue of which he is set apart from ordinary people and treated as endowed with supernatural, superhuman or at least exceptional powers or qualities."[63] Churchill, Gandhi, Mandela, and Hitler: did the 20th century produce anyone with more charisma than them? And like before, prisoner radicalization is still a double-edged sword: prison can produce both freedom fighters, who struggle for economic and social justice by nonviolent means, and terrorists, who use violence to cause a change in the social order.

Today, the mango tree and Gandhi's cell at the Yeravda Jail are national shrines and his writings on nonviolence are uniformly taught to the jail inmates.[64] Gandhi's enduring legacy, though, is the prison fast, and prisoners from all corners of the globe have followed his example by undertaking hunger strikes to bring attention to perceived social injustices.

The tactic was used to spectacular effect by the Irish Republican Army in 1981 when Republican prisoners at the Maze Prison near Belfast (also known as the H-Blocks) launched a hunger strike protesting the British government's revocation of a prisoner-of-war status for prisoners in Northern Ireland. The strike was led by twenty-seven-year-old Bobby Sands, then serving fourteen years for possession of a firearm while on an IRA mission. Sands began his fast on March 1 and decided that other prisoners should join the strike at staggered intervals to maximize publicity as they steadily deteriorated over several months. The prisoners, known as the "blanket men" for their refusal to wear anything but blankets, survived without food for up to seventy-three days. According to the British historian Michael Burleigh, the blanket men "knew that their emaciated images would be mentally blended with that of the crucified Savior, and that their funerals and wakes could be turned into IRA recruiting demonstrations."[65] On April 9, at the height of the hunger strike, Sands was elected to the British parliament on the Anti H-Block/Armagh Political Prisoner ticket. Then on May 1, after taking only water and salt for sixty-six days, Sands became the first of ten blanket men to die. Over one hundred thousand people lined the route of Sands's funeral procession. Thousands joined spontaneous anti-British marches in Paris, Milan, and Oslo, as Dublin and Belfast erupted into violence. Not only did Sands's death lead to a new surge of IRA recruitment, fund-raising and media attention, but it also sparked a campaign of momentous violence outside the prison walls, which would ultimately lead to a fundamental change in the criminal justice system in Northern Ireland. These historic events formed the basis for the peace process, culminating in the 1998 Belfast Good Friday Agreement. Today, Sands continues to loom large in the collective memory of Northern Ireland. His image appears in Sinn Fein recruitment posters and in a larger-than-life mural at the organization's headquarters. In France, streets and newborn babies are named after Bobby Sands, such is his legend.[66]

Inspired by the IRA, since 2000 several waves of hunger strikes have been launched against the use of isolation cells by Marxist revolutionaries in Turkish prisons. In what is considered the longest-running death fast in history, in 2002 more than a hundred female prisoners survived for as long as two hundred days without solid food, resulting in forty-five self-inflicted fatalities. "We do this to make life better for all humanity," said a death faster named Lale Colak before she slipped into a coma and died in an Istanbul hospital at the age of twenty-seven.[67]

Hunger strikes have been used for decades by prisoners in the United States, including a multiwave strike in 2011–2012 by a reported twelve thousand California prisoners in protest against overcrowding and the use of administrative segregation—an action joined by fasting protestors of the Occupy movement.[68] Hunger strikes have also extended to offshore facilities operated by the military. In the summer of 2005, at least two hundred Muslim detainees at Guantanamo initiated a two-wave hunger strike to protest the conditions of their confinement and a policy that allows them to be held for years without charge—referred to by Britain's highest judicial authority as "a legal black hole."[69] Official documents and confidential accounts indicate that the U.S. military subjected Guantanamo prisoners to such torture techniques as hooding and sleep deprivation, exposure to extreme temperatures, and psychological ploys meant to induce humiliation and fear, including the use of attack dogs.[70] Among those imprisoned at the time was Guantanamo detainee # 372, Said Ali al-Shihri, who organized the failed Christmas Day bombing plot of 2009.[71]

But this is not a book about suffering. Rather, it is about how prisoners use criminal cunning, collective resistance, and nihilism to incite terrorism against Western targets. Prison radicals have the ability to sway the course of history, as we have seen. Some are now engaged in what they perceive as a campaign that will influence the progression of Western history. Their campaign will eventually end—like all movements, the international jihad movement will have its apogee and its decline—but it may take many years before it reaches that point.[72] Until then, prisoners will fight, not through populist political movements of yesteryear, but through criminal conspiracies intended to render death by a thousand cuts. The Christmas Day plot and the 2001 attempt by Richard Reid to bring down an American Airlines flight between Paris and Miami with a shoebomb, both causing increased airport security and the victimization of millions of travelers; the Madrid train bombings of 2004; Al-Qaeda in Iraq and Al-Qaeda Central—all were led by men who radicalized behind bars. In the latter case, I refer to al-Qaeda's chief ideologue during the bin Laden years, Ayman al-Zawahiri, radicalized through torture in an Egyptian prison in the early 1980s following the assassination of Anwar Sadat.

People can become radicalized in any number of social networks: in mosques, universities, military barracks, sports clubs, brothels, libraries, barbershops, and Internet chat rooms. Those radicalized in prison tend to play for keeps—precisely for the reasons identified by the intelligence expert Charles Allen in his 2007 congressional testimony. By their very nature, prisons are intended to induce transformative experiences among inmates. Today's prisons are hotbeds for personal transformation due to the increasingly chaotic nature of prison life caused by the movement toward mass incarceration. Mass incarceration has increased the social marginalization of inmates and their desire for bonding, group identity, and spiritual guidance. These changes make prisons a better place to foment terrorism than any other social setting. At least that is what the gravitational force of history says. Since 2008, about two dozen Muslim Americans have been charged with terrorism-related offenses for joining or seeking training with militant groups abroad. Four of the most serious cases—culminating in suicide bombing, the murder of American military personnel, and the attempted bombing of a federal building—involved young men who had been radicalized in prison.[73]

In the pages ahead I explain how this threat has expanded within the secretive underground of prisoner subcultures through extremist interpretations of religious doctrines that inspire ideologies of intolerance, hatred, and violence. For Muslims, this often involves an alternative religious vision expressed in pious forms of "Prison Islam," which encompasses gang values and fierce intragang loyalties based on idiosyncratic interpretations of the Koran. For white supremacists, the vision is conveyed in the neo-paganism of Nazi dystopia.

A careful assessment of the problem requires both historic and ethnographic perspectives. We are required, then, to visit the worlds of such diverse prisoner subcultures as the Black Guerrilla Family, Jam'iyyat Ul-Islam Is-Saheeh, al-Qaeda of Europe, and the Aryan Brotherhood. The research shows that prison-based terrorists are radicalized in their early twenties, typically by cellmates or fellow gang members who possess qualities of charismatic leadership. Far from ubiquitous, the problem can often be traced to small prisoner networks inside specific institutions—New Folsom Prison in California, the Feltham Young Offenders Institution in Britain, Topas Prison in Spain, and Guantanamo in Cuba.

Terrorism is not prevalent among radical prisoners. In fact, the study shows that conversions to all types of religious faiths—including radical versions of Islam—are more likely to produce positive behavior among prisoners, rather than terrorism. This is consistent with the preponderance of criminological research indicating that religious beliefs have a pro-social and anticriminal impact on society.[74] Moving from radicalization to actual recruitment for terrorism is an extremely rare event. The criminologist Todd Clear has estimated the likelihood of a radicalized prisoner turning to terrorism at ten times greater than 1 in 2,500, or about the same chance as winning the lottery or getting struck by lightning. "To say that radicalization is remarkably rare is to say that it matters *not* as a substantive issue," he concludes, "but as a symbolic one . . . the *symbolic* importance of terrorism far exceeds its actual importance."[75] This, however, is sheer nonsense.

Symbolic terrorism is meant to send a message to audiences beyond the intended target. It typically involves secret midnight bombings of corporate offices, government buildings, synagogues, or mosques, and those actions tend to avoid casualties. For example, the Weather Underground was responsible for forty-five bombings in the United States between 1970 and 1977—targeting "symbols of American justice"—and they purposely and successfully avoided injuring anyone.[76] Symbolic terrorism is a form of "theater" in which terrorists want a lot of people watching, but not a lot of people dead.[77] The Madrid train bombings and the campaigns of Al-Qaeda in Iraq and Al-Qaeda Central, including the 9/11 attacks, were brazen acts of terrorism that caused catastrophic death and destruction. They were much more than symbolic acts of violence, as are other cases within the invisible history of prisoner radicalization.

During his imprisonment at the Missouri State Penitentiary at Jefferson City in 1964, James Earl Ray became loosely affiliated with the prison chapter of the Ku Klux Klan. His political ideas distorted by intravenous amphetamine abuse, Ray grew obsessed with the civil rights work of Martin Luther King and a prison rumor that the White Knights of the Mississippi Klan were willing to pay a $100,000 bounty for King's head.[78] Three years later, Ray escaped from Jefferson City and made his way to Memphis where on April 4, 1968, he assassinated King on the balcony of the Lorraine Motel. One escaped convict, one bullet, and the course of American history was radically altered—not symbolically but in a tangible and vital way. Only a tiny, infinitesimal fraction of prison converts to white supremacy faiths and to Islam—primarily, fresh converts, the newly pious, with an exaggerated sense of religiosity—turn radical beliefs into terrorist action. They are the spectacular few.

2

Islam in Prison

As with many lofty ideas, the restorative power of religion in prison began with a friendly conversation over a beer. In 1786, as Americans struggled with postwar economic depression, Benjamin Rush, a distinguished Philadelphia physician and a signer of the Declaration of Independence, came upon a group of "wheelbarrow men" cleaning the streets outside his house. Street cleaning was a requirement of inmates at Philadelphia's Walnut Street Jail under the recently enacted penal code of the Commonwealth of Pennsylvania, as was the wearing of a distinctive garb, a shaved head, and a wheelbarrow to push while working. Being curious, Rush offered the men mugs of molasses beer, and while talking with them Rush found that he not only had sympathy for their plight, but also respect for the dignity with which they bore their humiliation.[1]

As a result of this incident, Rush began to speak out against the penal laws. He first did so in a March 9, 1787, speech before a group of well-known Philadelphians belonging to the Society for Promoting Political Inquires, which held its meetings at the home of Rush's friend, eighty-one-year-old Benjamin Franklin. Influenced by the writings of the English prison reformer John Howard, who favored imprisonment for all criminals as a substitute for physical punishment, Rush advanced a radical proposition that would ultimately set a new international standard for penology—that "the only design of punishment is the reformation of the criminal."[2] Central to this proposition was the restorative power of religion. "Happy condition of human affairs," Rush proclaimed in his speech, "when humanity, philosophy and Christianity, shall unite their influence to teach men, that they are brethren; and to prevent their preying any longer upon each other!"[3] Believing that criminality was caused by the stresses of society, Rush recommended removing criminals from all harmful associations and inculcating them with moral principles from the Bible. Toward this end, Rush envisioned the construction of what he originally called a "house of repentance." His plan called for individual cells for the solitary confinement of prisoners, a room for worship conducted by a chaplain, and a garden for growing food "cultivated from their own hands"—all designed to create genuine regret and *penitence* in the criminal's heart. Thus was born the term *penitentiary*.[4]

Rush published his speech in an anonymous 1787 pamphlet—often attributed to Franklin, an inveterate prankster in his own pamphleteering—which led to the creation of the Philadelphia Society for Alleviating the Miseries of Public Prisons, comprised mainly of Quaker intellectuals.[5] It took the society more than thirty years to convince the Commonwealth of Pennsylvania to build the kind of prison envisioned by Rush. Yet build it did on farmland outside Philadelphia. When the massive Eastern State Penitentiary opened its doors in 1829 (known locally as Cherry Hill because its site had once been a cherry orchard), it was one of the largest public works projects of the new republic. A technological marvel, Eastern State featured central heating, flush toilets, and showers in each private cell—luxuries not even President Andrew Jackson could enjoy at the White House.[6] It would soon become the most famous prison in the world, leading to the creation of the penitentiary system—a system that sought to not simply punish prisoners but to move them toward spiritual redemption. Philosophically, the penitentiary was rooted in the inextricable relation between criminal rehabilitation and religion.

These early efforts to reform prisoners through Christianity were conducted in large homogeneous institutions primarily along the Eastern seaboard. As immigration to the United States expanded in the 20th century, the nation's prisons became more heterogeneous, leading to the introduction of new faiths into inmate populations. Because America was founded on a belief that freedom of worship cannot be infringed, a conflict eventually arose between what legally constituted an established religion and the individual's right to exercise it, a conflict that would torment generations of prison wardens to come. While scholarship on religion in the American prison would become vast and varied in the years ahead, for decades the role of Islam was airbrushed out of the historical record. That history is vital, however, to understanding the terrorist threat posed by prisoners today.

* * *

The emergence of Islam in American prisons can be traced to Timothy Drew, who was born to former slaves in 1886 on a Cherokee Indian reservation in Sampson, North Carolina.[7] What is known about him is based less on historical recollection than on the African tradition of mythmaking. By no means is this tradition a limitation because mythmaking deals with the critical human issue of self-identity. According to the legend, Timothy Drew's mother foresaw in him things divine. But when she died, Drew was turned over to an aunt who abused him until the boy ran away. It is said that he took up with a band of gypsies and then joined a crew of merchant sea-men at the age of sixteen. Several years later, Drew arrived in Egypt where, during a visit to the Pyramid of Cheops, he was introduced to Islam. The experience tested Drew's courage, it is told, and he emerged as Nobel Drew Ali. After reading the *Circle Seven Koran*, he dreamed of a religion "for the uplifting of fallen mankind," especially the "lost-found nation of American blacks." Upon awakening from his dream, he became the Prophet Nobel Drew Ali.

In 1912 or 1913, Drew Ali returned to the States and settled in Newark, New Jersey, where he founded the Canaanite Temple. After his introduc-tion to the writings of the Sudanese-Egyptian intellectual Duse Muhammad Ali, the editor of *The African Times and Orient Review*, which was a journal championing national liberation struggles and promoting solidarity among "nonwhites" around the world, Drew Ali's house of worship became known as the Moorish Science Temple. He preached a revolutionary doctrine hold-ing that black Americans are descended from the Moors, a North African tribe whose practice of Islam dates to their invasion of Spain in 711.[8] Their ancestors were the Canaanites, descendants of Ham, the son of Noah, whose progenies inhabited West Africa where they established the Moorish Empire that later ruled most of Europe and Asia. Africans who were brought to America as chattel slaves in the 16th century were Muslims; therefore, Drew Ali argued that the original religion of black Americans is Islam, not Chris-tianity. Slavery had erased this cultural memory, however, and blacks came to accept the label "Negro" and the conditions of bondage.[9] This racist social institution could have been avoided, Drew Ali argued, had blacks remem-bered their original identity as Moors.

For historical proof, Drew Ali cited the Black Laws of Virginia, which legally exempted Moroccan nationals (or Moors) from slavery. In 1774, the founding fathers of the Constitution had declared that only Negros were subject to slavery. Legally, then, Moors could not be counted as slaves. According to legend, George Washington was aware of the precedent established by the Black Laws and cut down the Moorish red flag flown by his slaves at Mount Vernon, so as to hide their identity.[10] Therefore, George Washington did not cut down the cherry tree, but the Moorish red flag. This example provided Drew Ali with the basis for his evolving *theodicy*, or a theology of correction. In 1916 Drew Ali and his followers moved to Chicago and six years later they founded the first Moorish Sci-ence Temple there. From then on, the Moroccan star and crescent, fezzes, the Moorish flag, the adoption of Islamic names, and the correction of "El" or "Bey" to the surname (meant to signify Moorish descent) all came to symbolize Moorish identity in America and membership in the Moorish Science Temple. Moorish Science would also play an instrumental role in the evolving view among many black Americans that they had an ancestral claim to Egypt.

As for Nobel Drew Ali, history would remember him as the first in a long line of iconic disenfranchised black men whose struggles against a white-dominated, racist society became the catalyst for new American religions based on Islam. A close look at these leaders reveals that they did not ascend from disconnected episodes of history; rather, one period flowed into another, each arising out of similar class and racial inequalities.

*   *   *

The Nation of Islam evolved from Moorish Science mythology, yet with a stronger emphasis on race. Its founder was an enigmatic figure named Wallace Dodd Fard (pronounced *FA-rod*) who arrived in Detroit in 1929 after serving a three-year sentence in California's San Quentin Prison for selling narcotics to an undercover policeman. By this time, Nobel Drew Ali was in jail on murder charges and Duse Muhammad Ali had founded the Universal Islamic Society of Detroit, which would come to influence the thinking of Wallace Fard (also known as Wali Fard Muhammad).[11] Fard, who claimed to have been born in Mecca in 1877 (though some scholars trace his birth to Southern California in 1896), began to attract the attention of poor blacks as he walked the streets selling fabrics and expounding a novel religious message blending tenants of traditional Islam with antiwhite contentions.[12] He presented himself as "the Prophet" and the reincarnation of Nobel Drew Ali; his soap-box preaching proclaimed that American Negroes were Asiatic-African descendants of the lost tribe of Shabazz from Mecca. According to Fard, these Negroes were "the cream of the planet," which had been captured, exploited, dehumanized, and enslaved.[13] Fard proclaimed that he had come to Detroit's ghettos to resurrect "the Lost-Found Nation of Islam in the Wilderness of North America."[14]

In 1930 or 1932, Fard established the first Nation of Islam mosque in downtown Detroit. Like Nobel Drew Ali, he expounded a religious theodicy, holding that Negroes were descendants of the original black humanity. By an extraordinary historical mistake, these descendants had produced the wicked white race. For Negroes to correct the white racism they encountered in everyday life, Fard argued that they must have a history that reversed the traditional account of African contributions to civilization. In order to do that, black Americans must reject Christianity and return to their ancestral faith in Islam. They must also have independence and a culture that stresses preparedness for protection of self and honor. It was from this premise that Fard created the Fruit of Islam, a martial arts-trained paramilitary unit that became the organization's security force.[15]

When Fard disappeared in 1934 the Nation of Islam was inherited by his tireless and loyal lieutenant, Elijah Muhammad (born as Elijah Poole). The Detroit temple now counted some eight thousand members; when Elijah Muhammad moved to Washington, D.C., in 1935, he opened a second temple. Muhammad moved to the south side of Chicago in 1940 where he opened a third temple; a fourth was opened in Milwaukee the same year. In 1942, the Nation of Islam began its first prison ministry in Petersburg, Virginia.[16]

By this time Elijah Muhammad was a prisoner himself. In 1942 he was sentenced to four years at the Federal Penitentiary in Milan, Michigan, for refusing induction during World War II. While in prison, Muhammad met other black draft resisters and engaged in an intense study of Islam's history and culture. Of special significance to him was the work of the Sierra Leone Creole scholar Edward Blyden (1832–1912) whose seminal 1888 work, *Christianity, Islam and the Negro Race*, argued that Islam was better suited to people of African descent than Christianity because of the lack of racial prejudice, the doctrine of brotherhood, and the value placed on learning in Islam.[17] Equally important was an observation Elijah Muhammad made about self-sufficiency in prison. Through prisoner labor and cooperation, he saw that the Milan facility was able to produce enough food and clothing to meet the needs of the inmate population. Upon his release in 1946, Muhammad returned to Chicago where he set out to redress the complex social problems arising from the Great Migration. Demonstrating an enhanced personal authority since his release from custody, Muhammad pushed for a goal of self-reliance within the Nation of Islam, eventually leading to the establishment of Muslim-owned farms, dairies, laundries, grocery stores, barbershops, transportation businesses, and a newspaper.[18] The prison ministry was also expanded to include an outreach program intended to show that convicted felons, alcoholics, drug addicts, and prostitutes occupied a special place in Nation of Islam doctrine.

In 1948, the outreach program attracted the attention of a twenty-three-year-old convict at Massachusetts's Concord Reformatory named Malcolm Little—later Malcolm X—whose contribution to the self-awareness of blacks and Muslims, both inside and outside prison, is immeasurable. (Both Nelson Mandela and Ayman al-Zawahiri would one day cite Malcolm X as a major influence.) His conversion to the Nation of Islam was aided by immediate family members. As Malcolm told his biographer, Alex Haley:

My brothers and sisters in Detroit and Chicago had all become converted to what they were being taught was the "natural religion for the
black man." . . . They all prayed for me to become converted while I was
in prison. They had decided that [Malcolm's younger brother] Reginald,
the latest convert, the one to whom I felt closest, would best know how to
approach me, since he knew me so well in the street life. . . . And [after the
conversion] anytime I got a chance to exchange words with a black brother
in stripes, I'd say, "My man! You ever heard about somebody named Mr.
Elijah Muhammad?"[19]

Malcolm was later transferred to Massachusetts's Norfolk Prison Colony where he undertook a rigorous course of independent study and self-
improvement. He read books by Kant, Nietzsche, and W. E. B. Du Bois and
was especially taken with Gandhi's struggle against British rule in India.[20]
In 1950 Malcolm began his da'wa, which was the process of "fishing for
converts" as it is known in the Nation of Islam. He converted a handful of
prisoners and began to agitate the Norfolk administration for their rights to
the dietary and medical restrictions common to the Muslim faith, as well
as the rights to have their cells facing east toward Mecca to accommodate
daily prayers. When the warden denied these requests, Malcolm threatened
to take their case to the U.S. office of the Egyptian consul, leading to the warden's capitulation. This incident led to Malcolm's first exposure to the media
and what may be the earliest known example of prisoner radicalization in
America. On April 20, 1950, the *Springfield Union* reported the Norfolk
controversy under the banner headline "Local Criminals, in Prison, Claim
Moslem Faith Now: Grow Beards, Won't Eat Pork, and Demand East-Facing
Cells to Facilitate 'Prayers to Allah.' "[21] Unlike Elijah Muhammad, who rarely
criticized the government following his stretch in prison, Malcolm would
bring a political consciousness to the practice of Islam, one that drew directly
from his personal experience as a prisoner. In sermons and public allocu-
tions, Malcolm would often use prison as a metaphor to describe the plight
of the world's black population, arguing that just as prisoners are expected
to rehabilitate themselves as a condition of release, blacks must transform
themselves as a condition for securing their freedom from oppression.

The Nation of Islam and the Moorish Science Temple experienced a slow
but steady growth in membership in U.S. prisons throughout the 1950s and
early 1960s. These prisoners were largely an enigma, however, due to their
unique cultural and religious traditions, many of which were alien to orthodox Islam.[22] Suffice it to say that these groups were far more American than
they were Islamic.[23] Moorish prisoners celebrated Friday as their Sabbath and

prayed facing east with hands raised, not prostrated. Nation members prayed the same way, though at one point Elijah Muhammad, angry with Arab Muslims, ordered his followers to pray toward Chicago. Neither group recited the Kalmia Shahabad, nor did they practice the Five Pillars of Islam. Both groups fasted during Christmas rather than at Ramadan, and other celebrations, such as the Prophet's birthday, were replaced with rituals specific to the black American experience.[24]

During these years wardens routinely denied Black Muslims the right to openly practice their faith on the ground that it threatened prison security. At issue were the Nation's belief in black supremacy and its distribution of publications urging defiance of prison authorities. This occurred against the background of a national investigation launched by the FBI director J. Edgar Hoover, who suspected the Moorish Science Temple of collaborating with the Japanese during World War II, leading the FBI to infiltrate the group.[25] For these reasons, then, the state itself played a role in politicizing Muslim prisoners over the dual issues of race and religion.[26] In the mid-1950s these tensions were intensified by the confrontational atmosphere of the newly evolving civil rights movement. At this juncture, wardens saw the first glimmers of radicalization in California prisons where Black Muslims were observed training each other in the martial arts and encouraging the use of violence when necessary to defend their religious rights to worship.[27]

Meanwhile, Elijah Muhammad had transformed the Nation of Islam into a broad-based religious movement with more than seventy thousand followers, a good number of them prisoners. When Malcolm X (released from prison in 1952) convinced the great heavyweight boxing champion Cassius Clay to convert to the Nation in 1964—and when the charismatic champ was christened Muhammad Ali by the Honorable Elijah Muhammad—"Black Muslim" became a household term in America. Then in August 1965, the Watts neighborhood of Los Angeles erupted in a momentous four-day riot. Hundreds of young blacks rampaged through the streets shouting, "Burn, baby, burn!" "Civil war!" "Remember Emmett Till!" According to the L.A. police chief, William Parker, the Watts rebellion was instigated by "Black Muslim ex-convicts who fomented general insurrection."[28]

That autumn, seven months after his assassination at New York's Audubon Ballroom, Grove Press released *The Autobiography of Malcolm X*, introducing a generation of readers to Malcolm's tortured journey from pimp to martyr and his final invective stemming from Malcolm's historic visit to Mecca "that only one force can dissolve racial hatred at its root—purified, nonsectarian Islam."[29] James Baldwin's *The Fire Next Time* (1963)—appraising the Nation of Islam and warning that violence would result if white America did not change its attitudes toward blacks—had become a national bestseller; while James Brown rode the top of the R&B charts with "Papa's Got a Brand New Bag." This was the stuff of legend—historic events that would crystallize black pride and radicalism.

Quite naturally, these events gave Black Muslims a formidable recruiting presence behind bars, especially in California, as revealed in the celebrated case of Eldridge Cleaver. Leroy Eldridge Cleaver, a former Los Angeles gang member, was twenty-five years old in 1958 when he began a two- to fourteen-year sentence at San Quentin for charges of assault with intent to murder stemming from the rape of a white woman.[30] Cleaver shared a cell with a prison boxing champion named Butterfly who had recently joined the Nation of Islam. "Butterfly had become a Black Muslim," Cleaver recalled, "and was chiefly responsible for teaching me the Black Muslim philosophy."[31] Over the next several years Cleaver distributed writings by Elijah Muhammad and Malcolm X and became a prodigious writer himself, publishing his first works in the Nation's prison newspaper. In 1963, the minister of San Quentin's Muslim mosque, Booker T. X. (Johnson), was killed by an officer in the prison's high-security Adjustment Center. With the endorsement of Elijah Muhammad's representative in Los Angeles, Cleaver became Johnson's successor and was instructed to impose a firm discipline on the members of the San Quentin mosque in order to avert Muslim-initiated violence following the killing of Booker T.X.

Some black inmates joined the Nation of Islam for its spiritual agenda, and others did so for its principled position on race. Neither of these appealed to Cleaver. Instead, he used the Nation to show California's prisoners that a radical convict political union could work with the outside world to change power relations within the prison, an insight that would later inspire the emergence of California's prison gang system. "To me" Cleaver later wrote, "the language and symbols of religion were nothing but weapons of war."[32] Predictably, authorities soon transferred Cleaver to Folsom Prison in an effort to control his agitation. There, the writing continued and Cleaver eventually found a way to smuggle his articles out of prison where they found a home in San Francisco's burgeoning underground press, including *Ramparts*, a sophisticated muckraker that became an early opponent of the Vietnam War. Cleaver also maintained his association with the Nation and would use these words to describe the organizational sophistication then common to "fishing for converts" among Black Muslims in California prisons:

Soledad, San Quentin, and Folsom were the prisons with the highest concentration of adherents to Islam. . . . Muslims in each prison had organized themselves into a Mosque, with a hierarchy patterned rigidly after the structure of the Mosques in the outside world. Each prison had its inmate minister, captain, Fruit of Islam. . . . During the exercise periods, it was not a rare sight to see several Muslims walking around the yard, each with a potential convert to whom he would be explaining the *Message to the Black Man* as taught by Elijah Muhammad.[33]

Scholars of the period argue that black prisoners were attracted to the Nation of Islam as part of a shifting pattern of deviant social exchanges that provided inmates with an explanation for their criminal behavior by removing individual guilt and shifting it to the oppression caused by white racism.[34] Less cynical observers contend that the Black Muslim faith provided prisoners a rationale for their status, and prisoner-to-prisoner efforts to break the vicious drug/crime cycle, in which many had been trapped, gave them a positive self-identity.[35] The disillusionment with hedonistic lifestyles certainly explains much of Islam's appeal among black prisoners of the era. Beginning in the mid-1960s, the Nation's prison ministry implemented programs to deal with self-destructive behavior, including basic education, "manhood" training concentrating on respect for women, responsible sexual behavior, and drug prevention and life skills management. Efforts also involved visits by evangelists who delivered books and literature to inmates. College correspondence courses were added as were classes in Arabic and Islamic history. Collect-calling services for inmates to telephone families were set up, and halfway houses and employment services were initiated to help reintegrate Muslim ex-cons back into their communities.[36] The net effect of these programs was to make the prison a less closed institution for African American inmates, thereby creating the opportunity for prisoners to develop identities imported from the outside world. It was from this distinctive racial and spiritual context that the U.S. prisoners' rights movement took root, eventually sprouting civil rights litigation challenging prison desegregation and inadequate conditions of confinement.[37]

Thanks to the self-improvement programs, and the emerging prisoners' rights movement, along with Elijah Muhammad's early leadership and the subsequent canonization of Malcolm X (their well-documented falling-out notwithstanding), by the mid-1960s Black Muslims represented the best organized and most articulate group of prisoners in the United States. As the penologist John Irwin recalled, "During the 1960s, Black Muslims became a sizable faction in many prisons, organizing themselves into distinctive groups characterized by a high degree of commitment and discipline among their members."[38] Advances were also being made on the legal front.

* * *

After a long string of prisoners' rights cases in the 1960s, the federal courts held that black supremacy alone was not sufficient to suppress the Black Muslim faith. The courts ruled that the Nation of Islam and Moorish Science Temple constituted established religions; therefore, Nation and Moorish prisoners were allowed the right to practice their religion with the same freedom and privileges as Catholics, Jews, and Protestants. These court decisions expanded religious freedoms for Black Muslims, thereby giving them the rights to receive uncensored religious literature in the mail, to hold group prayer meetings, to shave their heads and be served pork-free meals, and, in some cases, to be segregated from incarcerated "white devils."[39] The resolution of the Black Muslim case meant that the standards applied there must apply to any duly recognized religion, forcing wardens to provide equal protection for all inmates. Moreover, by the end of the 1960s Black Muslims had established a vital presence within the nation's prison system. Not only had they unified black inmate populations around the restorative power of religion, but with their emphasis on hard work and sobriety, Black Muslims also represented the era's prevailing philosophy of rehabilitation. The movement would reach its pinnacle in the late summer of 1971.

Beginning on September 9, 1971, Muslim prisoners swiftly organized themselves in order to protect forty-three guards taken hostage during the legendary Attica prison rebellion in upstate New York. Five grueling days later, during which time three prisoners were stabbed to death after being marked as snitches, twenty-nine prisoners and ten guards were killed by the crossfire of two hundred attacking New York State troopers in a bungled attempt to retake the facility. At this perilous moment, an agreement to end the siege was mediated by two Moorish Science prisoners, Carl Jones-El and Donald Noble, and a loquacious Nation prisoner from the Virgin Islands named Herbert Blyden X.[40] On September 15, the brother of a slain guard appeared on the CBS Evening News to tell Walter Cronkite that he "no longer considered inmates animals" after hearing that Black Muslims had helped save the hostages.[41] Nevertheless, afterward, the riot police roamed the Attica yard, beating and torturing scores of naked inmates, many of whom were seriously wounded.

The Attica rebellion opened a window onto the culture that produced it, revealing deep divisions in American attitudes toward race and imprisonment. Speaking to an NBC News anchorman, John Chancellor, on September 15, Senator Edmund Muskie (D-Maine), the front-runner in the democratic presidential primaries, said, "The Attica tragedy is more stark proof that something is terribly wrong with America. We have reached the point where men would rather die than live another day in America. When we are told there is no constituency for prison reform, we must become that constituency."[42] Two days later the Weather Underground launched a retaliatory strike on the New York Department of Corrections in Albany, exploding a bomb near the office of Commissioner Russell Oswald. The communiqué accompanying the attack blamed the Attica riot on Governor Nelson Rockefeller, claiming that the rebellion demonstrated "how a society run by white racists maintains its control with white supremacy being the main question white people have to face."[43] Later that day, in a taped conversation with an aide in the Oval Office, President Richard Nixon cynically described the Attica riot as "basically a black thing."[44]

Some blame was also directed toward the academy and its obligation for promoting prison reform. On October 3, the *New York Times* leveled a stinging indictment against the all-but-moribund state of academic criminology. "The inmates at Attica considered their conditions so intolerable," wrote a reviewer of Leon Radzinowicz and Marvin Wolfgang's *The Criminal in Society* (1971), "that they were willing to die to dramatize them. This seems a far cry from the analysis of prison conditions in this study (by Gresham M. Sykes). . . . The criminologists' studies seem to miss the strong racial and political elements of convicts' discontent."[45]

Completely overlooked in this national debate was the role of Islam. Yet at a time when 1960s activists were deserting politics to chant the mantras of new religious movements, the Black Muslims of Attica had asserted a courageous and profoundly constructive political stance by drawing on African American people's age-old resistance to racism and oppression, not unlike Gandhi's satyagraha struggle waged from an Indian prison four decades earlier. The Black Muslim faith was no longer an individual means of coping with the pains of imprisonment, but it was now a collective instrument of criminal justice peacemaking—peacemaking, it must be said, carried out under the conditions of a prison riot involving more than a thousand hostile felons armed with makeshift weapons. After Attica, wardens relaxed existing restrictions against practicing Islam, and Black Muslims became a stabilizing force in many prisons.[46] As Muslim identities intensified among black prisoners in the years ahead, the trend spilled over into the massive racial ghettos of Chicago, New York, and Los Angeles, affecting a symbiosis between the prison and street culture.[47] As a result, prison cellblocks began to mirror ghetto neighborhoods, complete with their own rituals of gang solidarity and rough justice.[48]

* * *

Meanwhile a different story was unfolding on the West Coast, one that would ultimately reverse the achievements of Islam behind bars and create a form of prison-based terrorism. Eldridge Cleaver was transferred from Folsom to Soledad Prison in 1966 and then paroled to San Francisco where, in the tradition of Malcolm X, he pursued a vision of severing all contact with the criminal underworld and becoming a valued member of the black community. "When I stepped out of Soledad State Prison into San Francisco in 1966," he would write, "I sat my feet down in the center of the Haight/Ashbury. I embraced it, wallowed in it."[49] Cleaver founded a Haight-area cultural center known as the Black House and became a staff writer at *Ramparts*. Further drawing on his prison experience, Cleaver quickly distinguished himself as a master of clandestine communications.

In February 1967, Cleaver appeared on a radio talk show and caught the attention of Huey P. Newton and Bobby Seale, founders of the Black Panther Party for Self-Defense. "We ran down to the radio station that night," Seale recalled. "Huey related to Eldridge as Malcolm X, coming out of prison. Eldridge could rap and . . . he could write. . . . This nigger could write. Huey couldn't write . . . but understood the need for a media."[50] Cleaver joined the Black Panthers and was appointed their Minister of Information. Together with other ex-cons, Cleaver began the party's mimeographed newspaper, *The Black Panther*, which rapidly grew to a circulation of more than one hundred thousand copies a week, the largest circulation of any of the Bay Area's underground broadsheets. As the paper's editor, Cleaver challenged the basic legitimacy of prisons, thereby echoing Malcolm's argument that convicts rarely feel an obligation to pay any debt to society because they feel *they* are the ones who have been wronged. An early issue of the paper carried the Panthers' ten-point program, including one adopted from the Black Muslims: "We want freedom for all believers in Islam in prison or in houses of correction."[51] Supporting Cleaver's efforts to establish a black revolutionary presence behind bars, Huey Newton declared that "as more blacks are put in prison, more black leaders will be made."[52] Although *The Black Panther* was banned from California prisons, it was nevertheless smuggled onto cellblocks where Cleaver's articles found a receptive audience.

But Cleaver was moving beyond that audience. Within a year of his release from prison, Cleaver lectured at Harvard, appeared on nationally televised talk shows, met with New York Senator Bobby Kennedy (whose face reminded Cleaver of a "nighttime burglar who had been in prison for at least ten years"), and built bridges with the Bay Area's white counterculture that were not insignificant to the success of the Black Panther Party.[53] On April 15, 1967—with the "Summer of Love" about to flower into psychedelic splendor—Cleaver joined a massive anti-Vietnam War protest through the streets of San Francisco to Kezar Stadium, where he appeared onstage with Coretta Scott King and Julian Bond to address a crowd of seventy-five thousand who had been warmed up earlier in the day by Country Joe and the Fish, Judy Collins, Big Brother and the Holding Company, and other bands.[54]

As his media skills developed, Cleaver transformed his legend into a cult. Recognizing the need for what Bobby Seale called "a centralized symbol of the leadership of black people," Cleaver arranged for a photographer to shoot an image of Huey Newton posing regally in a giant wicker chair, dressed in a black leather jacket and beret, with a shotgun in his right hand and a tribal spear in his left.[55] Along with the iconic image of Che Guevara, this photo became an essential symbol of the late 1960s that would grace every radical's wall from San Francisco to Paris.

On February 28, 1968, McGraw-Hill released *Soul on Ice*, Cleaver's prison memoir written mostly during his days at Folsom. As with *Malcolm X Speaks*, Cleaver's memoir was a work of spiritual autobiography that became a defining book of the times. "*Soul on Ice is* the sixties," wrote Ishmael Reed in the book's updated preface. "The smell of protest, anger, tear gas, and the sound of skull-cracking billy clubs, helicopters, and revolution is present in its pages."[56] *Soul on Ice* was as much an allegorical masterpiece on black masculinity as it was a concise description of the prevailing attitudes held by black convicts in America. It was also a bold repudiation of the Nation of Islam. Back in 1963, Cleaver and other Black Muslims at San Quentin and Folsom had separated themselves from the Nation in a dispute over financial support for legal fees involving Muslim cases in Los Angeles. The rifts deepened when Malcolm X announced his break from the Nation of Islam on March 8, 1964, citing the Nation's "rigid religious teachings" as a cause. Many black prisoners would follow his path, leading to Islam's precipitous decline. "At a secret meeting of the Muslims in Folsom [in 1965]," wrote Cleaver, "I announced that I was no longer a follower of Elijah Muhammad, that I was throwing my support behind Brother Malcolm. I urged everyone there to think the matter over and make a choice, because it was no longer possible to ride two horses at the same time."[57]

Soul on Ice sold more than a million copies after its release and the *New York Times* christened it 1968's Book of the Year, bringing Cleaver national recognition as the potential intellectual and political heir to Malcolm X.[58] Tall, handsome, and wickedly articulate, Cleaver would emerge as arguably the most charismatic black figure of the era. Accordingly, *Soul on Ice* was banned from California prisons. In his riveting chronicle of California's radical prison movement, Eric Cummins writes that *Soul on Ice* "slowly found its way back into Soledad, Folsom, and San Quentin prisons, anxiously anticipated and then secretly smuggled in. . . . The teachings San Quentin black prisoners wanted were less and less Muslim, except for the late speeches of Malcolm X. Cleaver commanded great respect inside the walls among the more radical black inmates."[59] One inmate of the era told Cummins that *Soul on Ice* gave rise to "a more terroristic style of political practice."[60]

The year 1968 also brought an expanding crisis of police repression against the Black Panthers and a concurrent shift toward urban terrorism in response. On April 6, as riots erupted across urban America in the aftermath of Martin Luther King's assassination two days earlier, Cleaver was involved in a spectacular shootout between the Black Panthers and the Oakland police department. "So we started the fight," Cleaver recalled years later to the historian Henry Louis Gates Jr.:

> There were fourteen of us. We went down into the area of Oakland where the violence was the worst, a few blocks away from where Huey Newton had killed that cop [Oakland policeman John Frey in 1967] so we dealt with them when they came upon us. We were well armed, and we had a shootout that lasted an hour and a half. I will tell anybody that that was the first experience of freedom I had. The repressive forces couldn't put their hand on me because we were shooting it out with them for one hour and a half. Three police officers got wounded. None of them got killed; I got wounded.[61]

When the shooting stopped, Cleaver emerged from the basement of a burning house, naked and bleeding with his arms in the air. Beside him was the young Panther Bobby Hutton, who moments later would be shot and killed by the police. Cleaver was arrested and taken to the Vacaville Medical Facility where he was treated for a buckshot wound to the foot and charged with violating his parole by being a felon in possession of a firearm, associating with other felons, and failing to cooperate with his parole officer. Public outcry over Bobby Hutton's death sparked a flurry of protests and a letter to the editor of the *New York Times*, which was signed by James Baldwin, Ossie Davis, Leroi Jones, Norman Mailer, and Susan Sontag. Confined to a wheelchair at Vacaville, Cleaver wrote a series of theoretical essays on American society, social change, and prison. In one, "The Decline of the Muslims," Cleaver reiterated the point that Black Muslims had become a minor force in prison following the split between Elijah Muhammad and Malcolm X.

"What black inmates now look to with rising hopes," Cleaver concluded, "is the cry for Black Power and an elaboration of its details in the name of Malcolm X."[62] In a sign of the times, after only nine weeks of incarceration Cleaver was released on $50,000 bail based on a court ruling that Cleaver had been arrested for political views expressed in his Kezar Stadium speech, rather than for his act of domestic terrorism: a ninety-minute gun battle with police officers.[63]

Throughout 1968, Cleaver continued his evolution from the black consciousness of his prison days, to the African American nationalism of the Black Panthers, to a broader Marxist interpretation of social revolution involving a coalition with white radicals. This, of course, made him especially vulnerable to law enforcement. On September 8, J. Edgar Hoover called the Panthers "the greatest threat to the internal security of the country," leading to his instigation of the infamous COINTELPRO against the Panthers—a series of covert and often illegal acts by the FBI with the explicit intent to "expose, disrupt, misdirect, discredit, or otherwise neutralize" activities of the movement.[64] On September 10, Huey Newton was convicted of manslaughter in the case of the Oakland police officer John Frey and was hauled off to San Quentin. The next day, Cleaver was invited to teach an experimental course on racism to three hundred students at the University of California, Berkeley, outraging then-California Governor Ronald Reagan. "If Eldridge Cleaver is allowed to teach our children," said Reagan, "they may come home one night and slit our throats."[65] Undaunted, Cleaver shot back at the governor in a letter: "Who in the fuck do you think you are, telling me I can't talk, telling the students they cannot have me deliver ten lectures? In fact, my desire now is to deliver *twenty* lectures."[66] The University of California board of regents voted to bar Cleaver from the campus, igniting a massive student protest and leading the faculty senate to vote 668 to 114 to defy the regents.[67] The lectures proceeded as planned.

Riding the waves of critical acclaim for *Soul on Ice*, Cleaver ran for president of the United States on the Peace and Freedom Party ticket with a rotating assemblage of white radicals as his running mate, including at one point the Yippie Jerry Rubin whose advice to teenagers for kicking off the revolution was "kill your parents."[68] Cleaver toured U.S. college campuses during the 1968 campaign, electrifying audiences with speeches on Vietnam and revolutionary change and ultimately receiving eighty-three thousand votes in the general election, despite the fact that Cleaver was only thirty-four years old and too young to run for president in the first place.[69] Cleaver told his audiences that he had no prospects of winning the election. "As a matter of fact," he declared, "if I were elected, I would not enter the White House. I would send a wrecking crew there to burn the motherfucker down."[70] Cleaver was still on parole, however, and in late November the courts overturned the decision granting him bail in the Oakland shoot-out. Facing a long prison term on six felony counts of assault with intent to kill police officers, and fearing that he would be murdered if he returned to prison, Cleaver jumped bail and fled the United States for a life of exile.

But his legacy as a prison radical would endure well into the next decade. "More than any other prisoner," Cummins concludes, "it had been Eldridge Cleaver who had drawn major sectors of the counterculture into the movement against California's prisons. Owing largely to this single charismatic convict, California became unique in the nation in the degree to which the prison movement came to dominate radical politics. . . . And more than any other book, it was *Soul on Ice* that had confused these cultural radicals into thinking convicts, all convicts, were their soul-mates and could be their leaders."[71]

Yet the saga of California's prison radicals had just begun. Although Cleaver was unquestionably a prison radical of historic significance—breaking important ground in terms of exporting social networks from the prison to the community, clandestine communications, and most certainly charismatic leadership—he came from an era (circa 1958 to 1966) when convicts still lived by the code of "do your own time." Prisoner radicalization had not yet hardened into a broad multicultural movement. That was about to change, ushering in unprecedented waves of turmoil that would lay the foundation for America's imprisonment binge of the late 1980s and beyond.

* * *

Three far-reaching developments would alter California prisons at the dawn of the 1970s, further diminishing Islam's influence among prisoners that began with Malcolm's break from the Nation of Islam. First was the emergence of inmate "study groups." In response to a revised section of the California penal code involving inmate rights to receive political literature in the mail, gangs as diverse as the Mexican Mafia, the newly formed Aryan Brotherhood of San Quentin, and the Black Guerrilla Family seized the opportunity and established their own secret educational networks. In this way, ordinary convicts were transformed into students of militancy, which brought a combination of criminal mentality and strident ideology into yard politics, often fueled by drugs. Imported reading material, a mainstay of convict ideology, accentuated the racial differences between prisoners, thereby amplifying the belligerent effects of gang rivalries. These rivalries were further intensified by a second development. On the heels of the Black Muslim cases of the late 1960s, other racial groups applied for expanded religious privileges, including the right to racial segregation. This marked the point at which the Aryan Brotherhood began to openly display Nazi tattoos, publicly intimidating blacks and Chicanos with their own "white is beautiful" and "black devil" argot.[72] Thus was born the political gangs of California prisons. And with them came an escalation of fights and yard attacks. The gangs led to an intensified radicalization among prisoners, creating the final development: a rapid increase in terrorist-related gang warfare.

On January 13, 1970, three Black Muslim prisoners were shot and killed on the exercise yard at Soledad by a tower guard attempting to break up a relatively minor fistfight between a Muslim and a member of the Aryan Brotherhood.[73] Three days later, a young, inexperienced white guard named John Mills was beaten and thrown to his death from the third tier of a close-custody cellblock in Soledad. The murder investigation focused on W. L. Nolen, one of the Muslims killed on January 13. In an earlier stretch at San Quentin, Nolen was the prison boxing champion and a close friend of a twenty-eight-year-old prisoner with an extensive disciplinary record named George Jackson, a member of the Capone Gang from Los Angeles then serving an indeterminate one-year-to-life sentence for a gas station robbery involving $70. Nolen and Jackson were members of a Soledad study group that combined Marxist ideology with martial arts training. (It would evolve into the revolutionary Black Guerrilla Family.) Jackson and two other black inmates were charged in the slaying of Officer Mills and they became known in the news as the Soledad Brothers. Picking up where Eldridge Cleaver left off, Jackson's "blood for blood" strategy of deadly retaliation would be seen by California's radical prisoners as the first shot fired in a class war to bring the prisons down from within. "He was a mean, rotten son of a bitch," recalled John Irwin, who was acquainted with Jackson through the prisoners' rights movement at San Quentin. "He was a bully. He did a lot of things which were in the right direction, but he also was an unscrupulous bully."[74]

The case against the Soledad Brothers was moved to San Francisco, and Jackson and the other two defendants were transferred under high security to San Quentin's Adjustment Center (AC, a prison within a maximum-security prison) to await trial. There, Jackson assembled a series of letters he had written to his family and lawyer dating back to 1964 (adding some written since the Soledad incident), telling his personal story of imprisonment and calling for convicts to unite with liberation armies of the world to wage urban guerrilla warfare as a means for effecting social change. Jackson's letters were published by Coward, McCann in the fall of 1970 as *Soledad Brother*, with a foreword by the French author and playwright Jean Genet. Jackson wrote with uncommon fury: "This monster—the monster they've engendered in me will return to torment its maker, from the grave, the pit, the profoundest pit. Hurl me into the next existence, the descent into hell won't turn me. . . . I'm going to charge them reparations in blood. I'm going to charge them like a mad-denned, wounded, rogue elephant, ears flared, trunk raised, and trumpet blaring. . . . War without terms."[75]

Although *Soledad Brother* was declared contraband for California's prisoners after its publication, in the free world it became a sensation and brought Jackson international acclaim among black militants, white activists, college students, and a veritable catalog of cultural icons including Jane Fonda, Pete Seeger, Noam Chomsky, Allen Ginsberg, Michel Foucault, Tom Hayden, Bob Dylan (whose 1971 single "George Jackson" recounted such bibliographic details as "He wouldn't take shit from no one/He wouldn't bow down or kneel/Authorities they hated him/Because he was just too real"), and the UCLA philosophy professor Angela Davis, a close personal friend of Jackson who would play a pivotal role in creating his legend. But more to the point is what happened inside California prisons.

After the Soledad incident, as George Jackson became a hero of mythical proportions among black convicts, the clandestine study groups of California prisons underwent a critical transition. No longer held in secret, they moved into the open—often en masse with fifty inmates or more—onto prison yards, thereby emboldening the gangs and making radicalization both easier for leaders to organize and ultimately more dangerous. Of this period, the sociologist James Aho writes that leaders of the American radical right "began to see the opportunity of winning into their fold the tough and violent cadres they need to further their revolution." As one leader said, "I brought 20 convicts out of San Quentin with me. They became 'Third Reich Missionaries.'"[76]

Even though he was confined to a high-security unit inside San Quentin, Jackson was able to tell a reporter from the *New York Times Magazine* that he was actively revolutionizing California's convicts "through education and study."[77] The tone of the "educational literature" imported into prisons was also becoming more dangerous because inmates were now receiving pamphlets not only calling for overt acts of prison revolt and the killing of guards, but also providing detailed instructions for manufacturing weapons and bombs. Prison had become a battleground for racial grievances. Inmate assaults against guards jumped from thirty-two systemwide in 1969 to eighty-four in 1973. Nine guards and twenty-four inmates would be killed in California prisons in 1970 and 1971.[78]

In July 1970, seven black inmates were charged in the stabbing death of another guard at Soledad. All seven were members of a black studies group. On August 7, George Jackson's seventeen-year-old brother, Jonathan, rose from his seat during a trial at the Marin County Hall of Justice in San Rafael, California, and announced, "All right, gentlemen, I'm takin' over." He drew a sawed-off shotgun from his coat and freed three black San Quentin prisoners standing trial—handing them pistols—and took a judge, a prosecutor, and three women jurors hostage, demanding the release of the Soledad Brothers. Jackson, the judge, and two prisoners were killed as they fled the courthouse. Authorities later determined that the sawed-off shotgun used in the blood-bath was purchased in Angela Davis's name, a crime punishable by death under California law. J. Edgar Hoover promptly designated Angela Davis the most wanted criminal in America, as support rallies for Davis broke out from Berkeley to Boston and then from East Berlin to Johannesburg, South Africa. "They want to send me to the death chamber to make a point," Davis would tell a reporter.[79] After her capture in New York on October 13, 1970, President Nixon went on national television to congratulate Hoover on the arrest. Two weeks later, Herbert Marcuse, celebrated Father of the New Left, filed an appeal with the California courts warning that "the case of Angela Davis has [only] served to intensify still further the hatred and hostility against radical dissent in this country."[80]

George Jackson was still in San Quentin's AC unit, awaiting trial for his role in the killing of Officer Mills at Soledad. By this point, Jackson had spent a total of seven years in solitary confinement for his long list of disciplinary infractions. Months of isolation in the AC unit, coupled with the recent death of his brother at the Marin County Courthouse and the capital murder charges facing his friend Angela Davis, may have pushed George Jackson to the psychological breaking point. Eric Cummins's interviews with prisoners who knew Jackson in the AC unit indicate that he spent hours sitting on his bunk with a folded blanket for a pillow at his back, his feet stretched across the commode, drinking cold coffee, smoking cigarettes, and feverishly using a pencil to write another book of letters calling for the creation of small-armed cells of revolutionaries capable of waging civil war against the U.S. government (published posthumously in 1972 as *Blood in My Eye*). In these pages, Jackson predicted that his death would evolve from a prison escape. The rest is well known.

On Saturday, August 21, 1971, Jackson used a smuggled Astra 9-mm semiautomatic pistol to free several black prisoners in adjoining cells, and he then took six officers and two white inmate tier-tenders hostage. Ten minutes later, Jackson bolted down the tier with the gun and a guard's keys in hand, then ran through the lobby and onto the yard, where he was killed by a single shot in the back by a gun-rail officer. When the dust settled, three guards and the two tier-tenders were found dead in Jackson's cell. They had been shot in the head, strangled with electrical cord, and their throats had been slit with razor blades. Two of the victims had their jugular veins gouged out with a pencil.

* * *

News of Jackson's death spread like fire across dry land. The next morning, when prisoners at Attica were released from their cells to line up for the march to breakfast, officers were greeted by somber inmates who moved silently and lined up in rows of two with a black convict at the head of each row. Many of them wore black armbands. They marched silently to the chow hall, grabbed their trays, and sat quietly at their tables but did not eat. What officers were witnessing was not only a day of mourning for George Jackson but also a protest against the official story of his death: that Jackson had somehow hidden the gun in his Afro hairdo after talking to his attorney in the San Quentin visiting area.[81] "The most direct effect of the George Jackson murder," wrote Howard Zinn in *A People's History of the United States*, "was the rebellion at Attica prison in September 1971—a rebellion that came from deep grievances but was raised to the boiling point by the news about George Jackson."[82]

Jackson's legacy is hard to calculate because he affected so many—politicians, wardens, and guards; prisoners, activists, and students; philosophers and poets. After the AC incident, San Quentin, Soledad, Folsom, and the Deuel Vocational Institute went on total lockdown. Enraged guards, determined to avenge the deaths at San Quentin and Attica, set out to destroy inmate black power, leading to a sinister alliance between guards and white racist prisoners. Inmates associated with Jackson were rounded up, often beaten, and isolated in San Quentin's AC unit, which became a prototype for the new high-technology "control unit" model of solitary confinement, leading first to the construction of the Security Housing Unit (SHU) at Pelican Bay, California, and then to the federal Administrative Maximum-Security Unit (ADMAX, or "Supermax") at Florence, Colorado, which would later be used to incarcerate al-Qaeda terrorists.

In their campaign to isolate radicals, California wardens cracked down on inmate contact with visitors and suppressed mail privileges and access to books. Around the time that the Rolling Stones immortalized Angela Davis in their tribute single "Sweet Black Angel," her writings became contraband in California prisons, along with those by Malcolm X. Governor Reagan and the legislature increased law-enforcement funding for investigating prison radicals and slashed budgets for education, counseling, vocational training and library services, marking the beginning of a national withdrawal from rehabilitation and a return to raw punishment. Within this context Richard Nixon exploited his association with crime control to win popular support. On October 23, 1972, the president told a New York audience, "You can be sure that the age of permissiveness is gone"—prefiguring the formation of the Drug Enforcement Administration (DEA) in 1973 and a dramatic expansion of the federal government's role in narcotics enforcement, thereby revitalizing Nixon's "war on drugs" and ultimately leading to historic rates of incarceration and the creation of a permanent American underclass.[83]

Inmate study groups retreated into the convict underground, thereby increasing the flow of contraband reading material into prisons and creating even more sophisticated forms of smuggling. After San Quentin and Attica, many radical inmates in America became little more than political gangsters with utterly no interest in spiritual redemption. By 1974—as heroin flooded the ghettos of Harlem, Los Angeles, and Oakland to meet the demands of returning Vietnam vets—the Nation of Islam also descended into a spiritual quagmire of thuggery and deceit. In April, San Francisco police arrested four members of the Black Self-Help Movement & Storage Company, a Nation of Islam outreach program for ex-cons, and charged them with twenty-three execution-style murders of white victims, leading to the longest criminal trial in California history. Each defendant was sentenced to life imprisonment, taking with them the last vestiges of hope for the prisoners' rights movement.[84] In this regard, *Soledad Brother*, the gold standard in smuggled convict literature, would create a new paradigm of prisoner radicalization— one in which George Jackson emerged as the black man's Nietzsche. "Forget that Westernized backward stuff about god," Jackson wrote.

I curse god, the whole idea of a benevolent supreme being is the product of a tortured, demented mind. It is a labored, mindless attempt to explain away ignorance, a tool to keep people of low mentality and no means of production in line. How could there be a *benevolent* supreme controlling a world like this? He would have to be malevolent, not benevolent. Look around you, evil rules supreme. God would be my enemy. The theory of a good, just god is a false idea, a thing for imbeciles and old women, and, of course, Negroes. It's a relic of the past when men made words and mindless defenses for such things as sea serpents, magic and flat earths.[85]

The most radical prison gang of all, the Black Guerrilla Family ("one of the most effective and deadly revolutionary forces in society," as the U.S. Justice Department would call it) and its various spin-offs, began to terrorize California institutions and strengthen its ties to militants on the outside.[86] When Donald DeFreeze of Soledad's "Black Cultural Association" study group escaped from prison in the spring of 1973 and formed the Symbionese Liberation Army with white BCA prison volunteers living in a Berkeley commune—and then with them committed assassination, bank robberies, murder, bombing, extortion, and the kidnapping of the newspaper heiress Patty Hearst—he completed the work begun by Eldridge Cleaver and George Jackson to establish convict links with terrorist groups of the free world.

The steps taken to rein in California's prison radicals in the early 1970s would come to dominate U.S. penal policy in the years ahead. Innovative programs that once helped prisoners succeed on parole—education, work release, and drug treatment—were severely reduced if not wiped out altogether. Federal law made drug offenders and prisoners serving life sentences ineligible for educational Pell grants. In 1994 Congress passed legislation totally barring inmates from higher education. Great works of literature were banished from prison libraries, leaving shelf upon shelf of juvenile fiction appealing to the lowest common denominator of convict mentality. Striped uniforms returned and chain gangs reappeared on the sides of rural highways, evoking images of the Southern penal farms modeled on the old slave plantation system. A section of President Bill Clinton's 1996 welfare-reform policy barred ex-convicts from receiving Medicaid, public housing, and Section 8 vouchers. These cutbacks fell disproportionately on young African American men at a time when incarceration rates for black males in the United States were skyrocketing.

All the while, criminologists kept their backs turned to the problem of prisoner radicalization, as they had done at Attica and San Quentin. Irwin argued that criminologists "lost contact with the prison after the mid-1960s . . . and shifted their attention from prisoners and criminals to police and the law."[87] Into this void came an abstract positivism locating the causes of crime in individual human deficiencies. This was the criminology of "denatured causes," as the prominent criminologist Jock Young would call it, "of defective individuals and deficit cultures. . . . It was a criminology which had lost contact with reality."[88] Out of this intellectual sinkhole arose a tendency to demonize and to deny the rationality of those branded as terrorists. Drawing on medical metaphors, terrorists became "pathological" or "infected" by radical ideas, a description that lies in stark contrast to research showing that terrorists are surprisingly normal in terms of mental health.[89]

No writer of the era pushed back against this ill-conceived notion better than George Jackson did. "The textbooks on criminology like to advance the idea that the prisoners are mentally defective," Jackson wrote in *Soledad Brother.* "There is only the merest suggestion that the system itself is at fault. Penologists regard prisons as asylums. . . . But what can we say about these asylums since *none* of the inmates are ever cured. Since in every instance they are sent out of the prison more damaged physically and mentally than when they entered. . . Do you continue to investigate the inmate? Where does administrative responsibility begin? [W]e can then burn *all* of the criminology and penology libraries and direct our attention where it will do some good."[90]

And when it was all said and done—when the repressive policies were in place, when rehabilitation was obliterated and reform no longer an option for prisoners, when criminals no longer mattered to criminologists, and inmate populations came to embody a sea of black and brown faces—Islam rose from the ruins to once again become a major force in American prisons.

3

Prisoner Radicalization after 9/11

Following the tumultuous era of Attica and the Soledad Brothers, the prison became a central institution in American society, integral to its politics, economy, and culture. Between 1976 and 2000, the United States built on average one new prison each week, and the number of incarcerated Americans increased tenfold. With more than 2.3 million inmates—mostly black and Hispanic—in federal and state prisons, America became the world's leading jailer, surpassing even China. Related to this unparalleled growth came a silencing of prisoners, brought on not only by the shrinking of individual identities within the sea of mass incarceration, but also by legislation banning prisoners with "anti-establishment" views from having access to the media.[1] There would be no iconic black men like Malcolm X, Eldridge Cleaver, or George Jackson during this era.[2] Nor would Black Nationalist groups create icons as they had done before. The radicalization of prisoners ratcheted down considerably during this period, but it still simmered on—to be ignited by 9/11 and the U.S. war on terrorism.

In the United States, prisoner radicalization is defined as "the process by which inmates adopt extreme views, including beliefs that violent measures need to be taken for political or religious purposes."[3] Researchers had little interest in the matter until after the 9/11 attacks. Central to this concern was the discovery of an al-Qaeda training manual entitled *Military Studies in the Jihad (Holy War) against the Tyrants*, seized during a 2000 police raid on a safe house in Manchester, England. Known in intelligence circles as the "Manchester document," the manual identified Western prisoners as candidates for conversion to Islam because they may harbor hostility toward their governments.[4] Prisons had certainly become a matter of interest to al-Qaeda. During a September 2000 interview on an Arab-language television station, Osama bin Laden issued a call for jihad in order to release the "brothers in jail everywhere."[5]

Since then, Islam has become the fastest growing religion among prisoners in Europe and North America.[6] France is especially instructive. Roughly 8 percent of the French population is Muslim, yet Muslims make up an astounding 80 percent of some French prisons.[7] Experts estimate that among those who seek religion while imprisoned in the United States, an equally astounding 80 percent turn to the Muslim faith.[8] The yearly number of conversions to Islam in municipal, state, and federal correctional institutions within the United States is estimated at 30,000 or perhaps as many as 40,000.[9] Based on these estimates, some 350,000 American prisoners have converted to Islam since 2001.

Although blacks still predominate in U.S. prisons, more Hispanics and whites are converting to the religion as well, contributing to a growing belief among prisoners that Christianity has failed to serve their needs. Meanwhile, Moorish Science Temple and the Nation of Islam (which moderated its racial views following the 1975 death of Elijah Muhammad and moved toward orthodox Islam, thereby giving it an international appeal) are now competing for followers with Sunni, Shiite, and Sufi strains of the religion—Sunni Islam being the largest faction. Nation and Moorish spin-off groups have also proliferated, leading to such esoteric Black Nationalist outfits as the 5% Nation of Islam, the Universal Zulu Nation, and the United Nuwaubian Nation of Moors. Since the early 1980s, gangs like the Vice Lords and the Gangster Disciples have sought recognition as "Muslim circles" so that they can hold their own worship services inside prison chapels. Wardens have commonly denied these requests, however, contending that the gangs were using religion as a front to commit crimes, recruit inmates, and intimidate other prisoners. This development has evolved into what chaplains call "Prison Islam," groups that are known for using religious medallions and tattoos, along with selective verses from the Koran, to draw recruits from gang subcultures. As tensions have grown between the various groups in recent years, Prison Islam factions have increasingly used violence and fierce intragroup loyalties to maintain internal security. For prisoners who follow Muslim teachings under these conditions, they discover only a gang's version of Islam, which has little to do with the true faith.

Events outside the prison have also brought about an evolutionary inmate movement that opposes Prison Islam and other forms of extremism. Starting in the early 1980s, the Nation of Islam began to reclaim some of the moral ground it had sacrificed during the mid-1970s by becoming more politically engaged. In the early 1990s, this activist impulse was propelled by the rise of urban hip-hop music and the release of Spike Lee's *Malcolm X*. Later selected for preservation by the Library of Congress for its cultural and historical significance, in 1992 the film was heralded as one of the great screen biographies of all time. "Celebrating the sweep of an American life," enthused the film critic Roger Ebert, "that bottomed out in prison before its hero reinvented himself."[10] Because Islam, prisons, and hip-hop share a deeply intertwined history, Muslim prisoners found new cultural spheres for recruiting inmates into their folds, thereby creating a resurgent interest in reinventing black manhood through Malcolm's brand of purified, nonsectarian Islam. The works of Malcolm X and Angela Davis once again became relevant to black prisoners in America, and then to the world. Of this black renaissance, the eminent African American scholar Manning Marable surmised that "Malcolm X represents the most important bridge between the American people and more than one billion Muslims throughout the world."[11] By the time the Arab Spring of 2011 rolled around, thousands of young Muslim inmates had become part of a global hip-hop generation—a generation that is caught up between many cultures and countries, with Islam serving as the means to transcend all of these cultures by subordinating them to a sacred identity.[12]

* * *

Due to the rapid growth of Islam behind bars, occurring against the backdrop of lingering post-9/11 fear, research on prisoner radicalization became a classic "hot button" issue, prompting the president of the American Society of Criminology to pronounce it a "difficult and contentious" area of study.[13] It is contentious, I would argue, precisely because it is difficult. Conducting primary research on prisoner radicalization is nearly impossible due to widespread official reluctance to allow researchers access to prisons, often for spurious reasons. My own efforts are a case in point. Prior to being granted permission to study Islamic extremism in California and Florida prisons, the New York State prison system instantly denied my research request with an automated e-mail reply, claiming that it did not have adequate resources to support the project. After a lengthy review, the Bureau of Prisons turned down the research, claiming that it was "too political." Another state denied all contact with prisoners because the research did not include the radicalization of Catholics, Protestants, and Buddhists.

Complicating matters, some of the world's most innovative thinkers on Islamic extremism have entered the fray with a fixed point of view. The acclaimed social anthropologist Scott Atran is the best example. In his sweeping international study, *Talking to the Enemy*, Atran identifies the role of prisoner radicalization in the formation of both Al-Qaeda in Iraq and the terrorist cell responsible for the Madrid train bombings. He argues that there are "many millions of people who express sympathy with Al Qaeda or other forms of violent political expression that support terrorism. There are, however, only some thousands who show willingness to actually commit violence. They almost invariably go on to violence in small groups . . . consisting mostly of friends and some kin within specific 'scenes': neighborhoods, schools, workplaces, common leisure activities and . . . online chat rooms."[14] Even though there are "many millions of people" who hold radical views and "some thousands" who will act on them, Atran ignores the lessons of Iraq and Madrid by suggesting that U.S. prisons are one "scene" we need not worry about. For Atran, concern about radicalized U.S. prisoners turning to terrorism is based on nothing more than "hype and hysteria."[15] Atran makes this assertion even though his research does not include a study of American prisoners, let alone their sympathy with al-Qaeda or their willingness to commit violence. There is no evidence that the anthropologist has even set foot inside a prison.

Given these problems, one can only report research claims and counter-claims and then cite the record. My own research shows that it is a mistake to glibly dismiss concerns about prisoner radicalization in the United States as "hype and hysteria." Nor should the United States ignore lessons from abroad. To the contrary, the same radicalizing forces are at work in American prisons as those working in European and Middle Eastern prisons—yet they operate on a different cultural frequency. I argue that the number of prisoners who actually graduate to terrorist acts are remarkably few, but their actions are nonetheless serious. Moreover, the radicalization of prisoners is a problem unlike any other faced by criminal justice administrators today—or at any other time in history.

Research on Islam in prison after 9/11 is divided into three warring camps. The first camp takes an alarmist stance, arguing that Western prisons have become incubators for radical Islam and terrorist ideology. One prominent study claims that because Islam feeds on resentment and anger all too preva-lent in American prisons, it poses a threat of "unknown magnitude to the national security of the U.S." because "*every* radicalized prisoner becomes a potential terrorist threat."[16] Similar concerns have been raised in Europe. In a report on the British prison system, the RAND Corporation found that "con-temporary violent Jihadists can and will seek out new recruits in the prison environment."[17] Another study shows that prisons are "an important recruit-ing ground for Islamic radicals in Britain, and perhaps the most sophisti-cated recruitment system for jihadis in Spain."[18] Still another researcher con-cludes that European prisons are an ideal setting for recruitment into Islamic terrorist networks. Just as prisons are "schools for crime," in which petty criminals "graduate" into more serious criminal careers, so, too, are prisons "universities" for advanced training in terrorism.[19]

The alarmist's message has found a sympathetic audience among poli-cymakers, including U.S. Senator Rand Paul (R-KY) who in 2011 cited the fact that many prisoners convert to Islam as a cause for blocking legislation that would make synthetic drugs illegal. There has been "much discussion in the Senate regarding combatting radical Islam," said the senator. "Notably, Islam is currently the fastest-growing religion among prisoners in the United States. Sending people—often young people—who may already come from broken homes and difficult family situations into a brutal prison environment is potentially a breeding ground for radicalization."[20]

Also supporting the alarmist view is Robert Hood, a former warden at the federal Supermax in Colorado. Among those within custody during his watch were the Unabomber Theodore Kaczynski; one of the Oklahoma City bombing accomplices, Terry Nichols; and the first World Trade Center bomber, Ramzi Yousef. The shoe-bomber Richard Reid was also there. "Is [prison] a breeding ground?" Hood rhetorically asked a reporter. "Without question I think that it is—it always has been." He further explained:

> Richard Reid—I spoke to him every day. Did he become radical—a radical Islamist—while in a U.K. prison? In my opinion, yes. If you look at those characteristics of conversion, he had a personal crisis, he couldn't handle himself very well in the prison setting and he was searching for identity. . . . If I was going to recruit someone, Richard Reid is the kind of guy you want to grab. There are some really susceptible people who want to find a cause, and they're all over the place. I'm not suggesting that all of them are going to fit these characteristics, but if you took 2.3 million inmates in the country, a good percentage of them would be susceptible.[21]

As compelling as it is, there are problems with the alarmist point of view. Anecdotes aside, it is based on research that lacks any depth of understanding about the nature of prisoner subcultures, the social processes of religious conversion, or the vulnerability of individuals to recruitment by terrorist organizations. These studies are also bereft of social science methodologies. There are no interviews with prisoners and they offer only scant evidence on the perceptions of wardens, guards, prison chaplains, and gang intelligence officers.

* * *

The second camp is more reassuring. It claims that Islam in prison does not pose a security threat. If anything, just the opposite is true. Islam is thought to have a moderating effect on prisoners, which plays an important role in prison security and rehabilitation. Once on the path to restructuring their lives—down to the way they eat, dress, form support systems, and divide their day into study, prayer, and reflection—Muslim prisoners have begun the reformation process, making them *less* of a recruiting target for terrorists than for other prisoners, and certainly less of a target than alienated street-corner youths of the urban ghetto. In his review of the literature, the religious historian Philip Jenkins concludes that "Islam is a major presence in American prisons, and many would say that this is a good thing because the Muslim influence can encourage people to get their lives together, to get off drink or drugs, to learn self-discipline."[22] Overall, my research supports this assessment. Islam in prison does more good than harm due to the *structure* and sense of *identity* it offers to young black men.

A major consequence of mass incarceration is that it has left thousands upon thousands of urban black males in prison for crimes they committed due to limited access to viable employment. In 1990, John Irwin and James Austin published an important study showing that most black men in prison had not finished high school, had no job skills, had never been steadily employed, and were unemployed at the time of their arrest.[23] In my interviews with young African American men who became Muslim converts in prison, I found that this lack of employment had created a more personal problem: many of them had never learned how to make good use of their time. Black Internet websites brim with the question "why are black people always late?" or offer explanations for "C.P. time" (colored people's time). From what I was told by the Muslim converts, time is not something to be capitalized upon in a low-income black community where job prospects are slim to nothing. Time is the enemy under these conditions, something to be wasted. When these men arrive in prison, again they find that their biggest enemy is time—the time they must serve until parole or, if they are serving a life sentence, the time until death. Aggravating this cultural problem are individual experiences of loss and suffering, and drug and alcohol abuse. These experiences can lead to an unstable, negative self-image and a resulting identity crisis.

Islam provides a remedy for these difficulties. It offers young black men a sense of identity and belonging in a like-minded community of abstemious believers; also the Islamic work ethic values self-discipline and the productive use of each period of the day—specifying segments for grooming, eating, studying, praying, and working to benefit the world or the hereafter ("inner jihad" as it is known in Orthodox Islam)—so Muslim prisoners learn to conquer time. It is often their greatest accomplishment. However, it is sometimes misconstrued as evidence of extremism. Positive changes in personal behavior like giving up smoking, drinking, and gambling are occasionally considered signs of radicalization instead of genuine attempts at self-discipline.

Suffice it to say that Islam in prison is often misunderstood. Other researchers have discovered aspects of the faith that are equally constructive.

One post-9/11 study in the reassuring camp unpacks the reform possibilities of Islam, suggesting that prisoner conversions to the Muslim faith can be explained by broad social forces including court intervention, the impact of race in America, the role of religion in the African American community, and the volatility of prisoner subcultures.[24] Another study found that most Muslim inmates convert to Islam while incarcerated and that there is no relationship between conversion and subsequent criminal behavior.[25] A study of chaplains in the Florida Department of Corrections found that Islamic conversion among African American female prisoners is uncommon due to their lack of familiarity with Islam, coupled with the fact that proselytizing is prohibited in Florida prisons.[26] In a study of inmates who converted to Islam in British prisons, researchers discovered that the Muslim faith provides converts with a moral framework from which to rebuild their lives.[27]

According to a national investigation of prisoner radicalization conducted in 2005, administrators insisted that there was no evidence of terrorist recruitment by Muslims in their prisons.[28] The finding is supported by a 2009 study indicating that officials in New York, Pennsylvania, Ohio, and Texas—states with large Muslim inmate populations—have seen no signs of prisoner radicalization whatsoever.[29] Further backing comes from a report by the Congressional Research Service, which has wide circulation within the government, indicating that of forty-three violent jihadist plots and attacks against the United States since 9/11, only one involved radicalization in prison.[30] Another study of 117 homegrown jihad terrorists in the United States and Britain found only seven cases in which prison had a significant impact on an individual's radicalization process.[31]

According to this body of research, the typical prison convert to Islam is a poor black man upset about racism, not Middle Eastern politics; it is also someone who became a Muslim to cope with the pains of imprisonment, not to fulfill a religious obligation to al-Qaeda. As one expert put it, "Al Qaeda is made up of a lot of upper-middle-class Saudis who are religiously offended by the American way of life. The boys in the hood are not offended by it. They want a piece of the American way of life."[32] Others contend that even if some Muslim prisoners were interested in joining the jihad, al-Qaeda recruiters would keep them at arm's length due to the fact that prisoners have extensive criminal records, have fingerprint files, and are inherently unreliable.

Although some prisoners become Muslim in name only, either to seek protection or to take advantage of dietary or meeting privileges, others undergo authentic conversions, which help them interact with other inmates in an optimistic manner. Whatever the motivation for conversion, Islam provides a self-imposed discipline on inmates that, in turn, gives prison authorities a convenient force in helping them maintain order. Islam in prison is not without its problems, so goes the argument, but such problems pale in comparison to the dangers posed by gangs like the Crips, the Bloods, Mara Salvatrucha (MS-13), and the Aryan Brotherhood.

This reassuring position has also found a receptive audience among professionals. Prison chaplains, particularly, claim that there are few documented cases of U.S. inmates joining a terrorist group while in prison. Their position was succinctly summarized in congressional testimony by Paul Rogers, a past president of the American Correctional Chaplains Association. "Regarding reports of prisons being infiltrated by terrorists or terrorist organizations via prison religious programs," he said, "these have been blown way out of proportion."[33] The president of the Islamic Division of the American Correctional Chaplains Association expressed a similar opinion in my interview with him, suggesting that prisoners act only in self-interest. "I've worked in Georgia prisons since 1975," he explained. "And I've met thousands of prisoners—thousands. I don't see where prisons would be a place for terrorist recruitment. Terrorism demands sacrifice and prisoners ain't ready to sacrifice anything. Most Islamic prisoners are just looking for protection and a place to belong."[34]

Yet research supporting the reassuring viewpoint has its own problems. The studies say little about the reasons for why Islam currently appeals to an unprecedented number of inmates in Western prisons. Because these studies concentrate exclusively on the positive aspects of Islam, they also fail to consider human factors that make Muslim prisoners vulnerable to extremist interpretations of Islam and potential recruitment by terrorist organizations. Reports appealing to the idea that concerns over prisoner radicalization are based on nothing more than "hype and hysteria" are especially shallow.

One study measured "jihad-based radicalization" by asking a reported 270 inmates only two questions: what were their opinions about the Iraq War? And what were their opinions about the war on terrorism? Unfavorable opinions were counted as support for jihad-based radicalization, which was found to be low. But the research failed to take into account the prisoners' religious backgrounds, so we learn nothing about the radicalization of Muslim inmates—the *only* inmates who recognize jihad. And even though the study purported to interrogate prisoner radicalization, the researchers curiously state that the purpose of their investigation "was *not* to discover . . . radicalized inmates poised to engage in terrorism after release."[35] (If research on "jihad-based radicalization" does not investigate the connection to Islamic terrorism, then what exactly is the study investigating? There are no other options.) Another study looked at radicalization through the rearview mirror by examining the backgrounds of homegrown terrorists to determine whether they had spent time in prison. Few had. Accordingly, the study did not explore the prison experiences that might have contributed to extremism and terrorist recruitment among those few, including their engagement with Islam or prison gangs. The authors simply state that "prison radicalization need not be seen as one of the top priorities at this time."[36] The analysis is two pages long.

Using a more attentive methodology, I offer a different perspective on the problem. My research indicates that while Islam is mainly a positive influence in prison, certain forces within the prison Muslim movement are aligned with the efforts of al-Qaeda and its associates to inspire convicts in the United States and Europe to conduct terrorist attacks on their own. This is a terrorist threat primarily fueled by the incarceration of inmates in disorderly, overcrowded maximum-security prisons—by mass incarceration itself. One reason for the discrepancy between this study and previous work is my access to prisoners, some of whom were affiliated with terrorist groups. There is a dearth of research based on direct contact with terrorists. The criminologist Andrew Silke suggests that the figure is as low as 1 percent of all published terrorism studies.[37] In the majority of studies on prisoner radicalization, researchers rely on second-hand documents, mostly produced by intelligence agencies, or they consult Internet resources, journalists' insights, academic publications, or government statistics.[38] I have done all of this, too. Yet in addition to having direct contact with terrorist prisoners, I interviewed inmates who had been sent to administrative segregation (the "hole") for attempting to radicalize other prisoners. These methods were supplemented with mail correspondence with radical prisoners; a review of their court documents, manifestos, and diaries; interviews with intelligence analysts and law enforcement officials who investigated these prisoners; and in some cases field visits to the neighborhoods where they had lived. In so doing, I attempt to imagine the texture of their lives—their criminal thinking styles, the prison organizations they came from, and the personal situations that set them on the pathway to political violence. This in-depth analysis is then used to validate several key assumptions of the terrorism literature.

* * *

My study belongs to a third camp of research on prisoner radicalization. This camp offers a more nuanced approach, arguing that prisoner radicalization occurs only under specific conditions of confinement. These studies rely exclusively on the perceptions of prison wardens, guards, chaplains, intelligence officers, and prisoners who have adopted radical religious beliefs.

To begin with, the federal government recognizes that prisoner radicalization is a problem that does exist in the United States. It is not an abstraction based on hype and hysteria. Prison officials have a stake in controlling the terrorist threat. In 2003 the director of the Federal Bureau of Prisons told Congress, "We know that inmates are particularly vulnerable to recruitment by terrorists and that we must guard against the spread of terrorism and extremist ideologies."[39] The circumstances supporting radicalization were spelled out by the government two years later. According to a landmark survey of some two thousand U.S. prisons conducted by the FBI in 2005 and 2006 (undertaken in response to the JIS case in California), the conditions essential to prisoner radicalization are as follows: (1) most cases of prisoner radicalization appear to be originated by domestic extremists with few or no foreign connections; (2) some radicalized Islamic inmates are current or former members of street or prison gangs, indicating an emerging "crossover" from gang members to Islamic extremists; and (3) radicalization activity levels appear to be higher in densely populated areas on the West Coast and in the northeastern United States.[40] After data from the survey were fully analyzed, the FBI added one more condition: (4) charismatic leadership may be the single most important contributing factor to prisoner radicalization.[41] Like all politics, all prisoner radicalization is local.

Criminologists have independently confirmed a number of these findings, beginning with the discovery of a crossover between prison gangs and Islamic extremism. The point is made abundantly clear in George Knox's study of a Michigan prison gang called the Melanic Islamic Palace of the Rising Sun. After interviewing Melanics (or "blacks" in Arabic), other prisoners, and guards, Knox found that the Melanics used their own brand of Islam to wage a holy war against other prisoners, culminating in a 1999 riot at the Chippewa Correctional Facility—two years before the 9/11 attacks.[42] More than anything, Knox found that the Melanics represented a mutating form of Prison Islam—small prison gangs who use coercion and selective Koranic verses to recruit new members. British researchers have made identical discoveries, indicating an important consistency with the alarmist point of view. That is, while prisoner radicalization is a global problem, the threat has progressed farther in Europe than it has in the United States, thus giving U.S. intelligence analysts the opportunity to learn from foreign cases.[43]

In 2006, a gang called the Muslim Boys began showing up at Britain's high-security Belmarsh Prison, where they became known as a criminal vanguard of religious extremists with ties to potentially more dangerous networks, including al-Qaeda.[44] A Home Office report stated that "violent Islamic extremists are terrorizing inmates . . . as they trawl for al-Qaeda recruits. They [Muslim Boys] force prisoners to accept the Muslim faith— those who refuse suffer assaults."[45] The gang's victims were reportedly slashed by razor blades and scalded with hot water.[46] Two years later, the independent researcher James Brandon warned that British prisons were at risk of becoming universities for terrorism due to a combination of "pull" factors (networks of Islamic prisoners who inculcate new arrivals into extremist worldviews by providing social and moral support) and "push" factors (the violent nature of prison life forces inmates to seek protection by joining gangs that espouse Islamist ideologies). Crucial to this dynamic are highly supportive friendship networks and the role of inmate leadership. Observing the complexity of radicalization, Brandon notes: "Many of the most influential extremists in prison are . . . charismatic individuals who have a reputation for consistently showing kindness and generosity towards other inmates."[47] Such warnings prompted the British Home Office to conduct a comprehensive overview of prisoner radicalization, leading to an influential report by a Cambridge University criminologist, Alison Liebling. According to Liebling, Islamic radicalization has become a matter of profound concern to staff and other inmates. A new generation of criminals has entered the high-security prisons of England and Wales, one characterized by "high numbers of Muslim prisoners [who are] disrupting established hierarchies."[48]

These findings mirror my investigation, which reflects a pattern of radicalization among Muslim gang members in California's overcrowded maximum-security prisons.[49] As one Shiite prisoner told me at the height of the Iraq War, "People are recruiting on the yard everyday. It's scandalous. Everybody's glorifying Osama bin Laden. But these Muslims come to Islam with the same gang mentality they had on the streets. Same red rags, same blue rags [symbols of the Crips and Bloods]. The mentality is pure ignorance driving terrorism. There is recruiting feeding on the broken spirit and ignorance."[50] Along with Muslim prisoners, I interviewed inmates affiliated with white supremacy gangs.[51] In both instances, radicalization was based on a prison gang model whereby inmates are radicalized through a process of one-on-one proselytizing by charismatic leaders.

I also learned something about the positive side of radicalization's double-edged sword, thus confirming the reassuring viewpoint. That is, an inmate-led counter-radicalization movement is now evolving from the same conditions that spawn prison extremism. These self-help groups may, in turn, provide a way to resolve the radicalization issue. Yet before that work is presented, there is another river to cross. Although some Western prisons have undoubtedly become fertile ground for extremism, criminologists have yet to show an empirical relationship between prisoner radicalization and terrorism. Without that evidence, prisoner radicalization is little more than a chimera—interesting perhaps, but a chimera nevertheless. It is to that evidence that we now turn.

4

The Spectacular Few

Attempting to understand the relationship between prisoner radicalization and terrorism brings to light two puzzles. The first relates to the criminological implications of the relationship. If radicalization is "the process by which inmates adopt extreme views, including beliefs that violent measures need to be taken for political or religious purposes,"[1] then it is not enough to simply discover that "extreme views" are held by convicts. Researchers must also take into account the social processes by which prisoners adopt such views and then explain how they translate their beliefs into violence. In and of itself, being a "prison radical" is not illegal and it does not pose an imminent threat to public safety. Radicalization is a threat only when it is encapsulated in criminal subcultures with the ideology and skill necessary to carry out an act of terrorism.[2] The surest way to understand the problem, then, is to look at cases in which violent measures have actually been taken, or attempted, by inmates for political and religious purposes. In other words, research must focus on specific *incidents* where radicalization has led to terrorism.[3]

The second puzzle involves the arrangement of events over time. There are three ways in which a prisoner can become involved in terrorism. The most likely way is for an inmate to wage a terrorist plot after he or she has been released (or has escaped) from prison. Less likely, a prisoner can devise a plot with a parolee who has been released from prison and/or with fellow travelers in the community. Less likely still, a prisoner can wage a terrorist plot from behind bars without assistance from outsiders. The first instance involves a time lag between a release from prison and the terrorist event; in the second instance there will be a time lag between the parolee's release from prison and the terrorist event. (In all other instances there will be a zero time lag because the prisoner has not been released.)

As such, the link between the occurrence of prisoner radicalization and the terrorist event is best conceptualized in terms of the theoretical perspective most attuned to temporal ordering: life-course criminology.[4] Life-course theory concentrates on a criminal's changing personal choices and life experiences over time, and it seeks to uncover trajectories or "turning points" that form critical periods in the process of violent development. In this way, becoming radicalized in prison is one of what may be *several* decisive life experiences—including those that may have occurred before and after imprisonment—in the process leading to terrorism.

One tool for exploring these life-changing experiences is a database of cases where prisoner radicalization has been linked to terrorism. The database features information on the backgrounds of terrorists, their radicalization, the nature of their terrorist plots, their competency in carrying out the plots, and the time lag between release from prison and the terrorist event.

* * *

The Prisoner Radicalization/Terrorism Database is displayed in appendix 1. It includes fifty-one domestic and international cases based on open sources such as prior research, prisoner memoirs, media accounts, government reports, and court documents. Cases were selected based on the FBI's definition of terrorism, which defines the crime as "a violent act or an act dangerous to human life in violation of the criminal laws . . . to intimidate or coerce a government, the civilian population, or any segment thereof, in the furtherance of political or social objectives."[5] The database is concerned only with cases where offenders were radicalized in prison and were subsequently involved in either an executed or attempted act of terrorism upon release or while in custody. In other words, the database represents a purposive sample of criminals who were not terrorists when they entered prison but who became terrorists upon release or during confinement.[6] While this database is tremendously useful, all terrorism databases contain flaws and this one is no exception. Its limitations are as follows.

First, sources used to construct the database were created for purposes other than the study of prisoner radicalization. Often missing in these sources was information on the offender's criminal background, education level, military training, incarceration history, gang involvement, and mental-health records.[7] Moreover, the database is limited by the vagaries of open-source reporting. Second, although the database includes both domestic and international cases, it is concerned only with attacks and threats against Western targets. Missing are terrorist attacks in such hotbeds of extremism as Pakistan, Sri Lanka, and the Middle East. As James Brandon observes, many modern Islamic terrorist movements in those parts of the world have been dominated and led by individuals who were radicalized in prison.[8] (To be sure, the originator of contemporary Islamism, Sayyid Qutb, wrote his manifesto, *Milestones*, after being tortured in an Egyptian prison.) Such a limitation has the dual effect of significantly underreporting incidents of radicalization and terrorism, while biasing the data toward democratic nations (especially the United States) where free media and open-source materials are more available than in nondemocratic countries. Finally, the database underreports terrorism's connection to prisoner radicalization for legal reasons. For example, case 20 in the database presents details on Mohammed Achraf, convicted of plotting to bomb Spain's National Court in 2004. Sources reveal that Achraf organized the operation while confined for credit-card fraud in a Spanish prison and was assisted by four other inmates, but their identities have never been disclosed by the courts. For these reasons, then, the database represents a conservative estimate of the problem at hand. Despite its shortcomings, the database can still be used to summarize incidents of prisoner radicalization and terrorism; condense into understandable forms the backgrounds of terrorists; designate where and how they were radicalized; identify inmate social networks that supported their terrorism; and show the extent to which terrorist tactics have evolved over time.

* * *

The cases cover a period of forty-three years. Cases are listed chronologically in appendix 1 by the year of the terrorist event, beginning with Eldridge Cleaver in 1968 (case 1) and ending with Joseph Davis in 2011 (case 51). While a few of the cases originated in prisons outside the West (though the targets were all Western), the majority of cases demonstrate that—although extremely rare—radicalization in prison and recruitment to terrorism can and does take place in the United States, Britain, France, and Spain. Typically working in small groups, these radicalized prisoners committed bombings, assassinations and murders, executions of police officers, airline hijackings, kidnappings, and bank robberies.

Background information is displayed in table 4.1. (All were men but one.) The figures in table 4.1 show that thirty-eight of the fifty-one cases (75 percent) occurred since 2001.[9] Contrary to research suggesting that there is virtually no relationship between prisoner radicalization and terrorism, these figures indicate a growing trend in the opposite direction. The largest increase in prison-based terrorist events over the past four decades has occurred since 9/11, mirroring a global trend in support for jihadist ideologies outside prison during the same period.[10] About 40 percent of the cases occurred between 2006 and 2009, with about half of those (nine out of twenty) taking place in 2009. This trend also squares with recent research. A study conducted by the RAND Corporation of forty-six post-9/11 terrorism incidents shows an increase in jihadist radicalization leading to criminal activity in the United States during the year 2009.[11]

The figures in table 4.1 show that most of the cases originated in U.S. prisons. The majority of the terrorists were African American or African; one-fourth were Caucasian; and the rest were of Arab or Hispanic ethnicity. The mean age at the time of the terrorist event was thirty-one years old, confirming research showing that terrorists tend to be somewhat older than

Table 4.1. Background characteristics of prisoners involved in terrorism (N = 51)

Year of attack/plan	N	(%)
1968–1974	3	6
1983–1986	2	4
1992–1995	6	12
1996–2000	2	4
2001–2005	16	31
2006–2009	20	40
2010–2011	2	4
Country of incarceration	**N**	**(%)**
United States	33	65
Britain	6	12
Spain	5	10
France	4	8
Jordan	1	2
Egypt	1	2
Yemen	1	2
Ethnicity	**N**	**(%)**
Caucasian	12	24
African American	18	35
African	14	28
Arab	5	10
Hispanic	2	4
Age at attack/plan	**N**	**(%)**
20–24	8	16
25–29	11	22
30–34	20	39
35–39	5	10
40–44	1	2
45–49	2	4
50 and over	2	4
Unknown	3	6
Mean age = 30.9		

common criminals.[12] More importantly, the finding indicates that prison-
based terrorists are somewhat older than other terrorists. In his seminal
study of four hundred Afghan mujahedeen, Marc Sageman found that the
average age for joining the jihad was 25.6 years old, some six years younger
than the prison-based terrorists.[13] Three of the terrorists were between forty
and forty-nine at the time of the event and two were over fifty—a finding
consistent with Robert Pape's equally influential study of 462 suicide bombers, which showed that some terrorists do not become active until they reach
their forties or fifties.[14]

* * *

I use the U.S. Justice Department's definition of prisoner radicalization ("the
process by which inmates adopt extreme views, including beliefs that violent
measures need to be taken for political or religious purposes"). One measure of this process is prisoner conversions to religions that may be perceived
as espousing ideologies of intolerance and violence. This would involve not
only radical interpretations of Islam but also a constellation of white supremacy faiths. Foremost among them is Christian Identity, which asserts that
Jews are the children of Satan, while white Aryans are the descendants of the
biblical tribes of ancient Israel and thus are God's chosen people. Because
they are God's chosen people, Identity adherents believe that whatever they
do is permissible. It is God's will working through them that motivates their
violence. Also included in the white supremacy pantheon are Odinism and
its Icelandic counterpart, Asatru—a pre-Christian pagan faith based on
Viking-era Norse mythology, calling for the return to a mythical age of the
Nordic gods.[15] Although statistics are incomplete, some officials contend that
Odinism/Asatru may be the fastest growing religion behind prison walls in
the United States.[16]

Prisoner conversions are summarized in table 4.2. Before the figures
are presented, I must state two points that will become a constant refrain
throughout this work. First, not all prisoners who follow these religious
paths are violent or oriented toward racism and intolerance. Sunni Islam,
the Nation of Islam, Moorish Science Temple, and Odinism/Asatru all have
the potential to empower the powerless and give one's life a higher meaning. There are more than three million Muslims in the United States, yet
fewer than one hundred of them have been indicted on terrorism-related
charges since 9/11.[17] It is estimated that only 1 in 24,000 Muslims has ever
been charged with being a homegrown terrorist in the United States.[18] The
same minute ratio applies to prisons. While as many as 350,000 U.S. inmates

may have converted to Islam since 9/11, only 20 of them were involved in terrorism. Once again, only a tiny, infinitesimal fraction of prison converts to white supremacy faiths and to Islam turn radical beliefs into terrorist action. Even so, some the most serious post-9/11 terrorist plots have involved men who were radicalized in prison. The cases are spectacular and they are few. Second, converting to a belief system that *does* espouse violence, and actually committing violence, may be related but they are not necessarily coterminous. Separate additional factors—occurring before and after incarceration—influence the execution of a violent act.[19]

That said, table 4.2 suggests that radical ideas can be found in various sects of Islam. It shows that 59 percent of the terrorists underwent a conversion to some form of Islam in prison: be it to the Nation of Islam, Moorish Science, Sunni Islam, Salafi Jihadist (the theology upon which al-Qaeda is based; the term means "the pious ancestors," and members seek to purify the Islamic religion of any innovations or practices that deviate from the 7th-century teachings of the Prophet Muhammad), or Prison Islam, which in the United States can include inmates who identify themselves as Salafi Jihadists.[20] This is consistent with a Department of Homeland Security report, which showed that the most significant terrorist threat to the United States and its interests abroad is a growing extremist movement motivated by Salafi theology.[21] It is also consistent with the RAND study, which showed that nearly all of the domestically radicalized terrorists indicted in the United States since 2001 have been Muslims or converts to Islam.[22] "What sets the global Salafi jihad apart from other terrorist organizations," Sageman helpfully notes, "is its violence against foreign non-Muslim governments and their populations in furtherance of Salafi objectives."[23] Unlike these previous investigations, however, table 4.2 reveals the importance of white supremacy in the terrorism equation. It shows that 18 percent of the terrorists converted to a white supremacy faith while in custody.

The prominence of Islam in these figures is explained by two intersecting historical forces leading to the global emergence of jihadist terrorism. From one direction arose puritanical fundamentalism, first witnessed as a terrorist manifestation in the 1979 takeover of the Grand Mosque in Mecca by some five hundred heavily armed Islamic militants. Essentially, jihadists explain reality by blaming social problems on the modern departure from religious morality and the promise of redemption (*hijrah*) through a return to the idealized global Muslim community (the *ummah*). In the face of Islam's decline vis-à-vis colonization, globalization, economic stagnation, and corrupt dictatorships sponsored by the United States and its allies, resentment against the West became widespread in Islam. Engaging with this resentment, many fundamentalists turned militant, as in the case of al-Qaeda. "Every Muslim," bin Laden would claim in a barefaced expression of the Salafi Jihadist doctrine, "hates Americans, hates Jews, and hates Christians. This is part of our belief and our religion."[24] The formal sanction to wage jihad—which is translated as "striving in the path of God"—is found in the Medina verses of the Koran, revealed to the Prophet Muhammad between 622 and 632 ce, which emphasize defense against nonbelievers (as opposed to the "milder" Mecca verses, 610-622 ce, which stress beliefs and the building of strength among Muslims). As the Islamic scholar Fawaz Gerges notes: "The journey of jihadist was transformed into an open-ended quest, a path that all Muslims needed to embark upon to emulate the Prophet of Islam. Bin Laden believed that his reference to the Prophet's journey or exodus from Mecca to Medina would resonate in the hearts and minds of those upon whom he was now calling."[25]

From another direction came the brotherhood—or the bonding of family and friends around puritanical values—indicating that Islamic militancy is not so much the result of a particular religious doctrine as it is the consequence of an individual's association with groups that espouse extremism and violence.[26] Quintan Wiktorowicz, a senior director for global engagement at the National Security Council in the Obama White House and the author of early pathbreaking work on Islamic militancy, found that socialization within radical Islamic groups is needed to indoctrinate individuals into the movement ideology so that they are willing to sacrifice themselves for a radical cause.[27] Sageman likewise discovered that group loyalty among the mujahedeen was the true inspiration for waging the jihad, even trumping their ideological commitment to a cause.[28] I interviewed a U.S. intelligence officer who explained the urge for bonding in terms of the global malaise of Muslim civilization. "I've lived all over the Middle East, Yemen, and Afghanistan," he said. "Life in that part of the world is so hideously boring that jihad actually becomes a form of entertainment for young people. They have no access to music or cars, they can't date or travel, and their schools offer nothing of practical value. Making jihad is like joining a soccer team. It's a way to belong."

Western leaders of the jihad clearly understand this need for belonging and have offered social networking via mosques, sports clubs, and Internet chat rooms as a path to radicalization replacing what was once found only on the battlefields of Southeast Asia. As table 4.2 shows, the post-9/11 appearance of this inclination entered Islamic subcultures of Western prisons sometime around the start of the Iraq War and peaked in 2009. Since then, it has been declining. But why was 2009 the peak year?

The political scientist Fuad Ajami contends that Osama bin Laden's star can be bracketed by the years 1998 through roughly 2009. This period covers al-Qaeda's 1998 twin bombings of the U.S. embassies in Kenya and Tanzania; the millennium bomb plots in Amman, Jordan, and Los Angeles (at the International airport) in 1999; the two attacks on U.S. naval ships in the Port of Aden, Yemen, in 2000 (USS *The Sullivans* and USS *Cole*); and then the mega-terrorism attack on 9/11. The wars in Afghanistan and Iraq, and the widespread Muslim outrage over civilian casualties caused by those wars, created a "single narrative" interpreting the wars as evidence of Western imperialism and hostility toward Islam. This gave bin Laden's organization a second wind and led to the creation of al-Qaeda–inspired homegrown cells. The upsurge in homegrown terrorism paralleled an intense al-Qaeda recruitment campaign—its number of propagandist videos increased from a single video issued in 2001 to ninety-seven videos released in 2007—which inspired attacks on Casablanca, Madrid, and London.[29] And then began a round of plots to take down commercial aircraft, culminating in the failed Christmas Day plot of 2009. After that, says Ajami, "the bin Laden legend dimmed and the cult of martyrdom lost its luster."[30] Prison radicals were not impervious to this trend. Yet this does not mean that terrorism has vanished. A Department of Homeland Security report indicates that attempted terrorist attacks in the United States reached an all-time high in 2010, many of which were small-scale actions involving improvised explosive devices, the most serious being the Times Square plot by Faisal Shahzad, who was supported by both the Pakistani Taliban and the Internet cleric Anwar al-Awalki.[31]

Table 4.2 also includes ten terrorists (20 percent of the sample) in the "no conversion" category. However, all of them were either Sunni extremists or Salafists when they entered prison. Sources indicate that these prisoners were nevertheless radicalized through their associations with fellow inmates and/ or their conditions of confinement. A well-known example is the man who assumed leadership control of al-Qaeda in the aftermath of bin Laden's death and is now the most wanted terrorist in the world. Dr. Ayman al-Zawahiri (case 15 in appendix 1) was imprisoned for three years at the Citadel, a 12th-century fortress prison in Cairo, for crimes on the periphery of the 1981 plot to assassinate the Egyptian president, Anwar Sadat. Because Zawahiri knew military officers who were directly involved in the assassination, he was subjected to severe punishment.[32] An Egyptian intelligence officer would later testify that he witnessed Zawahiri in the Citadel, "his head shaved, his dignity completely humiliated, undergoing all sorts of torture."[33] Already a Salafist when he entered prison, Zawahiri's ideology became even more extreme as a result of the torture, thought to include daily beatings with electrical cables, the use of attack dogs, and the "strappado" or "reverse hanging"—a form of torture that originated during the medieval Inquisition whereby the

Table 4.2. Radicalization characteristics of prisoners involved in terrorism (N = 51)

Prisoner religious conversions	N	(%)
Islam	8	15
Sunni Islam/Salafi Jihadist	13	26
Nation of Islam	1	2
Moorish Science Temple	2	4
Prison Islam (Salafi/Wahhabi)	6	12
Christian Identity	5	10
Odinism/Asatru/Thule	4	8
No conversion (already Sunni/Salafi)	10	20
Other (Marxism)	2	4
Age at conversion (approximate)	**N**	**(%)**
Under 20	5	
20–24	11	
25–29	11	
30–34	4	
35–39	1	
Unknown	8	
Not applicable	10	
Mean age = 24.7		
Place of conversion	**N**	**(%)**
United States	27	73
California	5	
Texas	4	
Pennsylvania	4	
New York	3	
Michigan	2	
Arizona	1	
Florida	1	
Washington	2	
Colorado	1	
Illinois	1	
New Jersey	1	
Bureau of Prisons	1	
U.S. military	1	
Unknown	1	
Britain	6	16
Young offender institution	4	
Adult prison	2	
Spain	2	5
France	3	8
Jordan	1	2
Suwaqah	1	
Not applicable	12	

inmate's hands are tied behind his back and he is suspended in the air with a rope attached to the wrists, dislocating both shoulders. This has led some analysts to view Zawahiri's terrorist career—including his role in 9/11—as an effort to exact revenge on Western allies of the Egyptian government for the treatment he endured in custody.[34] Lawrence Wright, the author of the Pulitzer Prize-winning book *The Looming Tower: Al Qaeda and the Road to 9/11*, makes the unflinching argument that "Zawahiri entered prison a surgeon. He came out a butcher."[35] Although Zawahiri's grievance against the West was different from the one motivating bin Laden—who once said he began thinking about attacking the West following the American-supported Israeli assault on Lebanon in 1982[36]—Wright's perspective provides insight into the event that triggered al-Qaeda's first attack against the United States. It also validates the significance of kinship networks.

In June 1998, the CIA apprehended four members of the Egyptian Islamic Jihad—a group then led by Zawahiri who had recently joined forces with bin Laden in Afghanistan —on charges of plotting to bomb the United States Embassy in Tirana, Albania. The Clinton administration pushed for extradition of the four men from Albania to stand trial in Egypt, where they were likely to be tortured. Among those indicted in the Albanian plot was Zawahiri's brother, Muhammad. Shortly thereafter, orders were given to activate al-Qaeda's East African sleeper cells, resulting in the simultaneous August 7 bombings of the U.S. embassies in Kenya and Tanzania, killing 213 and injuring some 4,500—most of whom were Muslims.[37]

Granted, being radicalized in a Middle Eastern prison involves a very different set of cultural processes than a prisoner would experience in the West. Arab prisons, in particular, are often recruitment centers where Islamists control entire cellblocks and groups like al-Qaeda build their ranks. As a Jordanian security expert said in 2006, "Things no longer end in prison anymore. In fact, increasingly they begin there."[38] The motivation for terrorism can also be different. Joining an insurgency against the infidel invasion of a Muslim country is, from the point of Islamic theology, a justifiable act (as when mujahedeen join battles in Bosnia, Chechnya, and Afghanistan). Yet one thing is constant across the cases. Table 4.2 shows that prison-based terrorism is inimically linked to inmate subcultures through religious extremism. Religious extremism can therefore be seen as an essential element for prisoners from different prisons in different cultures to create violence in similar ways. Both foreign and American jihadists, along with the white supremacists, all reject the compromises with liberal values and secular institutions that are made by most religious groups. All reject the norms secular society has imposed on religion—norms that keep religion a private affair rather than allowing it to enter public spaces. And all have replaced main-stream religious beliefs with a more vibrant theology that they see as part of their tradition's early beginnings.[39]

Table 4.2 further suggests that these subcultures have a strong appeal among younger inmates—those who may be most vulnerable to radical ideologies supporting terrorism.[40] In this study, the average age of conversion was 24.7.

Table 4.2 ends with information about the place of conversion. As expected, most conversions took place in U.S. prisons, primarily in state institutions. California led the way with five cases, followed by Texas and Pennsylvania (four each), New York (three), Michigan (two), Washington (two), and five states with one apiece. Six conversions occurred in British prisons; three took place in France, and two in Spain. Closer inspection of the place of conversion in appendix 1 reveals an important link between small inmate groups confined to specific penal institutions and incidents of radicalization and terrorism. This link reflects what is known about the clustering of international jihadists around friendship and kinship arrange-ments.[41] A study of 242 jihadi terrorists in Europe, for instance, found that most came from homogeneous social networks. Terrorists within these net-works were roughly the same age, came from the same place, and were fre-quently from the lower socioeconomic strata; many of them had criminal records, and they radicalized together with family or friends.[42] The clustering of terrorists within specific prisons is what the FBI director Robert Mueller refers to as "pockets of radicalization."[43]

An important example is Abu Musab al-Zarqawi (case 19), the founder of Al-Qaeda in Iraq. In his case, as in others to be examined in this book, the passage through criminality, the meeting of a charismatic individual in prison (an imam or gang leader), and finding a group of people ready to engage in a common form of violence, constitutes a discernible pathway to terrorism.[44] Zarqawi did not convert to Islam in prison (he was raised by a Sunni family in Jordan). Instead he underwent a religious *regeneration*, or the enthusiastic adoption of a belief system that had not been taken seri-ously before, or that had been abandoned out of skepticism or indifference.[45] According to Zarqawi's biographer, "It was in prison that his magnetism and strength appeared in a new light."[46] Prior to his incarceration at Jordan's high-security Suwaqah prison in 1996, Zarqawi's "reputation was that of a hood-lum with vague religious learning."[47] Zarqawi thrived under the harsh condi-tions of the desert prison where he received extensive religious instruction from a fellow prisoner named Abu Muhammad al-Maqdisis, a renowned Salafi scholar known for his prolific writings arguing, among other things, that bombings are heroic acts that bring solace to the hearts of Muslims.[48]

Based on Maqdisis's tutelage, Zarqawi developed the body of a fighter and the proselytizing techniques of a born-again zealot. "In prison," writes al-Qaeda expert Peter Bergen, "Zarqawi worked out maniacally, learned the Koran by heart, and gradually rose to become a jailhouse capo [that] other inmates learned to fear and to obey without question."[49] These organizational skills allowed Zarqawi to recruit a gang of ordinary criminals and drug addicts from the Suwaqah population that would later prove vital to his terrorist campaign in Iraq. Thousands would be killed through beheadings and the bombing of hotels, mosques, Shia shrines, and the United Nations headquarters.[50] "It is a sad irony," wrote the Pulitzer Prize–winning author James Risen in 2006, "that Zarqawi's jihadists were turning Iraq into a terrorist haven *after* the American invasion, not before it."[51]

The importance of a specific institution is even more apparent in Britain. According to the database, shoe-bomber Richard Reid, a Taliban member named Martin Mubanga, Sulayman Keeler of al-Muhajiroun ("the immigrants," designated a terrorist organization under U.K. law) and a would-be jihadist bomber named Kevin Gardner (cases 16, 17, 40, and 48, respectively)—all converted to Islam while serving time in Britain's young offender institutions.[52] In 1995 and 1992, respectively, Reid and Mubanga underwent conversions at the Feltham Young Offenders Institution, a notorious London-area prison for male juveniles renowned for its riots, gang violence, inmate suicides, and inept management.[53] And though he did not convert there (that would happen in an adult institution), as a teenager Muktar Ibrahim (case 26), the leader of the foiled London subway bombing plot of 2005, was incarcerated at several young offender institutions, including a bit at Feltham in 1992. The other British terrorist in the database is Mohammad al-Figari (case 29), convicted of attending a foreign terrorist training camp in 2006. Figari was radicalized by a prisoner named Mohammed Hamid, a charismatic Salafi preacher and former drug addict, who was also incarcerated at Feltham during the early 1990s. That the radicalization of all British terrorists in the database can be traced to England's young offender penal system suggests the presence not only of a distinctive social network of prisoners who became terrorists, but also of an ongoing social network. The point of departure for understanding this network is the Feltham Young Offenders Institution.[54] This trend has extended beyond the years covered in the database. In early 2012, Kenyan authorities prepared to put on trial a twenty-nine-year-old Islamic convert from Britain named Jermaine Grant for plotting to kill Western tourists. Grant is believed to have joined al-Shabaab in Somalia after being radicalized while at the Feltham Young Offenders Institution.[55]

A similar network was found in Spain. Scott Atran's meticulous study of the Madrid train bombings reveals that the plot was hatched by what he calls "a loosely-affiliated cluster of childhood friends, neighborhood homeboys, siblings, cousins, petty criminals, drug dealers and former prison cellmates."[56] Leading the pack was a thirty-four-year-old career criminal named Jamal Ahmidan (case 21), known as "el Chino" (the Chinaman) because of his narrow eyes. Following his release from a Spanish prison on charges of dealing heroin in the mid-1990s, Ahmidan—then a junkie himself—initially found religion in a Madrid mosque. By 2000, Ahmidan was back in custody, this time confined to the Madrid Center for Internment of Foreigners on charges of falsifying travel documents. It was here that Ahmidan met a fellow inmate, Jose Trashorras (case 24), who introduced Ahmidan to Salafist theology. Ahmidan escaped from detention on April 4, 2000, and fled to his home in Morocco where he was later arrested and locked up on a murder charge but was never brought to trial. Ahmidan's radicalization intensified during his time in the Moroccan prison and by the time he was released in mid-2003 the wars in Afghanistan and Iraq were in full swing, as were the Muslim insurgencies against them. Atran offers compelling confirmation of the connection between prisoner radicalization and terrorism and of the contagion effect the phenomenon brings with it. "The Chinaman especially identified with Abu Musab al-Zarqawi," he writes. "Like the Chinaman, Zarqawi had been a violent criminal and Jew-hater who radicalized to jihad in prison."[57]

A year later, using money from dealing Ecstasy and hash, the Chinaman singlehandedly financed the Madrid train bombings in protest against Spanish support for the Iraq War, while Trashorras played a supporting role by stealing explosives from a mining quarry. More than two hundred were killed and over a thousand were wounded, marking the deadliest terrorist assault in modern Spanish history. (And the most successful: a new Spanish government promptly announced its withdrawal of troops from Iraq.) On April 3, 2004, Ahmidan and six other plotters died in an apparent suicide explosion in a Madrid suburb. Sageman writes about a "jihadi cool" in Europe, or a cultural phenomenon in which "it is fashionable to emulate terrorists."[58] Indeed, later that year Spanish authorities arrested eighteen members of the Martyrs for Morocco (a North African Salafist group with ties to al-Qaeda) for plotting a sequel to the Madrid train bombings—a bombing attack on the Madrid headquarters of the National Court. Two Algerians, Mohamed Achraf and Abdel Bensmail (cases 20 and 22), had recruited for and planned the National Court plot while incarcerated at Topas Prison in the Salamanca Province of western Spain. Sources link Bensmail to the former French prisoner Allekema Lamari (case 23), another ringleader of the

Madrid train bombings who died alongside the Chinaman.[59] At least four other conspirators in the National Court plot were former Topas prisoners. Once again, radicalization led to terrorism through a circumscribed social network of prisoners linked to one institution—Topas Prison.

Several U.S. cases reveal the importance of social networks within specific prisons. In 2005, the JIS members Kevin James and Levar Washington (cases 27 and 28), both inmates at California's New Folsom Prison, waged their plot to commit mass murder at two Los Angeles army recruiting centers, and then attack the Israeli consulate and several synagogues. The JIS case is complex, involving more than a dozen prison gang members linked to L.A. street gangs, a story I will explore in greater detail in chapter 7. For now, there is another case of note, also involving a coalition of prison gang members and an interloper from the streets. First, a note on definitions is necessary. Debate on the distinction between terrorism and hate crime is long-standing. Hate crime is defined as an act of prejudicial violence based on race, religion, ethnicity, or sexual preference.[60] The following event conforms to that definition, but it also represents a violent crime intended to "intimidate a civilian population . . . in the furtherance of political objectives" associated with the American white supremacy movement, thus qualifying it as an act of domestic terrorism according to the FBI definition. Not all hate crimes are acts of terrorism; in fact, very few qualify. This is one of them.[61]

Lawrence Brewer and John King (cases 13 and 14) met in 1995 while serving time at the Beto Unit of the Texas prison system in Livingston. Considered a "gladiator school" for younger inmates, Beto was dominated by violent, racially segregated gangs. Outnumbered by blacks three to one, whites were pressed into gangs for their own survival. Brewer and King tried to join the Aryan Brotherhood for protection. (King would later claim that he did so after being gang-raped by black convicts.) But the ABs would have nothing to do with them, so they took up membership in the lesser-feared Confederate Knights of America and swore an oath of loyalty to the Ku Klux Klan. Inked up with Klan and Nazi tattoos—including one on King's arm displaying a black man hanging from a tree—they embraced the tenants of Christian Identity and adopted the belief that a race war was imminent. Brewer and King were paroled months apart in 1997 and met up in King's hometown of Jasper, Texas, where they began hanging out with a local racist named Shawn Berry. According to his biographer, "King returned to Jasper thinking he was a recruit in an underground war for the town's soul. In his heart, he thought he was a race hero in the making, a representative of a long and distinguished line of Aryan warriors, willing to put himself in the service of his race."[62]

On the night of June 7, 1998, a forty-nine-year-old black man named James Byrd accepted a ride from Berry, Brewer, and King, who had spent the day drinking. Rather than taking Byrd home, the three men took Byrd to a remote country road, beat him with a ball bat and tire iron, urinated on his body, chained him by his ankles to their pickup truck, and dragged him for three miles, with Byrd holding his head up to indicate that he was alive throughout most of the ordeal. Byrd died after his right arm and head were severed from his body upon striking a concrete abutment. After dumping Byrd's body in front of an African American cemetery, the three men went to a barbeque and continued partying.

Widely considered one of the most merciless crimes of the late American 20th century (it led to the Federal Matthew Shepard and James Byrd Jr. Hate Crimes Prevention Act signed into federal law by President Obama in 2009), several aspects of the Jasper murder resonate deeply with the southern tradition of lynching. These traits not only include mutilation, decapitation, and revelry—such as a picnic or barbeque, during or after the event—but also signify an overt act intended to degrade the black community of Jasper by dumping the butchered corpse of James Byrd in front of the town's African American cemetery. Consistent with the FBI's definition of terrorism, then, the killing of James Byrd by neo-Nazi ex-convicts from the Texas prison system was "a violent act or an act dangerous to human life in violation of the criminal laws . . . to intimidate or coerce a government, the civilian population, or any segment thereof, in the furtherance of political or social objectives."[63] Still again, the source of terrorism can be traced to an inmate network inside a specific prison: the Beto Unit.

The database shows that no U.S. prison has created more terrorists than the one operated by the military at Guantanamo Bay. One was the Afghan Abdullah Mehsud (case 25, known at the camp as Said Mohammed Alam Shah). As a teenager, Mehsud lost a leg when he stepped on a land mine left over from the anti-Soviet war and was fitted with prosthesis. He was later forced into Taliban conscription; however, due to his missing leg, he was held out of combat and assigned a desk job. Mehsud, along with the Afghan Abdullah Rasoul (case 31) and the Saudi Said Ali al-Shihri (case 35), were taken into U.S. custody in Afghanistan and Pakistan during the early years of the war on terrorism and detained as enemy combatants at Guantanamo. These cases illustrate the conclusive point about prisoner radicalization: in each instance the prisoners were eventually released from Guantanamo after the government failed to uncover any evidence of potential terrorism. That is, they were not terrorists when they entered prison but they became terrorists upon release.[64]

Similar to the treatment of Ayman al-Zawahiri at the hands of the Egyptians—and the violence that would ensue—the U.S. military subjected Guantanamo prisoners to what has been obliquely termed "torture-based techniques" as part of an "enhanced interrogation" protocol intended to gather intelligence on future attacks against America, though little useful intelligence was gathered at Guantanamo.[65] According to media accounts of victim statements and official documents obtained through the Freedom of Information Act, these techniques involved widespread beatings; solitary confinement in over-air-conditioned cells where prisoners were stripped naked and exposed to loud rock and hip-hop music, strobe lighting, and sustained noise from tape recordings of crying babies and American television commercials; prolonged sleep deprivation; and various forms of personal humiliation— from forcing prisoners to soil themselves to the use of attack dogs and sexual abuse.[66] A 2003 report by the International Red Cross indicates that the techniques also included deliberate desecrations of the Koran, "excessive isolation" of detainees, and the absence of a policy for the release of those who did not belong in prison.[67] The report cited "a worrying deterioration in the psychological health of a large number of the detainees because of uncertainty about their fate."[68] According to a leaked document by a Guantanamo intelligence officer involved with interrogations, the techniques nurtured an "intense hatred for Americans that was festering in the cellblocks [which served] as a bond for the captives."[69]

Upon his release in 2004, Abdullah Mehsud was repatriated to Afghanistan where he rejoined his Taliban unit. Mehsud's final Guantanamo assessment stated that he "did not pose a future threat." To the contrary: Mehsud had been radicalized by Guantanamo. Having never committed an act of terrorism before, he set about making jihadist videos and organized a Taliban division to fight U.S. troops. Mehsud then planned and carried out a bold attack on Pakistan's interior minister, killing thirty-one people. Then he oversaw the kidnapping of two Chinese engineers affiliated with coalition forces. And finally, in 2007, Mehsud blew himself up in a suicide attack against the Pakistani Army. His martyrdom was hailed in an audio message by Osama bin Laden.[70]

Abdullah Rasoul was transferred from Guantanamo to Afghan custody in 2007 and was then locked up in the American-built wing of the Pul-e-Charkhi prison. When Rasoul emerged from custody he became an operations officer for the Taliban in southern Afghanistan where he led a series of attacks against U.S. and British forces.

Said Ali al-Shihri was released to the Saudis on November 9, 2007, after his military tribunal determined that the "detainee has no knowledge of terrorist organizations or activities."[71] But he soon would: Shihri had been radicalized by Guantanamo. Upon his return to Riyadh, Shihri entered a government-sponsored de-radicalization program, but less than a year later he escaped with other high-profile Saudi al-Qaeda operatives. Shihri traveled to neighboring Yemen, bin Laden's ancestral home, where he became a commander of al-Qaeda's Yemen branch (soon to become Al-Qaeda in the Arabian Peninsula [AQAP]). Using the official title "Secretary General of the Al-Qaida Organization in Saudi Arabia," Shihri's first act of terrorism came in September 2008, when he participated in the car bombing of the U.S. embassy in Yemen's capital, Sana, killing sixteen. Later that year he killed six Christian missionaries in Yemen. Then, in 2009, Shihri led the Christmas Day bombing attack on America.[72]

A year later, and nearly two years after he signed an executive order to close the facility, President Obama called Guantanamo "the number one recruitment tool" used by jihadists, because "it's become a symbol."[73] Not only is Guantanamo a symbol for many Muslims of American hypocrisy, confirming the contempt they believe the United States holds for them, but it is also for the intelligence community a symbol of the existential threat posed by prisoner radicalization. In 2003, a CIA officer familiar with interrogation techniques at Guantanamo told the journalist Seymour Hersh, "If we captured some people who weren't terrorists when we got them, they are now."[74] Seven years later, Obama's National Intelligence Director warned the president that Guantanamo may be producing terrorists rather than reforming them.[75]

*　*　*

Terrorism scholars are well aware of the debate between Bruce Hoffman and Marc Sageman over the nature of the terrorist threat against the West.[76] The debate has generated extensive interest because Hoffman and Sageman represent two of the most respected voices on the threat posed by al-Qaeda. Hoffman is the director of the Center for Peace and Security Studies at Georgetown University and a former award-winning scholar-in-residence at the CIA following 9/11. Sageman, a forensic psychiatrist who acts as the first-ever scholar-in-residence on terrorism matters for the New York City Police Department, is a former CIA operations officer in Islamabad where he had worked closely with the Afghan mujahedeen. Both have published definitive academic works on terrorism.

Hoffman argues that al-Qaeda is, and will continue to be, the major threat to Western interests. Sageman contends that the main threat no longer comes from al-Qaeda but from the bottom up—from radicalized individuals and groups who meet and plot in informal social networks (what Sageman terms "leaderless jihad"). According to the *New York Times*, the dustup between Hoffman and Sageman represents more than an academic dispute over ideas; rather, it symbolizes "the battle for influence and resources in Western counterterrorism policy."[77]

Hoffman's assessment is based on the global influence of al-Qaeda and the vitality of its organizational command structure. If Hoffman is correct, then counterterrorism policy must focus on military efforts to destroy al-Qaeda's central leadership along with its infrastructure of training camps and finance and communication systems, thereby eliminating the potential for Western Muslims to travel to Afghanistan, Pakistan, Yemen, and Somalia in order to receive terrorist training and return home with orders and expertise to strike local targets. Sageman sees al-Qaeda not as a static command-and-control organization but as an evolving threat that is now being driven by the Internet. The Internet has enabled a new generation of terrorist wannabes ("jihobbyists" as some call them). They are simply "a bunch of guys"— friends, roommates, or classmates—who undergo the process of radicalization together. If Sageman is correct, then counterterrorism policy must focus on law enforcement surveillance of suspicious e-mail and cellphone traffic, social-network messaging, and the like. Some analysts have dismissed this debate as trivial, arguing that both views are credible. Table 4.3 considers the debate as it relates to prison-based terrorism.

In the United States, 80 percent of the terrorists belonged to homegrown groups. Yet some of them were inspired by al-Qaeda, even though they did not travel abroad for training. Examples include JIS out of New Folsom Prison—who actually called themselves "Al-Qaeda of California"— and Luqman Ameen Abdullah's Ummah (cases 41 and 42), charged with fencing stolen goods, illegal gun dealing, and plotting to bomb the 2006 Super Bowl in Detroit. Abdullah would later die in a shootout with the FBI. Likewise, Michael Finton (case 44) thought he was working with al-Qaeda operatives when he parked a truck loaded with a ton of explosives in front of the Paul Findley Federal Building in downtown Springfield, Illinois, in 2009. Once Finton was out of range of the blast zone, he attempted to detonate the bomb with a cellphone. However, the explosives were fake, supplied by the FBI to catch Finton trying to carry out an act of terrorism. Also, three of the so-called Newburgh Four—charged with a planned bomb attack on two synagogues in the Riverdale section of the Bronx and the simultaneous shooting down of military aircraft over Newburgh in 2009 (cases 43, 45, and 47)—were influenced by a police informant who

Table 4.3. Characteristics of terrorism or threatened terrorism (N = 51)

Country	Types of Organizations	
	International group*	Homegrown group*
United States (34 terrorists)	7	27
Britain (6)	4	2
Spain (5)	5	0
France (4)	4	0
Jordan (I)	I	0
Egypt (I)	I	0
	Nature of Plots		
	Executed	Operational	Aspirational
United States (34)	23	4	7
Britain (6)	0	4	2
Spain (5)	3	0	2
France (4)	4	0	0
Jordan (I)	I	0	0
Egypt (I)	I	0	0
	32	8	II

* Number of terrorists reported

claimed affiliation with the terrorist organization Jaish-e-Mohammed, based in Pakistan.

The remaining cases show a clear international connection. They represent the richest test of the Hoffman/Sageman debate. Sageman contends that Hoffman overlooks his main point, namely, "that the threat from al-Qaeda and it progeny has evolved over time."[78] In the realm of tactics, vivid evidence of this evolvement appeared only days after bin Laden's death when, in an apparent reprisal strike, an al-Qaeda-linked terrorist walked into a popular tourist café in Marrakesh, Morocco, wearing a "hippie wig" and carrying a guitar and two bags packed with explosives. The blast killed seventeen, including French and Swiss tourists.[79] Hippie clothing and hairstyles are Western symbols of freedom and respect for individual rights. To appear that way is a far cry from the stern, clean-shaven, Arab-looking businessmen who boarded U.S. flights on the morning of 9/11. A similar agility is evidenced in the prison-based terrorists with international connections. In fact, these cases represent innovations in the field of terrorism.

In addition to the former Guantanamo detainees, the international cases include Jeff Fort (case 5), the leader of El Rukn (Arabic for "stones")—a notorious black street gang from the south side of Chicago. Throughout the 1980s, El Rukn used its own version of Moorish Science to promote gang activity at the Stateville and Joliet maximum-security prisons in Illinois, representing the earliest known example of Prison Islam. By 1986, Fort was doing time for drug trafficking at the Federal Correctional Center in Bastrop, Texas, where he continued to control El Rukn's activities from his cell. From this operational base, Fort developed ties with representatives of the Libyan dictator Moammar Gadhafi in order to commit unspecified acts of terrorism, most likely in downtown Chicago. During the planning stages, Fort used a prison telephone to arrange a $2.5 million payment from the Libyans, a conversation that was taped by authorities. After an El Rukn member bought a hand-held rocket launcher from undercover FBI agents, the conspiracy came to an ignominious end, leading to the conviction of Fort and others on terrorism charges. Even so, it was the first time a convict used a prison telephone to mobilize gang members and foreign nationals into a terrorist plot against the United States.

In 1994, Aqil Collins (case 8), an ex-offender from a California juvenile boot camp who had converted to Sunni Islam while in custody, traveled to Afghanistan where he trained with Afghan Arabs who would later become early members of al-Qaeda—predating the well-known "American Taliban" John Walker Lindh by a decade.

After his radicalization and release from a Minnesota prison in 2009, the Somali American Farah Mohamed Beledi (case 50), traveled to Somalia where he joined forces with al-Shabaab, thus leading to his federal indictment on terrorism charges back in Minneapolis. Two years later, at a peace-keeping base in Mogadishu, Beledi became the first prison-based terrorist with U.S. citizenship to blow himself up in a suicide bombing, killing two African Union troops and a government official. For law enforcement, the fact that a former American prisoner had engaged in a suicide operation in Somalia raised the possibility that suicide bombings could start taking place in the United States (most likely, in Minneapolis).

Hoffman argues that al-Qaeda is "much like a shark, which must keep moving forward, no matter how slowly or incrementally, or die."[80] The shark moves slowly but it remains a shark. Sageman contends that the shark has evolved into a barracuda. And the barracuda may evolve into a crocodile or perhaps become a squid. Over time, al-Qaeda's prison-based progeny have evolved in a similar way. The necessity for evolvement in terrorist tactics has long been recognized by al-Qaeda. As bin Laden once told an al-Qaeda associate, attacks on the scale of 9/11 could never be replicated and would have to be replaced with alternative tactics.[81]

Due to a greater degree of alienation among European Muslims, Sageman argues that there have been far more homegrown Islamic terrorists in Europe than in the United States. Table 4.3 does not bear this out with respect to prison-based terrorists. Of the six British terrorists, four were affiliated with international organizations (cases 16, 17, 26, and 40). All four of the French terrorists were associated with either the Algerian-based Armed Islamic Group, known by its French acronym GIA, or the Partisans of Victory, also a Salafist group (cases 9-12). And all five of the Spanish terrorists were either Moroccan émigrés or Algerian Salafists loosely affiliated with both al-Qaeda and GIA (cases 20-24). Further evidence of an international connection between the prison-based terrorists is found in the distinguished investigation of the French security expert Jean-Charles Brisard. According to his research, back in 1997 the head of the Spanish cell that would later become al-Qaeda of Europe, Abu Dahdah, sent $11,000 to Abu Mohammed al-Maqdisis while he was confined with Abu Musab al-Zarqawi at the Suwaqah prison in Jordan.[82]

This is another trend that has extended beyond the years that are covered in the database. In 2012, a series of brutal slayings transfixed France and raised renewed concern about the role of prisoner radicalization in the development of a new generation of Islamic terrorists. Beginning on March 11, Mohammed Merah, a twenty-three-year-old Frenchman of Algerian descent, went on a three-day shooting spree in southwestern France and killed seven, including three children at a Jewish school, representing France's deadliest terrorist attack since 1995. Prior to being killed in a police shootout, Merah claimed that he was affiliated with al-Qaeda and that the killings were meant to avenge the suffering of Palestinian children and to protest French intervention abroad. Initial reports indicated that Merah had a lengthy criminal record and that it was during one of his stints in prison that he became politicized into Salafi ideology. Even though Merah ultimately acted alone in the killings, after his release from prison he traveled to Afghanistan and Pakistan where he is thought to have received terrorist training.[83] Nicolas Sarkozy, the French president at the time, immediately instructed Ministry of Justice officials to investigate the promotion of Islamic extremism in French prisons. Described as "hardly a new problem," the New York Times concluded that "nearly every French proponent of fundamentalist or jihadi thinking has been radicalized in French prisons."[84]

In the main, the database comes down on the side of Sageman's assessment, though Hoffman's analysis should not be ignored by any means. Prison-based terrorists have evolved over time, as they continue to evolve, with respect to both organization and tactics. Yet the most significant evolvement has occurred among terrorists with links to international groups, including al-Qaeda and its affiliates. The majority of prison-based terrorists do not have formal ties with global Salafi networks, but they nevertheless draw inspiration from speeches, fatwas, and manifestos distributed by al-Qaeda and its associates over the Internet—which is notable because prisoners are routinely denied Internet access, suggesting that these materials are being smuggled into prisons via clandestine inmate communications systems. Perhaps most important, the database shows that prison-based terrorists emerge from pockets of radicalization that are loosely connected to each other through a chain of informal social networks. While Hoffman says nothing about informal networks, Sageman contends that post-9/11 terrorist groups are composed of "a bunch of guys" that go through the radicalizing process together. The same dynamic seems to be playing out between prisoners, indicating that the appropriate counterterrorism response is in the development of intelligence gathered by frontline prison staff, including prison intelligence officers, guards, counselors, and chaplains. Intelligence is the primary weapon in the fight against terrorism and the best intelligence comes from those closest to the source of provocation.

* * *

Researching incidents of prisoner radicalization and terrorism has been called a "daunting task."[85] The most daunting task is the cataloguing of terrorist criminality. Some of the cases considered here—like that of Michael Finton—have played a role in only one terrorist event. Others, most notably Zarqawi and Zawahiri, have been involved in terrorist campaigns involving dozens of events (killing and wounding tens of thousands it must be said), making it impossible to squeeze all pertinent information into a database. For those involved in multiple events, then, table 4.3 offers a summary estimate of their overall competence. The Nature of Plots section is organized into the categories Executed, Operational, or Aspirational. Executed means that the plot was carried out. Operational means that the offender had the means to execute a plot but it was aborted for one reason or another. Aspirational indicates that the offender had the motive to carry out an act of terrorism but lacked the operational resources to do so.

In the majority of cases (thirty-two out of fifty-one, or 63 percent), a terrorist event was executed, representing a fairly sophisticated level of criminal competence. Sixteen percent of the cases were operational and 21 percent were aspirational. The U.S. figures are significant given this criticism of prisoner radicalization by the criminologist James Austin: "Let us remind ourselves that the number of actual cases in which terrorist acts have been led by released U.S. prisoners who were radicalized while incarcerated is zero. . . . Existing intelligence and self-regulating prisoner control systems—coupled with the general *lack of competence* to become an effective terrorist cell—make the whole issue mute and unworthy of serious inquiry."[86]

According to table 4.3, the number of cases in which executed terrorist acts have been led by released or incarcerated U.S. prisoners who were radicalized in prison is at least twenty-three (some were involved in multiple events), accounting for 70 percent of the U.S. cases.[87] Fourteen cases have occurred since 9/11. True, some of the operational and aspirational plots are characterized by criminal incompetence. At least one, the Newburgh Four plot to shoot down military aircraft with stinger missiles, may have been delusional. But if "effective terrorist cells" refers to autonomous underground groups that attack government or civilian targets, then terrorists radicalized in U.S. prisons are competent more often than not.

To say that there have been no "actual cases" of terrorism by radicalized U.S. prisoners is to turn a blind eye on the Jasper murder and the multiple terrorist attacks against U.S. and other Western targets by the former Guantanamo detainees. The argument asks us to ignore Eldridge Cleaver's 1968 shootout with the Oakland police and his alleged instigation of the 1971 Marin County Courthouse massacre while in exile.[88] It also asks us to disregard Cleaver's behind-the-scenes involvement in two airline hijackings committed by the Black Panthers in the early 1970s.[89] It asks us to overlook George Jackson's killing of guards and inmates at San Quentin (case 2). It asks us to take no notice of the leading role of Donald DeFreeze (case 3) in the SLA's assassination of the Oakland School Superintendent Marcus Foster; several bank robberies and the killing of a bank clerk; the bombing of the Emeryville, California, police station; the kidnapping and raping of Patty Hearst; and a two-hour gun battle with Los Angeles police officers where he met his end.[90] It asks us to close our eyes to Farah Mohamed Beledi's suicide bombing and recent cases of terrorism committed in the name of Prison Islam, as well as acts of terrorism carried out by ex-prisoners affiliated with the radical right. These cases include the following.

As a founding member of the Order, considered by the FBI as the most competent domestic terrorist group it has ever faced, Gary Yarbrough (case 4)—who as a member of the Aryan Brotherhood converted to Christian Identity in the Arizona State Prison through the evangelizing efforts of the Aryan Nations prison ministry—took part in counterfeiting, assassination, and several spectacular 1984 Brinks armored-truck robberies, one of which netted more than $3.6 million, the largest overland robbery in American history at the time. As James Aho notes, Yarbrough was "not your standard criminal."[91]

As founding members of the Aryan Republican Army (ARA), the focal point of one of the most extensive FBI terrorism investigations of the 1990s, Richard Guthrie and Peter Langan (cases 6 and 7)—both prison converts to Christian Identity—robbed twenty-two Midwestern banks and distributed their robbery proceeds throughout the terrorist underground. Researchers have marshaled a wealth of evidence showing that a portion of the ARA's robbery money ended up in the hands of Timothy McVeigh, who used it to finance the Oklahoma City bombing.[92]

In 2001, Leo Felton (case 18)—a six-foot-seven, 225-pound biracial prison convert to the White Order of Thule at Attica (a bizarre mixture of Odinism/Asatru, Nazi occultism, and myths about the Order)—committed counterfeiting and the armed robbery of a Boston bank in order to finance an attack against the U.S. Holocaust Museum in Washington, D.C., meant to ignite a "holy race war." Felton did not bomb the museum but proceeds from the bank robbery were used to buy composite materials for the attack, including ammonium nitrate fertilizer (also used by McVeigh in Oklahoma City). Therefore, the bank robbery—committed "by force and violence" according to the federal indictment against Felton—was executed "in the furtherance of a political objective," thus fitting the FBI's definition of terrorism.[93]

In 2007, an Aryan Circle leader named Dennis Clem and his AC girlfriend, Tonya "Little Feather" Smith (cases 30 and 33)—Clem was a Texas prison convert to Odinism/Asatru and Smith was converted to Wicca in a Texas women's prison—committed multiple homicides while on a methamphetamine binge across the South, including the killing of two Louisiana police detectives. In 2008, Howard Cain, Eric Floyd, and Levon Warner (cases 36, 37, and 39), all converts to Prison Islam, committed bank robbery and the murder of a Philadelphia police officer.

These cases are few in number and largely unknown to the public. Nevertheless, they show that acts of prison-based terrorism are a reality in the United States, just as they are a reality abroad. Not only that, but the cases represent some of the most spectacular instances of terrorist-oriented criminality in recent memory. They matter because prison has been largely overlooked as an operational base for terrorist recruitment and organizing. Only by understanding this potential threat can counterterrorism officials take steps to train intelligence officers and prison staff about the warning signs of an imminent attack.

* * *

Finally, table 4.4 shows the elapsed time between an offender's approximate month and year of release from custody and a terrorist event. For those involved in multiple events, the time lag signifies the time between release and the first event.

Table 4.4. Time lag between prison release and terrorism (N = 51)

	0	<1 yr.	1–2 yrs.	3–5 yrs.	6–10 yrs.	>10 yrs.	Not known	Mean yrs.
United States (32)	6	7	7	4	1	2	5	2.6
Britain (6)			1	1	3	1		7.4
Spain (5)			3	2				2.4
France (4)	1		2				1	1
Jordan (1)			1					—
Egypt (1)							1	—

In six U.S. cases, there was no time lag (zero) because the terrorist plots were waged from prison. In addition to Jeff Fort's Libyan conspiracy, conducted from the federal prison at Bastrop, Texas, these include the George Jackson case; the JIS plot waged by Kevin James from New Folsom Prison; Eric Floyd's 2008 bank robbery and murder of a police officer while living in a Philadelphia halfway house (case 37); and Mohammad Bassir's conspiracy to kill FBI agents and bomb the Detroit Super Bowl, piloted from a Michigan prison (case 42).

Table 4.4 shows that nearly one-fourth of the U.S. cases occurred within months of release from prison. Leo Felton's crime spree to fund the Holocaust Museum bombing began one month after his release from New Jersey's Northern State Prison. Donald DeFreeze organized the Marcus Foster assassination seven months after escaping from Soledad (he simply walked away from his job in the prison boiler room). The Jasper murder took place some nine months after Brewer and King were paroled from the Beto Unit in Texas. Six months after his release from Guantanamo, Abdullah Mehsud organized his kidnapping of the Chinese engineers. Two months after Abdullah Rasoul was released from Guantanamo, he waged his attacks against U.S. and British forces. Said Ali al-Shihri joined al-Qaeda and bombed the U.S. embassy in Yemen within a year of his release from Guantanamo. At Kevin James's behest, six months into his parole from New Folsom Prison, Levar Washington recruited three others into the JIS plot and began robbing gas stations to raise money for the attacks.

In all, almost 40 percent of the terrorist events took place while a U.S. prisoner was either in custody or had been on the streets for less than one year. Another 24 percent occurred within two years; 12 percent occurred within three to five years; and the rest between six and ten years or more. In the United States, the mean lag time between release from prison and the terrorist event was 2.6 years. This compares to Britain (at 7.4 years) in a way that is not favorable to U.S. security.

Moreover, there are three ways in which a prisoner can become involved in terrorism, and all three have occurred in the United States. Inmates have launched terrorist plots after being released (or escaping) from prison. They have waged plots in collaboration with parolees and coconspirators in the community. And they have waged plots from prison cells without help from outsiders. No matter the method, once a prisoner is radicalized it does not take an excessive amount of time before those beliefs are transformed into violence.

* * *

What we have here, then, is evidence of fifty-one people who were not terrorists when they went to prison but became terrorists as a result of their prison experiences. What do we know of these experiences? In the most obvious cases, they involved torture. In other cases they involved prison conditions that were chaotic and violent. And in still other cases the open sources used to construct the database are silent on the matter. And what do we know of the prisoners who became terrorists? We know that they were typically radicalized during their early twenties; that they are predominantly black; and that they became involved in terrorism around the age of thirty. In the United States, these terrorists belong primarily to small homegrown groups that are often motivated by foreign organizations, including al-Qaeda; European jihadists are more likely to be affiliated with international groups. We know that the peak years of their terrorism coincided with the U.S.-led war in Iraq. We know that their terrorism is inimically linked to prisoner subcultures through religious extremism—the most serious being the threat posed by Prison Islam and a growing extremist movement motivated by Salafi-Jihadist theology. We also know that social networks matter in prison just as they matter to jihadist groups in the free world and that prison-based terrorism has evolved over time, from bank robberies and police shootouts to suicide bombings. Finally, we know that these terrorists exhibit a fairly sophisticated level of criminal competence, and the time frame between radicalization and commission of a terrorist act is measured in a few short years, if not months.

What we don't know is the relative importance of imprisonment as compared to other life-changing experiences. Therefore, in the following chapter I draw four paradigmatic U.S. cases from the database and examine them under the lens of life-course theory. That analysis provides a social context for understanding how a stretch in prison contributed to a radicalization process that led to bona fide acts of terrorism during the post-9/11 era. While radicalizing in prison is certainly important, it is only one of several key turning points along the pathway to terrorism.

5

Pathways to Terrorism

Addressing a Singapore conference during the early days of the Obama administration, U.S. Defense Secretary Robert Gates warned that the West was vulnerable to a dual threat of al-Qaeda terrorism from both European and American recruits. He added his concern that there also was "the development of violent, extremist networks" within Western nations.[1] This assessment is valuable because it draws attention to both international and domestic dangers posed by Islamic extremists. Yet the assessment does not go far enough—entirely overlooked is the white supremacy movement. In fact, the major domestic terrorism unit in the United States, the Department of Homeland Security (DHS), abandoned its efforts to gather intelligence on white supremacy groups in 2009 following a firestorm of criticism by lawmakers of the political right who accused the DHS of painting all conservatives as potential domestic terrorists.[2] Domestic plots are not included in the presidential daily briefings on terrorism or in interagency threat assessments within the federal government.[3] This is a big mistake—at least that is what history suggests. Racist antigovernment groups have been responsible for nearly all of the successful terrorist attacks in America since the early 1980s.[4] After years of dormancy, the movement is experiencing a revival brought on by the election of President Obama, rising unemployment, and the contentious debate over U.S. immigration policy. The bombing of government buildings and the killing of scores of young people at a summer camp in Norway during the summer of 2011 has, however, focused new attention around the world on the subculture of right-wing activists, stimulating debate over the focus of counterterrorism policy.

Four emerging threats are examined in the following cases. One looks at the white supremacy movement and another examines the threat posed by Somali gangs. In 2009, forty-two people were indicted on terrorist-related crimes in the United States, fourteen of them for recruiting Somalis into jihad.[5] The other two cases interrogate the threat of lone-wolf terrorists—one influenced by Prison Islam and the other inspired by an Internet-recruiting campaign by Anwar al-Awlaki.

A case-study approach is appropriate here because it not only has the ability to analyze a small number of cases, but also has the capacity to discover the sequence of individual trajectories, or "turning points," leading to terrorism. The case-study approach also can examine the extent to which these turning points were embedded in experiences deriving from prison social networks, clandestine communication systems, radical religious beliefs, and leadership competences—all of which can enable the transformation of an individual's violent tendencies into terrorist causes. The sociologist Howard Becker argues that case studies focus on process, or "the temporal dimension in which phenomena occur in specific settings."[6] According to Becker, social processes form a narrative analysis that has a story to tell. As we shall see, there is considerable variance in what is known about the following stories. That is a problem common to all terrorism research and it is unfortunate because the lack of available information prevents the writing of biographies that can reveal the underlying causes of radicalization. "Until we can answer basic questions about the trajectories radicalized individuals have followed," observes the veteran terrorism scholar Brian Jenkins, "our ability to understand and counter radicalization will be severely limited."[7] Yet to the extent that processes of radicalization contained within the subsequent accounts are similar across time and place, then perhaps something may be said about the common denominators of prison-based terrorism.

* * *

Ruben Luis Leon Shumpert (case 32) was born in Seattle, Washington, in 1977 to a Hispanic mother and an African American father. Reflecting on his upbringing in a court filing years later, Shumpert wrote, "My life has been peppered with substance abuse, crime, and hardships so severe it would have completely destroyed most people."[8] Emblematic of his adaptation to these hardships, when Shumpert was twelve years old he bought a gun and tattooed a large cross on his arm demonstrating his love for Jesus. Although Shumpert claimed that his background "neither defines [him] nor is it a contributing factor to [his] current situation," these two personal obsessions—guns and religion—would play a crucial role in what lay ahead for him.

As a teenager, Shumpert was arrested and remanded to juvenile detention on a firearms violation. With his release, the stage was set for a series of life-course events that would become turning points along Shumpert's pathway to terrorism. These events were made possible by four interrelated social networks.

Network 1: The Prison. According to Shumpert's statement to the court, by the age of twenty he had become a prosperous Seattle drug dealer. He bought expensive cars, assault rifles, and a house complete with surveillance

cameras.[9] In 1998, Shumpert was arrested and convicted of drug trafficking and sentenced to the Monroe State Prison near Everett, Washington. He
learned to cut hair in prison, and he is likely to have associated mainly with
other minority inmates. Shortly before his release on August 6, 2002, Shumpert converted from the Catholic faith to Sunni Islam. Like most Islamic converts, Shumpert chose a Muslim name to mark his new symbolic birth to the
religion: Amir Abdul Muhaimeen. He was then twenty-five years old.

Network 2: The Barbershop. Returning to Seattle, Shumpert gave up
substance abuse and drug dealing and vowed to stay away from guns. He
quickly became destitute and homeless, though, and sought shelter in a local
mosque. There he met a man who owned the Crescent Cuts Barbershop,
located in a ramshackle two-story building at 7821 Rainier Avenue South—
a low-income black community on the city's south side. Shumpert went to
work at Crescent Cuts (Crescent being the symbol of Islam), thereby put-
ting to use both the skill and the religion he had learned in prison. As in
many African American communities, the barbershop was a neighborhood
gathering place. According to a federal court document, "The shop served
as a casual meeting place for . . . like-minded individuals, mostly African
American men with criminal histories who had converted to Islam, either in
prison or after contact later with prison converts."[10] Sensing the potential for
terrorist recruitment among these prison-based Muslims in the year following 9/11, the Seattle office of the FBI developed an undercover informant—a
convicted felon who was paid $3,000 a month by the FBI—to monitor activi-
ties inside the barbershop.[11]

According to FBI testimony, "conversations at the barber shop often
turned to militancy and the need to be ready for jihad against the 'kafir,' or
non-believers. The acquisition of firearms was a frequent topic of conversation in that connection."[12] Among those involved in these conversations were
members of a local Somali street gang. There are no fewer than three versions of Shumpert's radicalization; it is possible that all three played a role.
A source close to Shumpert insists that it was through the Somali gang that
Shumpert was introduced to the Takfir wal Hijrah movement (the *takfir* doctrine involves declaring other Muslims to be apostates), a breakaway group
from Egypt's Muslim Brotherhood that would also influence both Ayman
al-Zawahiri and the Madrid train-bomber Jamal Ahmidan, the Chinaman.[13]
The FBI, however, asserted that Shumpert was radicalized by an older Somali
American named Abraham Sheik Mohamed, thought to be a moderate Salafist and former member of a terrorist group in Somalia, who was then the
presiding imam at Rainier Valley's Abu-Bakr Mosque.[14] For his part, Shumpert claimed that he was introduced to "radical Islam" by the FBI informant.[15]

The investigation went on for three years (from 2002 to 2005), during which time Shumpert became more attuned to world events and emerged as the most outspoken member of the barbershop group. He was also its most religiously devout. By this point Shumpert typically dressed in a white robe, wore a Muslim prayer cap and a beard, and had developed a prayer mark or a "raisin" in the middle of his forehead, the mark of a pious Muslim who grinds his forehead into the ground during prayer. Shumpert also got married, became a father, opened a homeless shelter, and conducted clothing drives for the poor. He also took part in interfaith dialogues at several churches and synagogues, and he volunteered at a shelter for troubled youth. Shumpert was an asset to his community. "I went from forcefully taking from people to quietly giving to people," as he would write.[16] Yet on one occasion Shumpert gave the FBI informant a counterfeit $100 bill. At another time, he sold the informant a handgun. Meanwhile, barbershop discussions about the war in Iraq were likely at fever pitch. Shumpert described his grievance like this: "Look at Iraq. Nineteen extremists kill over 3,000 Americans on 9/11 and over 30,000 Iraqis are killed as an indirect result. . . . The extremist commits an act of terror and the Muslim community always pays the price. So, many of us, in many different ways, have joined the fight against this evil ideology."[17] For Shumpert, the root cause of post-9/11 terrorism was terrorism perpetrated by the United States of America.

At length, Shumpert met several men who had recently returned from Chechnya. They gave Shumpert some jihadist videos (praising the 9/11 hijackers, the Taliban, al-Qaeda, and Chechen suicide bombers) and Shumpert began showing these videos to his customers at Crescent Cuts, including children as young as eleven years old.[18] According to the informant, as these videos played the group adopted the rallying cry "Black Hawk Down!' in reference to the shooting down in 1993 of a U.S. military helicopter in Somalia and the killing of its crew. Shumpert also made available to his customers such terrorist training manuals as *The Terrorist's Cookbook* and *The Minimanual of the Urban Guerrilla*.[19] With his grievance at an all-time high and reminiscent of the Chinaman's attitude prior to the bombings in Madrid, Shumpert announced that he was going to Iraq to fight alongside Abu Musab al-Zarqawi.[20] Yet before he could do so, on April 15, 2005, Shumpert was arrested for beating a man during a barbershop dispute and was locked up in Seattle's King County Jail. Before Shumpert could post bail, the FBI unsealed charges in federal court accusing him of passing counterfeit money and being a felon in possession of a firearm. The FBI then opened a second investigation, this one charging Shumpert with inciting terrorism and conducting military training inside the barbershop.

Network 3: The Jail. The FBI questioned Shumpert about his involvement with al-Qaeda and Osama bin Laden and about his intentions to carry out terrorist attacks against the United States. This proved fruitless for the FBI and its terrorism investigation of Shumpert ground to a halt. Meanwhile, scores of Seattle residents came to Shumpert's defense. Some signed a petition supporting leniency, and others wrote letters to the U.S. Attorney, saying that Shumpert was a positive influence in their community. This, too, came to no avail. Shumpert was still looking at a two-year federal prison sentence, leading Shumpert to take his most drastic step toward terrorism. In King County, Shumpert met a group of Somali inmates who advised him to accept a plea agreement, pleading guilty on the counterfeiting charge in exchange for dropping the assault and firearms violations, allowing Shumpert to be released on bond so that he could flee America and join the cause of jihad in Somalia.[21] He would do just that.

On May 20, 2006, after a year in custody, Shumpert was released on his own recognizance and ordered to reside in a halfway house until his sentencing on July 9. Reporters would later claim that Shumpert was ordered to surrender his passport as well; yet there is no indication that he did so or even that Shumpert had a passport.[22] A more likely scenario is provided by terrorists who were later associated with Shumpert. They contend that, while at the halfway house, Shumpert used his former jailhouse contacts to acquire a forged passport.[23] When Shumpert failed to appear for his July sentencing, the FBI raided a Somali grocery that once housed Crescent Cuts in an unsuccessful attempt to arrest him.

Network 4: The Transnational Terrorist Community. Shumpert had already jumped bail and fled the country, flying to Somalia via Dubai. Upon his arrival at the Mogadishu airport, Shumpert was met by members of al-Shabaab, a militia of violent Islamist guerrillas at war against Somalia's weak U.S.-backed transitional government because it is not based on Islam. In 2007, al-Shabaab established a strict *shariah* code (Islamic law) and, to enable recruitment, its own media division featuring jihadist videos complete with English rap lyrics. A year later, they were joined by al-Qaeda terrorists wanted in connection with the 1998 embassy bombings in Kenya and Tanzania. At this point, al-Shabaab and al-Qaeda become one. "We are negotiating how we can unite into one [with al-Qaeda]," said a senior al-Shabaab leader at the time. "We will take our orders from Sheik Osama bin Laden because we are his students."[24] Accordingly, al-Shabaab was designated as a terrorist organization by the U.S. State Department.[25] Renowned for its "summary justice" against government officials and innocent Sufi Muslims, al-Shabaab had in recent years committed a series of arsons, bombings, kidnappings, beheadings, amputations, and a mortar attack against a plane carrying a U.S. congressman.[26] Soon al-Shabaab would wage an assassination attempt against U.S. Secretary of State Hillary Clinton during her 2008 visit to Nairobi, Kenya.[27]

In preparation for jihad, al-Shabaab arranged for Shumpert to purchase an AK-47 assault rifle and took him to a training camp where he was issued the Shabaab insignia to wear on his uniform—the patch featured a green circle with a yellow banner on top reading, in Arabic, "the Movement of the Shabaab Mujahideen." The center of the image includes a map of the Horn of Africa, an open Koran, and two crossed AK-47s. For Shumpert, it could have been a personal medallion.

Shumpert was not the only American Muslim recruited by al-Shabaab during these years—yet he was the only American recruit who was *not* a Somali—representing a recruiting innovation for al-Shabaab. Between 2007 and 2009, at least twenty young Somali American men left Minnesota to attend al-Shabaab's training camps.[28] On October 29, 2007, Shirwa Ahmed, a twenty-seven-year-old Somali American college student from Minneapolis, blew himself up near Mogadishu in one of five simultaneous suicide bombings attributed to al-Shabaab, thereby becoming the first American suicide bomber anywhere.[29] It is conceivable that Shumpert used the same pipeline that brought Ahmed from Minnesota to Somalia and that would later bring the Minneapolis suicide bomber Farah Mohamed Beledi (case 50).[30]

On November 18, 2007, Shumpert placed a call from Somalia to an FBI special agent, Robert Walby, in Seattle, taunting Walby by saying that he was in Somalia and would not be returning to the United States. In the background, Walby could hear men chanting "Allah Akbar" ("God is Great"), often used by jihadists as a terrorist battle cry. On November 27, Shumpert placed a second call to Walby, this time making a direct threat, saying that he and the agent were now sworn enemies. "He then added," Walby testified, "that he and his Muslim associates would destroy everything the United States stood for."[31]

The rest of the story is sketchy. According to a Shabaab statement, sometime in 2008 Shumpert's brigade traveled to Adale, about 150 kilometers north of Mogadishu, where Shumpert was shot in the back during a battle with Ethiopian soldiers and evacuated with the wounded to Mogadishu for treatment.[32] After his recovery in early 2009, the militia retreated to a forest near Mogadishu. Within al-Shabaab's ranks at this point was a counterterrorism informant attached to AFRICOM, the U.S. military command for Africa.

While living in the forest, a small group boarded a boat during another fight with Ethiopian rivals, destination unknown. Acting on intelligence from the informant, the group was targeted by a U.S. rocket attack, killing three. Soon after, Joseph Lieberman, the chairman of the Senate Homeland Security Committee, announced that Ruben Shumpert was among the dead.[33]

Three features of Shumpert's story resonate with the major takeaways from the database analysis. First, Shumpert's association with al-Shabaab occurred at the height of the Iraq War, during the peak years of prison-based terrorism, suggesting that Shumpert was part of a global anti-Western terrorist movement rooted in the prison experience. Evidence of this movement is found in an al-Shabaab interview with Ayman al-Zawahiri on the fourth anniversary of 9/11. "I take this opportunity to address our prisoners," said Zawahiri. "We have not forgotten you. We are still committed to the debt of your salvation . . . until we shatter your shackles."[34] Al-Shabaab would shatter the shackles of Ruben Shumpert and set him free to fight jihad in Somalia. Second, each of the social networks that Shumpert was involved with—from the prison to the barbershop; from the jail to al-Shabaab—served to facilitate the transformation of Shumpert's existing violent tendencies into a terrorist cause. Radicalization behind bars was not his only pathway to terrorism. Finally, although Shumpert's pathway was inspired by several religious orientations, it was the amorphous social movement called the Salafi-Jihad that led him to terrorism.

* * *

Another takeaway from the database is that, as incredible as it may seem, inmates are capable of waging terrorist plots from behind bars without assistance from outsiders. Such a tactic has long been common knowledge among prisoners. Prison intelligence officers routinely discover inmate plots to send crude explosive devices to governors, congressmen, and even presidents, yet none of them have been successful. Al-Qaeda tacticians are fully aware of this potential. In 2011, New York City police arrested a Muslim convert who had used an al-Qaeda article called "How to Build a Bomb in the Kitchen of Your Mom" to construct a pipe bomb using match heads, Christmas lights, and a converted clock, yet it, too, was unsuccessful.[35] The following case represents a classic example of prison terrorism that achieved its desired results.

Marc Harold Ramsey (case 38) was born to a Caucasian mother and an African American father in Detroit on March 1, 1969. The couple divorced a year later, leaving the infant with his mother in their Detroit home. As he grew up, two behavioral patterns emerged that would ultimately play a crucial role in Ramsey's criminality. On one hand, Ramsey developed an intense interest in military affairs; on the other, he came to resolve family problems with violence. The latter problem first arose in 1977 when eight-year-old Ramsey set his mother's house on fire in an attempt to kill his abusive stepfather as he slept. Still, Ramsey was an outstanding student and an accomplished athlete. At thirteen, he was accepted into a military academy where he earned straight A's; later, Ramsey became an all-state baseball player. During these years Ramsey also maintained contact with his biological father, a Vietnam War veteran who worked as a nuclear engineer for the U.S. Department of Energy in Maryland.[36]

Following in his father's footsteps, after graduating from high school Ramsey enlisted in the Air Force. Yet trouble soon darkened his door. Unable to manage his financial affairs, Ramsey began writing bad checks and was arrested for larceny. Prior to his trial, he went AWOL, only to be captured and court-martialed for desertion. After serving three years in a military brig, Ramsey returned to his Air Force duties but once again fell on hard times when his three-year-old daughter was killed in a drive-by shooting in East Chicago, Indiana. Again he went AWOL and tracked down the man who murdered his daughter with the intent of killing him. And with that, the stage was set for Ramsey's entry into a terrorism trajectory that occurred within two social networks.

Network 1: The Prison. As a result of Ramsey's decision to avenge his daughter's death, he was sentenced to twenty-two years in the Indiana Department of Correction on kidnapping charges. It was here that Ramsey was introduced to the Moorish Science Temple. "I made a tour of nearly all the prisons in Indiana," Ramsey recalled. "And at each one I ran into more and more brothers who taught me about Moorish Science."[37] Accordingly, at the age of twenty-five he converted through the proselytizing efforts of a Moorish elder. In this tradition, Marc Harold Ramsey became Akeem Ramsey El.

In prison, Ramsey gained the reputation of a devout Muslim with an avid interest in military history. His views were shaped by the writings of Malcolm X and Louis Farrakhan, as well as newspaper articles and television coverage of America's role in the Middle East. Like many observers of Middle Eastern affairs, Ramsey found America's involvement in the region to be fraught with contradiction. "The 'do as I say not as I do' approach by our government loathes me [*sic*]," he explained. "The only nation in the world to ever use an atomic bomb on another country wants to tell another country you can't. Not you *should* not use one but you *cannot* even have the technology. And I don't even [want to] begin the issue of US supporting violations of international law committed by Israel."[38]

Ramsey became known to the U.S. Secret Service during the presidency of George W. Bush. Writing from an Indiana prison, Ramsey sent Bush and Vice President Dick Cheney a series of threatening letters, fulminating about their mishandling of Middle Eastern affairs. "He is on record with us and he is known as a prolific letter writer," a Secret Service spokesman would later say.[39] It was also during this time that Ramsey's father became critically ill due to his exposure to Agent Orange in Vietnam. Ramsey would later explain that his father's illness was "very important in the motives of some of my actions."[40]

Network 2: The Jail. Ramsey was released from prison in 2006, and he then relocated to Denver, Colorado. On September 17, 2007, however, Ramsey was arrested for felony menacing, second-degree assault, and being a fugitive from justice. Unable to post a $350,000 bond, Ramsey was locked up in the Arapahoe County Detention Center where he was subsequently charged with assaulting another prisoner and a guard, making Ramsey a high-security inmate.[41]

A year later, a U.S. Army scientist committed suicide as federal prosecutors were preparing to indict him in connection with the 2001 anthrax mailings that killed five people in the aftermath of 9/11. This event, which gained national media attention, had an intense effect on the already politically conscious Marc Ramsey, taking him far beyond the traditions of Moorish Science.

On August 20, 2008, Ramsey wrote a letter to the presumptive Republican presidential candidate John McCain. Before sealing it, Ramsey placed a white powder substance inside the envelope. He mailed the letter to McCain's campaign headquarters in Centennial, Colorado, and he affixed his name, inmate number, and location of the jail on the envelope—as required on all outgoing mail from the facility.

At 3 p.m. the following day, Ramsey's letter arrived at the headquarters (the Senator was in Sedona, Arizona, that day). "Senator McCain, IFF [*sic*] you are reading this then you are already DEAD!" the letter began. "Unless of course you can't or don't breathe." The letter attacked the government because it had taken care of McCain—an injured Vietnam War vet—but not of Ramsey's ailing father who had served in Vietnam during the same period as McCain. "You're not the only one that was in the jungle, buddy," Ramsey wrote. "When election time comes we're going to need somebody to take care of the soldiers. Not somebody who wants another war."[42] Ramsey's letter —signed "Allahu Akbar, Akeem Ramsey El"—was a terrorist threat veiled in war protest.

The Secret Service was notified, prompting a twelve-hour HAZMAT alert involving more than a hundred officials from the FBI, the National Guard, the Arapahoe County Sheriff's Office, and the U.S. Postal Service. Five

McCain staff members were taken to area hospitals as a precautionary measure and twelve were quarantined. Testing later determined that the white substance inside the envelope was not anthrax or another lethal substance; however, the identity of the substance was never disclosed.

The Secret Service quickly traced the letter to inmate Akeem Ramsey El at the Arapahoe County Detention Center, due to the simple fact that his name and address were on the envelope. On August 22, a Denver television crew was allowed to interview Ramsey inside a holding pen at the jail. Speaking straight into the camera, Ramsey said that he was "a terrorist sympathizer." Ramsey later gave a more detailed explanation for his crime. "The VA [Veterans Administration] would do nothing [for my father]. It was then that I believed, as I still do, that something must be done. Soldiers were being returned home from Iraq every day in the same condition as my father or worse. . . . Vietnam strikes 40 years later and Senator McCain was trying to [use] Vietnam as a springboard to the Oval Office."[43] In 2009 Ramsey was sentenced to thirty months in federal prison on terrorism charges related to his executed threat against McCain.[44]

Not only does Marc Ramsey represent a classic case of the stand-alone prison terrorist but his pathway classically demonstrates the importance of inmate leadership. In his case, as with Abu Musab al-Zarqawi at Jordan's Suwaqah prison a decade earlier, Ramsey's passage through criminality led to the meeting of an inmate imam (the Moorish elder in Indiana), which served as a crucial first step along his pathway to terrorism. Ramsey's case is also consistent with other features of the database. His violence was triggered by events surrounding the Iraq War; by moving beyond Moorish Science teachings—Nobel Drew Ali said nothing about the use of political violence—he embraced a form of Prison Islam. His tactic, the use of imitation anthrax, is another innovation in the field of prison-based terrorism.

* * *

The next case also resonates with the database analysis. It highlights the roles of extremist religion and inmate social networks as crucial to the radicalization process in the peak years of prison-based terrorism. But it is distinguished from the preceding two cases due to the outstanding question it raises for national security.

Shawn Robert Adolf (his real name, case 34) was born in 1974, probably in Greeley, Colorado. Other than being Caucasian, nothing more is known of his early life.[45] Court records show that Adolf's first criminal offense occurred in 1993 when he pled guilty to two burglary charges in Weld County,

Colorado. In time, two social networks would provide turning points for his pathway to terrorism.

Network 1: The Prison. In 1997, a Denver court sentenced twenty-three-year-old Adolf to eight years in state prison for possession/sales of a controlled substance, weapons charges, and grand theft. Sources indicate that by the time Adolf entered prison he was a member of the Sons of Silence, a "1%" motorcycle gang based in Colorado Springs. (Within biker subcultures, it is believed that 99 percent live within the boundaries of the law; the remaining 1 percent is the outlaw element.) According to gang investigators, in prison the Sons of Silence are linked via the methamphetamine trade to both the Aryan Brotherhood and the Aryan Nations; the latter was an influential neo-Nazi organization classified as a terrorist threat by the FBI.[46] Investigators also agree that religion plays an important role in the meaning and purpose of these white supremacy groups, indicating that Adolf was influenced by either Christian Identity or Odinism/Asatru. An Aryan Nations prison gang member summarized these influences in an interview with a researcher from the Southern Poverty Law Center: "Most of the guys are into Asatru, but then we also have guys who are into Christian Identity, so it varies. Overall, it's about brotherhood. It's about blood, not religion. Well, actually, dope comes first. The meth. Then the brotherhood. That's the reality."[47]

Network 2: The Domestic Terrorist Organization. Adolf was paroled in 2001 but was soon arrested in Weld County on two third-degree assault charges. Known to local law enforcement as Shawn "Trouble" Adolf, he was released on bail and told to follow orders from his parole officer. Court records show that by 2007 Adolf had eight warrants out for him on various felonies around Colorado, including burglary, aggravated motor vehicle theft, and skipping out on a $1 million bond. One of these crimes involved the theft of a travel trailer, which served as Adolf's home and mobile meth lab as he moved from campground to campground through Colorado and Texas, possibly with his wife. (Records show that one Shawn R. Adolf and Sarah Williamson were issued a marriage license on July 18, 2007.[48]) Adolf was placed on the most-wanted list of the Weld County Sheriff's Department, prompting an investigator to say she feared that Adolf would eventually kill a police officer. "I've been a cop for 18 years," she said, "and he was not your typical bad guy."[49]

In the summer of 2008, several thousand federal and local law-enforcement agents descended on downtown Denver in preparation for massive protest marches and traffic jams at the Democratic National Convention. Their primary concern was that Senator Barack Obama's nomination would draw tens of thousands of demonstrators, including antiwar protestors and anarchists carrying on the widespread vandalism and window smashing that marked the 1999 World Trade Organization conference in Seattle. "The magnitude of the event has expanded," said the Denver mayor John Hickenlooper three weeks before the convention. "It's bigger and more profound than we expected. . . . What worries me is we don't know what we don't know."[50] These were not idle words. On the eve of the convention, it became clear that local officials were unprepared for the task before them. Of the security arrangements, one local journalist remarked, "It makes you think something is about to happen." Another journalist called the security situation "a cluster-fuck."[51] Denver streets represented a full-on police state, complete with miles of concrete barricades, black-clad SWAT teams, hovering helicopters, horse-mounted police in riot gear, and designated "freedom cages" set up to accommodate the right to free speech. As it turns out, none of this was necessary for preventing the convention's most serious threat.

At 1:37 a.m., on August 24, the day before the convention began, a lone police officer in the Denver suburb of Aurora spotted a blue Dodge pickup driving erratically. The officer pulled the truck over and, while checking the identification of the driver, twenty-eight-year-old Tharin Gartrell, discovered that the driver's license was suspended and that Gartrell was on probation for possessing methamphetamine. Inside the truck, the officer found what appeared to be a mobile meth lab, along with ammunition, a bulletproof vest, fake ID cards, wigs, walkie-talkies, and two bolt-action rifles, one being a loaded Ruger Mark II .22-250-caliber field rifle with a hunting scope and bipod shooting stand attached—a weapon commonly used in the West for killing prairie dogs and other disease-carrying pests. Gartrell was arrested and questioned about the weapons. He said he had no knowledge of the guns but that the truck belonged to his cousin, Shawn Adolf.

Adolf was arrested a short time later after jumping out of a sixth-story hotel window and breaking his ankle. When taken into custody, Adolf was wearing a Sons of Silence t-shirt, body armor, and a ring emblazed with a swastika. Around one wrist he wore a handcuff key. Adolf admitted to being under the influence of methamphetamine.[52] An underage female, who had taken drugs with Adolf and his gang at the hotel, told investigators that Adolf had talked about killing Senator Obama. "No nigger should ever live in the White House," he said.[53] A third man—an Aryan Nations member as was Gartrell—also rolled over on Adolf, telling the Secret Service that Adolf had threatened to kill Obama on a prior occasion. Adolf had come to Denver, he said, to "go out in a blaze of glory" by killing Obama with a sniper rifle and telescopic scope from a distance of 750 yards during Obama's acceptance speech at Denver's Mile High Stadium on August 28, the fortieth anniversary of Martin Luther King's historic "I Have a Dream" speech.[54] The assassination was to be a "suicide mission" whereby Adolf would hide the Ruger rifle inside a hollowed-out television video camera, a method he had learned about in *The Bodyguard*, the 1992 Kevin Costner and Whitney Houston movie.

Moreover, the Secret Service had enough evidence to establish probable cause to believe that the three Aryan Nations members were conspiring to kill Barack Obama—a terrorist conspiracy with significant precedent in the database. During the 1992 presidential race, Richard Guthrie and Peter Langan (cases 6 and 7) were pursued by the Secret Service for plotting to assassinate President George H. Bush during a campaign swing through Georgia. Guthrie and Langan were affiliated with the Aryan Nations of Ohio at the time, and both had converted to Christian Identity in prison years earlier.[55] Likewise, after converting to Identity at the Arizona State Prison, Gary Yarbrough (case 4) would play a role in the Order's 1984 assassination of the Jewish radio talk show host Alan Berg in Denver.

Adolf's weapon, the Ruger rifle, also has a long history of use by violent extremists of the radical right. Richard Wayne Snell of the revolutionary white supremacist group the Covenant, the Sword and the Arm of the Lord, used a Mini-14 Ruger to kill a black state trooper in southwestern Arkansas in 1984, and he then fought it out with police across the border in Oklahoma. Snell was a movement hero in the eyes of Timothy McVeigh; Snell was executed on April 19, 1995, the same day McVeigh bombed the Oklahoma City Federal Building. McVeigh owned a .223-caliber Ruger assault rifle and the Aryan Republican Army committed its bank robberies with the same piece of weaponry.[56] Not only is the gun dependable and easy to load and fire, but it also has achieved nothing less than a fetishism within the American radical right: the weapon has been endowed with an aura based on its reverent status. It was reportedly for this very reason that the perpetrator of the mass killing spree in Norway, Anders Behring Breivik, chose as his weapon the Ruger .233-caliber assault rifle. In his 1,500-page manifesto, which was discovered after the attacks, Breivik wrote that he resorted to the assault rifle after discovering that he could not purchase enough ammonium nitrate fertilizer to build a weapon of mass effect terrorism like the one used by McVeigh in Oklahoma City. "Times are changing," Breivik wrote, "and the possibilities which were available to us during the time of Mr. Timothy McVeigh are no longer present."[57] Breivik's lawyer would later say that his client believed the massacre was necessary to save Norway and Europe from Muslims and to punish politicians who had embraced multiculturalism.

Shawn Adolf was locked up in the Arapahoe County Detention Center on a $1 million bond. On November 6, 2009, he pled guilty to federal weapons charges in connection with his assassination attempt against Barack Obama, and he faces up to thirty years in federal prison. As of 2011, Adolf was incarcerated in the Bent County Correctional Facility in southern Colorado. His actions in Denver reverberate with a number of characteristics familiar to other white supremacists in the database, none more obvious than his fanatical dedication to a cause—a necessary precondition for terrorism. Yarbrough, once again, was "not your standard criminal."[58] Following Langan's dramatic 1996 shootout with the FBI, leading to his capture, an agent said, "Someone who pulls a gun on twenty-two FBI agents is one nasty character. One nasty dude."[59] Shawn Adolf "was not your typical bad guy."

Shortly after the Norway massacres, President Obama released an updated national counterterrorism strategy. Although al-Qaeda was still considered the primary threat to U.S. security, the administration had clearly revisited the white supremacy issue. "Throughout our history," Obama wrote, "misguided groups—including international and domestic terrorist organizations, neo-Nazis and anti-Semitic groups—have engaged in horrific violence to kill our citizens and threaten our way of life. . . . As a government, we are working to prevent all types of extremism that leads to violence."[60] Crucial to this prevention strategy, as the Adolf case shows, is a clear understanding of the social networks that support prisoner radicalization and terrorism.

* * * *

Essentially, the debate over prisoner radicalization turns on a matter of logic. Criminologists who find no threats are working from a deductive model by attempting to estimate the *prevalence* of radicalization within the general U.S. prison population. With that population now soaring above the two million mark, this approach is like looking for a needle in the haystack. Criminologists who do recognize a threat work from an inductive model by focusing on actual *incidents* of prisoner radicalization and terrorism. They begin with a handful of needles and try to find consistencies in how they were made.

This research has discovered several consistencies, beginning with the importance of extremist religion as part of a cycle of ideologically motivated violence. This is not necessarily a direct cause-and-effect relationship where a young man goes off to prison, converts to a radical religion, and then becomes a terrorist. Prisons do not manufacture terrorists like a factory; if so, they are doing a lousy job. The process is more complicated than that. It seems to begin with conversion to a religious ideology that the convert himself may not fully understand. This is followed by other decisive turning points—both inside prison and out—that are sequenced yet progressive, with one turning point leading to another. Such an idea was eloquently theorized decades ago by Albert Cohen:

> The history of a violent incident is the history of an interaction process. The intention and the capacity for violence do not pop out, like a candy bar out of a vending machine. They take shape over time. One event calls forth, inhibits, or deflects another; it invites, provokes, abets, tempts, counsels, soothes, or turns away wrath. Every violent episode, whether it is an altercation between friends, a mugging, or a riot is the product of such an interactive history.[61]

Robert Sampson and John Laub, the winners of the 2011 Stockholm Prize in Criminology for their work on life-course theory, apply such an interactive process to the influence of prison, arguing that "the effect of confinement may be indirect and operative in a developmental, cumulative process that reproduces itself over time. . . . Its indirect effect may well be criminogenic (positive) as structural labeling theorists have long argued."[62] From the life-course perspective, Ruben Shumpert is seen as a common criminal who would have never become involved with the transnational terrorist organization al-Shabaab had he not gone to jail, because there he met Somali inmates who were sympathetic to their cause. For it was through these jailed Somalis that Shumpert not only took up the jihadist banner, but also obtained the forged passport that allowed him to become an international fugitive. This was a major turning point for Shumpert but it was not his only one. Shumpert may have never gone to jail in the first place were it not for the associations he formed at the barbershop; the most important association he formed was with an FBI informant. It follows that Shumpert may have never gone to work at the Islamic barbershop had he not converted to Islam in prison. And Shumpert may have never converted to Islam in prison had he not been dealing with substance abuse issues upon his arrival there. An often overlooked aspect of Sageman's research is that some mujahedeen had prior histories of drug abuse and had joined the jihad specifically to abandon their hedonistic lifestyles. "This was the appeal of Salafi Islam for many of the converts," Sageman concludes. "However, after joining the jihad, they returned to petty crime—without the drug abuse—in support of the cause."[63]

Yet Shumpert's involvements with these social networks do not tell the whole story of his pathway to terrorism. According to a 2006 poll by the Pew Research Center, some 5 percent of American Muslims expressed a positive view of al-Qaeda, due mainly to their disapproval of the Iraq War.[64] Shumpert was one of them. Shumpert was profoundly affected by the war because he saw it as an assault on Islam. This is a common theme among Shumpert's generation of anti-American jihadists, one that is documented time and again in terrorism research. J. M. Berger, for one, argues that the U.S. invasion of Iraq on the basis of unfounded claims about weapons of mass destruction "has provided jihadist ideologues with all the ammunition they need to deflect the question of 'who started' [the war]. No future change in the course of U.S. policy can fully erase the impact of that mistake."[65]

Sampson and Laub leave no doubt about the potential influence of such sociopolitical events on adult criminality. "The idea is that turning points in the adult life course matter," they argue, "and that a change in life direction may stem from macro-level events largely beyond individual control (e.g., *war*, depression, natural disaster, revolutions)."[66] Evidence gathered by New York University's Center on Law and Security shows that the Iraq War served as a recruiting tool for al-Qaeda, increasing the number of fatal attacks by jihadists around the world by more than one-third in the three years following the invasion of Iraq.[67] Shumpert's terrorist development was, therefore, a combination of turning points involving micro- and macro-level events, a phenomenon acknowledged in research showing that there is not a single "conveyer belt" to terrorism. Rather, the radicalization process involves a complex interaction of multiple pathways, including personal victimization, political grievance, and the influence of radical group dynamics.[68] A similar pattern is found in the other cases as well.

Marc Ramsey would have never waged his anthrax hoax against John McCain had McCain not stepped onto the world stage as a U.S. presidential candidate. This brought McCain's Vietnam War record into sharp relief against Ramsey's feelings about his father's failing health as a result of Vietnam. The personal became the political for Marc Ramsey—who had a personal history of solving family problems with violence—and that was his major turning point toward terrorism. Yet were he not confined to jails and prisons for his entire adult life, thereby depriving him of social bonding with noncriminals, Ramsey may have never begun his threatening letter-writing campaign against public officials. And had he not abandoned the basic teachings of Moorish Science and set out on his own path of Prison Islam, Ramsey may have never acted upon his intense hatred of U.S. Middle Eastern policy and its consequences for Muslims.

Like Shumpert and Ramsey, Shawn Adolf was a career criminal whose pathway to terrorism was fomented in the crucible of a macro-level political event: the ascendency of Barack Obama. Yet Adolf is distinguished from the others due to the unresolved question his criminality raises for U.S. security: how does an assassination attempt against America's first black president form? In Adolf's case, it began in prison when he joined the Aryan Nations with its racist religious creed. This was Adolf's first turning point. His second turning point occurred by dint of the fact that Adolf's affiliation with this domestic terrorist organization not only endured beyond his time in prison but also more than likely intensified due to Adolf's chronic and persistent use of methamphetamine. This is all too reminiscent of James Earl Ray's behavior leading up to the assassination of Martin Luther King.

But Adolf does share a final characteristic with the others. In each case, there was a long-lasting relationship between a terrorist-in-waiting and law enforcement officials. Shumpert was known to the Seattle FBI for nearly five years before he fled the country to join al-Shabaab, leading one to question whether Shumpert was encouraged and therefore entrapped by overly zealous FBI agents. Ramsey's string of vitriolic prison letters to politicians was well known to the Secret Service years before he became a high-profile inmate at the Denver jail. Adolf's violent tendencies had been feared by the Weld County Sheriff's Department for the better part of a decade. In other words, in each case law enforcement had ample warning of the terrorist event to come. Conceivably, preventive measures could have been taken. All of this raises a compelling question: to what extent does the socially imbalanced relationship between would-be terrorists and law-enforcement officials constitute a developmental process that can be generalized to other cases of terrorism?

* * *

For years, prisoners have used what James Aho calls the *politics of righteousness* as justification for ideologically motivated violence. It is nothing new. This research provides no evidence suggesting that terrorism is widespread among radicalized prisoners (it is not prevalent). To be sure, the identification of only fifty-one terrorists out of millions of inmates who have passed through prisons over the past half-century belies an obsession with the spectacular few. Then again, this is logical. Research shows that recruitment methods used by terrorists are not designed to yield a high number of recruits.[69] In general terms, this study does support security concerns about the prison as an operational base for radicalization and terrorism. The research shows that the largest increase in terrorist incidents committed by radicalized prisoners has occurred since the 9/11 attacks—a period paralleling the remarkable growth of Islam behind bars. It is also an era marked by public indifference about the terrorist threat posed by white supremacists.

Prison-based terrorists are typically radicalized during their early twenties through friendship and kinship networks featuring charismatic leaders. Others are radicalized through torture. In the United States, these terrorists belong primarily to small homegrown groups yet they are often motivated by foreign organizations, including al-Qaeda, highlighting the trouble with using such formulaic distinctions as "international" and "homegrown" terrorism. Shumpert's participation in international terrorist activity, for instance, would have never been possible without the help of homegrown extremists.

Prison-based terrorists exhibit a reputable level of competence in carrying out their attacks. A clashing viewpoint suggests that U.S. prisoners are criminally incompetent and have never executed a successful act of terrorism. The criticism is not only factually mistaken but it represents a myopic view of the global threat posed by the radicalization of contemporary prison populations. Recent developments indicate that national security concerns must extend beyond U.S. prisons.

Events occurring in foreign prisons have created serious challenges to American-led NATO military operations in Southeast Asia, the Middle East, and Africa. There have been several prison breaks in Yemen in recent years, leading to the escape of more than sixty inmates, including al-Qaeda members, some of whom were involved in the USS *Cole* attack.[70] According to a report by the Combatting Terrorism Center at West Point, Iraq's prison system has become the new cradle of jihadist propaganda, leading to the reconstitution of Al-Qaeda in Iraq following the death of Abu Musab al-Zarqawi.[71] Afghanistan's prison population has exploded, from six hundred prisoners in 2001 to about nineteen thousand in 2011, creating appalling conditions of confinement and widespread detainee abuse.[72] A 2011 report by the United Nations found evidence of routine human rights abuses and torture at detention centers in Afghanistan; in some cases, detainees were beaten with rubber hoses, hung from hooks, and had their genitals twisted to extract confessions.[73] There has also been a rash of escapes. Two bold Taliban attacks on Afghanistan's Sarposa Prison in 2008 and 2010 freed nearly 1,400 insurgents.[74] Another five hundred Taliban broke out of a Kandahar prison in 2011. The threat posed by Pakistan's prisons is even more ominous. The nation's prison system has the capacity to hold around twenty thousand convicts, yet they currently incarcerate close to one hundred thousand, of whom half are Islamic extremists linked to the Taliban or al-Qaeda. Children as young as ten years old are mixed in with hardened criminals and religious militants, creating the potential for a new generation of jihadists to carry on bin Laden's ideas for years to come.[75]

There is for Americans, however, an even more compelling case to be made about the global reach of prisoner radicalization. Osama bin Laden's chosen biographer has described Ayman al-Zawahiri—radicalized not in a U.S. prison but in an Egyptian prison—as the "real brains" behind al-Qaeda, an analysis that appeared in numerous post-9/11 accounts.[76] Some twenty years elapsed between Zawahiri's torture in Egyptian custody and his terrorist campaign against America. This significant time lag is not a cause to dismiss Zawahiri's three years in Egypt's notorious prisons. To the contrary, it only confirms Sampson and Laub's argument that the criminogenic effect of confinement is a "cumulative process" that reproduces itself over time. For ex-convicts, the prison experience lingers for the rest of their lives.

* * *

But that was al-Qaeda of old and today the West faces another kind of enemy—the lone-wolf terrorist, an unaffiliated individual who nevertheless often draws on beliefs and ideologies of validation generated and transmitted by extremist movements.[77] "The biggest concern we have right now," said President Obama in an interview shortly before the tenth anniversary of 9/11, "is the lone wolf terrorist."[78] It is exemplified in the final case discussed here, Carlos Bledsoe (case 49).[79]

Carlos Leon Bledsoe was born to middle-class African American parents of Baptist persuasion in Memphis, Tennessee, on July 9, 1985. In his youth, Bledsoe attended school and church and worked a series of menial jobs. He also admired the work of Martin Luther King and had hung a picture of the great civil rights leader on his bedroom wall. But then he drifted toward the gang life, leading to several school suspensions. After graduating from high school, Bledsoe left Memphis for Nashville where he enrolled at Tennessee State University. In 2003, prior to his eighteenth birthday and while still a student at Tennessee State, Bledsoe's emerging criminality became more violent. He was arrested for possession of a chrome-plated set of brass knuckles, which he had used to pulverize a woman's car window after she rammed into a vehicle Bledsoe was riding in. As Bledsoe smashed out the window, he shouted, "Bitch, I'm gonna kill you. . . . Get out. . . . I'm gonna kill you when I get your address." The case was processed out of court by juvenile authorities.

A year later, during a routine traffic stop Bledsoe was found with some marijuana, two shotguns, a switchblade knife, and a Russian-made SKS semiautomatic rifle with a chambered bullet. Facing a fourteen-year sentence on weapons charges, Bledsoe was given a plea arrangement whereby all but the switchblade violation was dropped in exchange for one year of probation. Curiously, the switchblade charge was dismissed and Bledsoe was never assigned a probation officer. Even so, the experience frightened Bledsoe and he set out to change his life. He found new friends and began an intense study of religion. Questioning his Baptist faith, Bledsoe was initially drawn to Judaism. He visited a couple of orthodox synagogues and was given some pamphlets to read but was turned away, because, in Bledsoe's telling of it, he was black. So he turned to Islam and converted to the faith at Nashville's al-Farooq mosque in 2004 when he was nineteen. Shortly thereafter, the picture of Martin Luther King came down from his wall.

By 2007, Bledsoe had become an observant Muslim and had legally changed his name to Abdulhakim Mujahid Muhammad. (The middle name, Mujahid, or "holy warrior," is not a common name among Muslims.[80]) Yet he had changed more than his name. In September, Bledsoe flew to Yemen, arriving there on the sixth anniversary of 9/11. He found a job teaching English at a British school in Aden, South Yemen, studied Arabic and Islamic law, and entered into an arranged marriage with a local woman. Who Bledsoe met during his time in Aden is the subject of debate, but in a subsequent letter to the press he discussed the influence of a terrorist network, stating that he was "asked many times to carry out a martyrdom operation in America."[81]

On November 14, 2008, Bledsoe was arrested at a roadside checkpoint for failing to carry the proper government documents for his travel. Found in his possession was a fake Somali passport, an explosives manual, a cellphone with numbers for wanted terrorists in Saudi Arabia, and a computer jump drive containing literature from Anwar al-Awlaki, the Yemen-based American Islamic cleric. Awlaki had been released from a Yemen prison a year earlier for his involvement in an al-Qaeda plot to kidnap a U.S. military attaché and he was then beginning to have a major influence on English-speaking jihadists internationally, including the would-be Illinois courthouse bomber Michael Finton, the underwear bomber Umar Farouk Abdulmutallab, and Nidal Hasan whose November 2009 massacre at Fort Hood, Texas, would come to define *opposition to the U.S. military* as the new face of lone-wolf terrorism in America.[82]

Bledsoe's plan had been to travel to Somalia for training in bomb building, perhaps with al-Shabaab, but he ended up imprisoned in Yemen's Political Security Organization, where he was interviewed by representatives from the U.S. embassy. According to Bledsoe's later statement to the court, he was also interviewed by an FBI agent. During his months in custody, Bledsoe met fellow Muslim detainees from Germany, Britain, Somalia, and Cameroon. Some were allegedly beaten, tortured, and sodomized by their interrogators in Bledsoe's presence. Although Bledsoe was an extremist before his imprisonment, the experience amplified his violent tendencies and brought him to a turning point. As Bledsoe later told a psychiatrist, his time in the Yemen prison provoked him to launch a jihad against America.

Bledsoe was deported to the United States in January 2009, purportedly through the intervention of the U.S. Justice Department, and he resettled with his father in Memphis where he went to work in his family's tour-bus company. Sources indicate that Bledsoe was placed on a terrorism watch list once he landed in the United States.[83] Other sources indicate that the FBI's Joint Terrorism Task Force had investigated him. In any event, several months later Bledsoe moved to Little Rock, Arkansas, where he opened a new office for the family business. On May 20, CNN reported the story of a foiled terrorist attack on New York synagogues and military aircraft by men who had converted to Islam in prison (cases 43, 45, and 47). It was around this time that Bledsoe's plan for killing took shape. Bledsoe made a martyrdom video for his wife back in Yemen, stockpiled ammunition, bought several firearms, and took target practice at a construction site. One of the guns he purchased was a .22-caliber rifle, bought over the counter at a Wal-Mart. Bledsoe would claim that the reason he made this purchase was to determine whether the FBI was following him. When Wal-Mart did not put a hold on the firearm purchase, Bledsoe was home free to pursue two ideas. "Plan A" was to assassinate three Jewish rabbis with Molotov cocktails. "Plan B" was to assassinate U.S. military personnel. He chose the latter.

On June 1, Bledsoe loaded his black Ford Explorer with six hundred rounds of ammunition, homemade silencers, the .22 rifle, and his SKS semiautomatic carbine. He drove to a Little Rock army recruiting center where he spotted two soldiers in fatigues smoking cigarettes near the entrance. Bledsoe opened fire from his vehicle, spending multiple rounds from the semiautomatic, killing one soldier and wounding another. Bledsoe sped away, intent on making the 150-mile drive to Memphis where he would switch cars, but he made a wrong turn into a construction zone where he was captured by a patrolman. As Bledsoe was being placed in the cruiser, he told the officer, "It's a war going on against Muslims, and that's why I did it!"

On January 12, 2010, with images of the underwear bomber still flashing on television screens across America, Bledsoe sent the presiding judge in his case a letter pleading guilty to one count of capital murder and fifteen counts of terrorist acts. "I'm affiliated with al-Qaeda in the Arabian Peninsula (al-Qaeda in Yemen)," he wrote. "This was a Jihadi attack on infidel forces." Months later, AQAP's English-language online magazine, *Inspire*, acknowledged the organization's strategic shift to lone-wolf terrorism by encouraging American Muslims to "fight jihad on U.S. soil," rather than attempting to travel overseas for training. The article extolled the virtues of random shootings and praised the killings by Nidal Hasan and Abdulhakim Mujahid Muhammad. As of 2011, Bledsoe was locked in solitary confinement at an Arkansas county jail after attacking a guard with a metal shank. As Bledsoe stabbed the guard, he shouted, "I got your white boy ass. Allah!"

* * *

The gestation period between Bledsoe's radicalization in a Yemen prison and his act of terrorism in Arkansas was roughly five months, shorter than Ayman al-Zawahiri's by an order of magnitude. (The human carnage left behind was also distinguished by an order of magnitude.) What is most at issue here is intention, however, not time lapses. Bledsoe's moral outrage over the treatment of Muslims in Yemen led him to make the ideological leap to armed jihad in America. Little Rock was to have been only the beginning. Armed with hundreds of rounds of ammunition, multiple firearms, a box of Molotov cocktails, and cellphones, Bledsoe's plan had been to commit mass murder at army recruiting centers from Memphis to Richmond, Kentucky, and then to go on to the nation's capital. From there his plan was to bomb synagogues throughout the northeast. Bledsoe is hardly unique. Shumpert's intention was to assist al-Shabaab in its ruthless campaign of summary justice against U.S.-supported government officials and Sufi Muslims in Somalia. The purpose of Marc Ramsey's anthrax hoax was to obstruct a U.S. presidential campaign. Shawn Adolf wanted nothing less than to kill Barack Obama. A common denominator propelled each man's trajectory toward terrorism: each had, in one way or another, been radicalized through prison social networks. Shumpert and his Somali homeboys in the King County Jail, Ramsey and the Moorish brothers of the Indiana prisons, Adolf and the Aryan Nations of Colorado, Bledsoe and the tortured Muslims in Yemen— all of these social networks facilitated the transformation of violent propensities into terrorist causes.

Along with a sense of brotherhood and a compelling ideology disseminated through folk knowledge, literature, videos, and (for Bledsoe) the Internet, what these social networks offered their supporters were two long-standing psychological preconditions for mass killing, used to spectacular effect by Hitler and Goebbels: the dehumanization of the victim and the symbolic elevation of the executioner to a position of moral sanctity.[84] Internalizing these preconditions, extremists began to think of themselves as soldiers. The verbal dehumanization of the "other" is evident in Shumpert's fight not against American citizens but against "everything America stood for." Ramsey addressed his victim as if he were "already DEAD." Adolf wanted to prevent a "nigger" from occupying the White House by killing him with a weapon made for the eradication of vermin. Bledsoe didn't stick a white male guard but his "white boy ass," followed immediately by the invocation "Allah!"— or the symbolic elevation of his violence to an expression of moral sanctity. Other verbal cues of moral sanctity: Bledsoe's "Jihadi attack on infidel forces" was retaliation against a "war against Muslims"; Adolf wanted to "go out in a blaze of glory" on the anniversary of Martin Luther King's famous civil rights speech; U.S. Middle Eastern policy "loathed" Ramsey (don't even get him started on Israel), signing off with the battle cry, "Allahu Akbar"; Shumpert was locked in a life-or-death battle against an "evil ideology."

Overall, the case studies indicate that terrorism is triggered by internal turning points revolving around individual grievances, and by external turning points beyond the individual's control. All of this is encapsulated in social networks. Social networks provide both an underlying structure and a grammar for extremists to connect with one another. In each case, social networks were there when criminals recruited themselves into the role of terrorists as a personal response to evolving world events, offering support, resources, and, in the case of Shumpert and Bledsoe, traditional knowledge on local customs in strange and distant lands. Social networks provide the pathways for moving from individual grievances to identification with radical political agendas to the abandonment of politics for violence exclusively. In the end, then, it is not just time that matters but timing and who you hang out with, both literally and virtually. And it is for this reason that life-course criminology matters to the study of terrorism. It provides a portal through which we may understand how people *evolve* into terrorists.

Life-course criminology may also provide a better understanding of how prisoners evolve into radicals. What prison conditions would inspire an inmate to set foot on the pathway to radicalization? Previous research offers few answers; ironically, what is usually missing from these studies is an investigation of prisons themselves. That subject is taken up next through an ethnographic study of prisoners who converted to Islam and white supremacy faiths while in custody. An ethnographic approach also allows for a more thorough investigation of the strategies employed by prison radicals to convert individual grievances into collective action: kinship networks, clandestine communication systems, and charismatic leadership.

6

The Riddle of Radicalization

In history, design and aesthetic, Folsom Prison is quintessentially American. Built with granite rock by inmate labor in the late 1870s, Folsom State Prison is nestled against a series of dry, rolling hills along the American River some thirty miles east of Sacramento in a town appropriately named Represa, California. The huge sun-bleached fortress has a way of intimidating all comers. "Its physical appearance is frowning and terrible," recalled a former inmate. "Its buildings are low-squatting, resembling the lines of a bull dog."[1]Another prisoner called Folsom "the citadel of suffering. It is gray—a dull, lifeless gray. . . . An oppressive sense of doom radiates outward from the blocks of stone."[2] A legendary roster of criminals has spent time in there: the Hell's Angels founder Sonny Barger, the Black Panther Eldridge Cleaver, the Soledad Brother George Jackson, 1960s icons Timothy Leary and Charles Manson, the R&B/funk musician Rick James, the rap mogul Suge Knight, and the Menendez brothers, to name a few. Its history of violence is incandescent. Over the years convicts have killed and maimed an untold number of guards, and hundreds of prisoners have perished at the hands of other inmates. Between 1895 and 1937, ninety-three condemned men were hung in an underground Death House.[3]

In the eyes of most people, though, the prison is known for a legendary cultural event that occurred there on the morning of Saturday, January 13, 1968: the making of *Johnny Cash at Folsom Prison*—Cash's live concert played before a thousand prisoners in the dining hall. It was a mighty show, as history records, featuring such laments on confinement and cold regret as "Folsom Prison Blues," "I Got Stripes," "Busted," "Cocaine Blues," the mournful "I Still Miss Someone," "Green, Green Grass of Home," a hanging song called "25 Minutes to Go" and the closer, "Greystone Chapel," a cry of sin and redemption written by a Folsom prisoner named Glen Sherley, who sat nearby the stage. "There's a Greystone Chapel here in Folsom," Cash sang in his lonesome baritone: "A house of worship in this den of sin." "Cash was singing from inside the place where American law and order and American hell met," wrote the music critic Mikal Gilmore of the concert, "and nobody else in popular music could match him for radical nerve or compassion."[4]

Released in the summer of 1968, Cash's masterpiece would go on to sell millions and become one of popular music's essential albums. Not only did the album represent a milestone for Johnny Cash the performer but it established Cash as the nation's leading public figure on prison reform, drawing the support of such powerful law-and-order hardliners as Richard Nixon, Ronald Reagan, and the Reverend Billy Graham. His advocacy took numerous forms, from writing letters to prisoners, to taking phone calls from death-row inmates (Cash spoke to Gary Gilmore, the brother of Mikal, prior to his 1977 execution at the Utah State Prison), to acting on prisoners' behalf to win their parole, to arguing their cases before reporters and politicians, including a 1972 meeting with President Nixon in the Oval Office. (To appreciate the historical significance of this meeting, imagine Barack Obama and the multiplatinum rapper Lil' Wayne holding an Oval Office discussion on mandatory minimum sentencing.) On July 26 of that year, Cash testified before the Congressional Subcommittee on National Penitentiaries. After recounting horrendous stories of rape and suicide within prison, Cash called for sweeping reforms to eliminate unequal sentencing and to establish an advisory panel that would recommend standards for state prisons. "Unless people begin to care about prisoners, all of the money in the world will not help," he told the committee. "People have to care in order for prison reform to come about."[5]

Cash's success as a reformer was due in large part to wider reforms then taking place within the American prisoners' rights movement. These reforms—many of which originated in California prior to the George Jackson incident at San Quentin—included greater access to religious services; the establishment of inmate councils, grievance procedures and reform-oriented classification systems; and job-training programs and inmate treatment.[6] Folsom Prison was a model of reform during this period. In 1968, each prisoner at Folsom lived in his own cell. Nearly all of the inmates were involved in educational or vocational training classes. Most released from the prison did not come back.[7] Wardens wrote books on penology and experts from around the world visited Represa to learn how officials kept recidivism at such admirably low levels. Even more remarkable, these reforms weathered the storms of rebellion common to the era. On November 3, 1970, 2,100 of Folsom's 2,400 prisoners went on a work strike protesting a wide range of issues, leading to a full-scale lockdown. Nineteen days later the strike was peacefully settled through negotiations between the warden and four outside representatives selected by the prisoners, two of whom were ex-convicts. One was the Black Panther Huey Newton, imprisoned at San Quentin from 1968 to 1970 for his killing of the Oakland police officer. The other was the penologist John Irwin of San Francisco State University, who did a five-year term for armed robbery at Soledad (1952–1957) before going on to become one of the nation's foremost advocates of prison reform.[8]

In actuality, the successes at Folsom were premised upon a belief in rehabilitation stretching from the humanistic principles of Enlightenment expounded by intellectuals in Benjamin Franklin's Philadelphia salon, to Elijah Muhammad's prison ministry outreach in Chicago, to the grooves of *Johnny Cash at Folsom Prison*. When asked by a reporter in the mid-1970s if he was becoming a political radical, Cash emphatically replied,

> No, I sure don't. I look at it the other way: I'm just tryin' to be a good Christian. . . . If you take the words of Jesus literally and apply them to our everyday life, you discover that the greatest fulfillment you'll ever find really does lie in giving. And that's why I do things like the prison concerts.[9]

Cash continued to perform in prisons well into the 1970s, including a return to Folsom in 1977. But then the epoch of American prison reform drew to a close; the concerts stopped and so did Cash's advocacy work. By the time Ronald Reagan was elected president in 1980, American prison reform was little more than a memory.

* * *

California prisons underwent profound changes during the Reagan years and beyond due to mass incarceration caused by tough mandatory minimum-sentencing laws, an increase in drug-related offenses, the re-incarceration of parolees for minor technical violations, and California's draconian "three-strikes" legislation, which required the courts to hand out twenty-year to life terms for third-time convicted felons. Between 1976 and 2006, California's prison population grew more than eightfold—from roughly 20,000 to nearly 176,000—creating the greatest prison-overcrowding problem in American history.[10] Concomitantly, and consistent with the post-Attica neglect of prisoners by criminologists, studies of prisons and convicts dwindled to nearly nothing. Researchers who stayed connected to the prison would, however, document a range of negative consequences that occurred when prisons fill beyond capacity. Chronic idleness and confinement in spaces that are occupied by too many people increase the number of social interactions that inmates have that involve uncertainty and problems in mental

reasoning. Add to this the increased risk of victimization and predatory violence accompanying overcrowding, and prisoners experience heightened
stress levels that aggravate interpersonal instability in an already dangerous
world where errors in social judgment can be fatal.[11]

Against this backdrop came the widespread emergence of gangs. Inmate-
on-inmate violence soared at Folsom in the early 1980s when the Aryan
Brotherhood seized control of the drug trade and protection rackets from
black and Hispanic gangs. The gangs brought a primitive racial tribalism to
Folsom, one in which blacks, whites, and Mexicans formed their own standing armies, each exaggerated by a bizarre spiritualism that often accompanies
secret-society crime networks. In the trenchant words of a prisoner named
Kenneth Hartman, Folsom was transformed from a rigid, orderly world into
a dystopian nightmare:

> This is the era that would be described as a "riot in slow motion." Rifle fire
> ricochets through the buildings every day. The sight of guards running by
> with bleeding victims on gurneys barely raises an eyebrow. Outside the
> prison, the local ambulance companies line up for the daily carnage, the
> routine business to come bleeding through the East Gate. The local news
> announces the weekly and monthly tally—who is winning the race war,
> how many whites have been dispatched—as a regular feature of the nightly
> broadcast. Folsom Prison is written up in regional and national publica-
> tions, touted as the bloodiest joint in America.[12]

Today Folsom Prison houses high-security inmates serving long sentences or those who were considered management problems at other facilities. The institution is severely overcrowded, with 4,427 inmates living in
spaces designed to hold 1,800.[13] Most of the inmates (about two-thirds)
are African Americans and Latinos, mainly from big cities (60 percent
from Los Angeles) and mostly unemployed prior to incarceration. About
two-thirds have been incarcerated before.[14] Over half read at or below the
third-grade level or are "marginally literate" by normal educational standards.[15] Every cell at the prison is double-bunked by race, and another
five hundred inmates are double-bunked by race in hallways (called "bad
beds"), leading to the dining hall where the Man in Black had recorded
his work of genius. But entertaining convicts is also a thing of the past.
(In 2008, a Johnny Cash fortieth-anniversary tribute concert sponsored
by the Prison Fellowship Ministries had to be scrapped for security reasons.) Cellblocks teem with violence, resulting in fifteen to twenty serious assaults per week.[16] An estimated 80 percent of the prisoners have

histories of intravenous drug abuse, and they continue to share tainted needles while incarcerated.[17] Mental illness is extensive and the suicide rate is twice the national average. An unimaginable 40 percent of the prisoners are infected with hepatitis C—a condition that, under California penal policy, cannot be treated until an inmate's liver begins to malfunction.[18] The prison's medical facility, once a pillar of health care, is under federal receivership after the courts ruled that it violated constitutional standards of cruel and unusual punishment.[19] In a Supreme Court case upholding this judgment, *Brown v. Plata*, Justice Stephen Breyer described conditions in California's prisons as "horrendous," citing evidence of prisoners "found hanged to death in holding tanks where observation windows are obscured with smeared feces, and discovered catatonic in pools of their own urine after spending nights locked in small cages."[20] There is a critical staff shortage at Folsom and serious morale problems. With punishment (or incapacitation) now the prevailing rationale for incarceration, funding for rehabilitation and work programs has been slashed to pieces, so prisoners spend their days doing little more than cruising the yard and bangin' Crip, Blood, Mexican Mafia, Aryan Brotherhood. Overcrowding has paralyzed wardens from transferring troublemakers out of the institution, increasing gang tensions.[21] Seven out of ten inmates released from the prison return within three years, representing the highest recidivism rate in the nation. Even the state's prison commissioner has described the place as a "powder keg" at risk of exploding.[22]

This powder keg of incarceration can be summed up in two photographs. One illustrates the structural problems at Folsom. The other illuminates a corresponding human factor that becomes the overriding catalyst to prison violence.

The first image shows the conditions of confinement caused by overcrowding in the California Department of Corrections and Rehabilitation, where prisoners are stacked like cordwood on row after row of triple bunks—with only a few feet of floor space separating one bunk from another—and no meaningful activity to sustain them. John Irwin called this the warehouse prison.[23] The inmates are idle and racially segregated into *cultural communes*, which heighten the emphasis on ethnic identities. A consequence of warehousing, the cultural commune is a deviant social contrivance through which its members displace their anger and rage. They displace it outwardly toward rival communes, downwardly toward communes of the weak and wretched, and upwardly toward authorities responsible for their miserable situation. In his majority opinion in *Brown v. Plata*, Supreme Court Associate Justice Anthony Kennedy argued that California prisons are actually criminogenic,

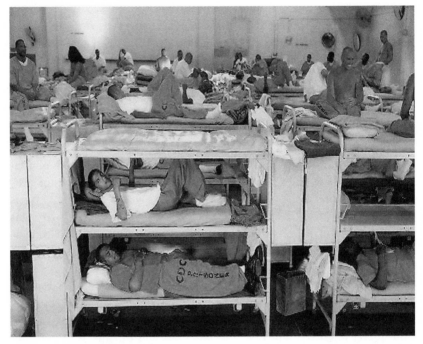

Overcrowding in a California prison.

that is, likely to produce crime.[24] There is, then, an amputation of that which was once capable of growth at Folsom Prison. It has entered the Dark Ages of penology—where charismatic convict preachers trawl for new recruits from the legions of dead souls. It is the perfect storm for prisoner radicalization.

The second image shows what happens under these conditions. In this harrowing photograph, a California prison gang member is seen with an elaborate mark of a swastika tattooed in a ring around his neck. His nose is broken from a fistfight, and his eyes are ulcerated from the ravages of methamphetamine and hepatitis C. Essentially, this is a human being with nothing to lose.

California's experiment with mass incarceration has been described as one of the great policy failures of our times.[25] Indeed, criminologists who study failed prisons need only look at Folsom for a model. Understanding this failure has broad implications for how we think about prisoner radicalization. To be sure, even though Folsom may be a worst-case scenario, its problems can be generalized to other American prisons. Mandatory-sentencing guidelines and a rising number of drug-related convictions are factors in a continued growth of inmates held in federal and state prisons in the United States.

Nearly all of these prisons are overcrowded with minorities making up over 60 percent of the U.S. prison population.[26] Within three years of their release, approximately 65 percent of former prisoners are rearrested, a recidivism rate that calls into question the effectiveness, if not the validity, of America's prisons. Violence, poor medical and mental-health care, and numerous other failures plague these prisons. And what happens inside prisons does not stay inside prisons, because a reported 95 percent of inmates are eventually released back into society, ill-prepared to lead productive lives and thereby jeopardizing public safety.[27] California is unique in the sense that its prison crisis has reached critical mass with the 2011 Supreme Court decision in *Brown v. Plata*. In effect, the Court's judgment required California to reduce its prison population by roughly 46,000 inmates within two years: this decision represents the most significant prison conditions case since the prisoners' rights movement of the late 1960s. California played a central role in that movement just as it is playing a central role in the movement toward mass incarceration.

On one level, it is a wonder that California prisons do not create radical inmates by the thousands. Given the reprehensible conditions of their confinement—which if present in a country like Iran would lead to charges

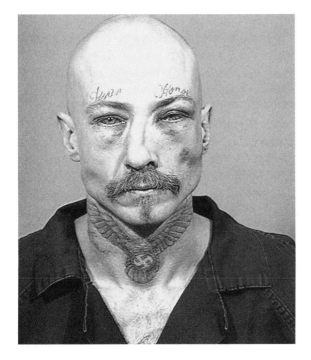

White supremacist gang member in a California prison.

of torture and human rights abuses—most inmates *should* find themselves with nothing left to lose, who in their desperation turn to hate and violence. Yet, on another level, not only does mass incarceration provide a context for understanding the inner lives of prisoners who adopt extremist views, but as the following analysis shows, it also offers a remedy. This is the riddle of radicalization, a puzzle whose answer can be found in the combined efforts of prison chaplains and inmate leaders who have created a system to steer prisoners away from radical interpretations of religious ideology.

* * *

In 2006 and 2007, I conducted a study of prisoner radicalization sponsored by the National Institute of Justice.[28] The work included approximately 140 hours of interviews with fifteen prison chaplains, nine gang intelligence officers, and thirty prisoners in Florida and California, including inmates at Folsom Prison and New Folsom Prison, built in 1986 as part of California's multibillion-dollar prison construction boom, when twenty-two new prisons were opened between 1980 and the early 1990s.[29]

The interviews with inmates took place during open yard hours inside prison chapels. Each interview lasted roughly ninety minutes and was conducted one-on-one with no guards, chaplains, or other inmates present. Tape recorders were prohibited so the data were collected in field notes. The prisoners ranged in age from nineteen to sixty-three, and their ethnicities included African American, Latino, Native American, and Caucasian. All of the prisoners were serving time for violent crimes, ranging from aggravated assault, kidnapping, and armed robbery to homicide. Their sentences stretched from ten years to life. Most came from urban areas and were involved in gangs prior to their confinement. About two-thirds belonged to a prison gang. The criterion for selection into the study was a conversion to a non-Judeo-Christian religion while in prison. Prisoners had undergone conversions to Islam (traditional and American versions), Hinduism, Native American faiths, Black Hebrew Israelism (a black supremacy group), those preferred by white supremacists (i.e., Odinism/Asatru, Teutonic Wicca, and Christian Identity), and secular humanism based on the traditions of self-help and men's consciousness raising. Many of the inmates had experienced multiple conversions. For example, it wasn't unusual to find a black inmate who came to prison with no religious background but then became a Baptist, followed by a conversion to the Nation of Islam, followed by a conversion to Sunni Islam. I also studied the role of prison gangs in inmates' spiritual lives.

My research found that:

1. Although only a very small percentage of converts turns radical beliefs into terrorist action, radicalization does pose a terrorist threat under certain conditions—in overcrowded maximum-security prisons with few rehabilitation programs and a shortage of chaplains to provide guidance for those seeking religion. Gang intelligence officers in Florida and California reported having uncovered potential terrorist plots inside such prisons.
2. Virtually all of the prisoners I interviewed said that their religious conversions occurred at a point in their incarceration when they felt they had no purpose in life and lacked a sense of belonging.[30]
3. Prisoners who convert to new religions are primarily searching for meaning and identity. They are often serial converters. Muslims, especially, tend to "float" between groups. In most cases, a conversion has a positive effect on rehabilitation.
4. Prisoners convert to various faiths through friendship and kinship networks (cellmates, family, or fellow gang members) or through independent study and reflection. Some are assisted by prison chaplains.
5. Radicalization is linked to prison gangs.
6. Inmate leadership is the most important factor in prisoner radicalization.

Marc Sageman contends that the most urgent issue facing terrorism researchers is not to explain why terrorism happens but to explain why more people who live in the same social networks do not commit terrorism.[31] Folsom Prison and New Folsom Prison provide a natural laboratory for testing this issue. New Folsom also houses high-security inmates serving long sentences or those who were considered management problems at other prisons. It is a huge complex, situated on 1,200 acres adjacent to Folsom Prison. It is also severely overcrowded with a population of 3,300 living in spaces designed for 1,788, some five hundred of whom are double-bunked in the gymnasium. And like Folsom, New Folsom is a violent, racially segregated, gang-riddled institution with serious suicide and drug problems, epidemic levels of hepatitis C, formidable staff shortages, cataclysmic management failures, and a near-total lack of state-supported treatment. It, too, is a powder keg of incarceration, which begs the rhetorical question once posed by George Jackson. "Why," he asked in *Soledad Brother*, "do California joints produce more Bunchy Carters and Eldridge Cleavers than those over the rest of the country?"[32] Oratorical flourishes aside, however, New Folsom differs from Folsom in one important respect: it has produced a full-blown terrorist threat in the form of Jam'iyyat Ul-Islam Is-Saheeh, or JIS. In a 2006 interview, an FBI spokesman, John Miller, remarked, "I think if you look at the JIS case, of all the terrorist plots since 9/11, it is probably the one that operationally was closest to actually occurring."[33]

Because Folsom Prison has produced no known terrorist cell (neither Cleaver nor Jackson were radicalized at Folsom but at San Quentin; in fact, Cleaver was transferred to Folsom in an effort to curtail his influence on other prisoners), it provides a ready-made pool of inmates for a control group that can be used to compare prisoners who converted to the same religious faiths, under the same prison conditions, as those involved in an actual terrorist plot. The control group therefore constitutes a group of inmates "making the same noise" as terrorists but that do not act on their radical beliefs—an approach comparable to that used by Wiktorowicz in his pioneering study of defections from the radical Muhajiroun of Britain.[34] A comparison of these groups has the potential to provide significant information about the social context in which networks of radicalization develop within multicultural prison populations. This information may then be used to understand better not only Islamic radicals like Ruben Shumpert, Marc Ramsey, and Carlos Bledsoe but also neo-Nazis like Shawn Adolf.

* * *

Dostoyevsky famously argued that "the degree of civilization in a society can be judged by entering its prisons." Entering California prisons can reveal something equally important about the possibility of solving problems organically, from the bottom up. Take the treatment of Jewish prisoners, for example, one of the least-understood groups in all of American penology.

Folsom is what John Irwin called "the Big House"—a huge, gothic-style tier-and-catwalk structure—with one place of worship on the mainline: Greystone Chapel. Three chaplains work there. One is a rabbi who wears a yarmulke, openly conducts services on the holidays, and counsels Jewish inmates, all the while mixing freely with other prisoners including Muslims, Hindus, and white pagans. Despite all of the problems at Folsom— and they are severe, to be sure—there is a noticeable sense of tolerance among the prisoners who spend their days at Greystone Chapel. That is the whole point of religion in prison: to accept everyone, including Jews. "Most Jewish inmates feel abandoned," said the rabbi in an interview, "so they go into hiding. Jews will hide among the Nazi gangs, which is actually the safest place for them to hide. If you have a rabbi [on staff] then Jews will come out of hiding and five times as many Jews will show up in the prison population."

There are reasons for this level of acceptance. Greystone Chapel is an inviting place, immaculately maintained by inmate custodians. Its walls are covered with prisoner artwork that celebrate Native American, Muslim, Jewish, and Christian traditions. These works include a famous mural above the pulpit called "The Prisoner's Last Supper." The mural is featured as the institution's main attraction at the Folsom State Prison Historical Museum, along with larger-than-life images of Johnny Cash standing before the East Gate. There is a set routine in the chapel, including schedules for each religion extending into evenings, weekends, and holidays. This makes the chapel a busy place with a constant flow of prisoners passing through each day, attending services, study groups, or counseling sessions with chaplains and inmate volunteers. Essentially, the collective commitment of chaplains and prisoners to authentic transformational experiences—organized around an institutional tradition of religious tolerance and diversity at Folsom Prison— makes Greystone Chapel the safest area in an otherwise perilous place. It is an area where people "care about prison reform" and it also serves to maintain order on the yard. Because of this, the chaplaincy is supported by higher-level authorities, all the way up to the warden.

In stark contrast, New Folsom is a modern "correctional institution" without walls, bars, gun-rails, or any of the other distinguishing features of a prison. There is also no history, no conventional order, and no predictability. Yet it is known for having some of the most sophisticated technology of any prison on Earth. The institution boasts everything from perimeter motion detectors, ground-sweeping radar, and biometric screening of inmates to "ballistocardkiograms" that can detect a prisoner's heartbeat, and machines capable of smelling smuggled contraband. Guards dress in black ninja-type uniforms with Kevlar vests, ball caps, and sunglasses. They carry an assortment of Tasers, stun guns, pepper spray, billy clubs, tear-gas canisters, and, in some areas, mini-14- and 9-millimeter rifles. "Now, instead of rats, cockroaches . . . and danger," Irwin said of these advances, "you've got this clean, spacious, high-tech prison. But [it] comes down to the same thing—cruel and unusual punishment."[35] Remarkably, though, despite these high-tech advances the California prison system does not have a computerized management information system. "We have no computer system in place to monitor inmates," said the department's chief of security in an interview at his Sacramento office (ironically, only a short drive from Silicon Valley and the corporate offices of Microsoft). "We have no technical sophistication. We have only paper files or we rely on cellphone calls."

New Folsom has three yards, each with its own chapel. Moving between yards requires walking through three security gates to leave one yard, taking ground transportation through two sally ports to reach the next yard, and then passing through three more security gates to enter that yard. This trip can take an hour or more depending on traffic. New Folsom is also staffed by three chaplains, yet as a chaplain said, "Multiple yards means that a chaplain's presence gets spread around. So the chaplain tends to lose influence on any particular yard. That's when the gangs move in." New Folsom has a Jewish population as well. But as another chaplain told me, "They all go underground because of the Nazi Low Riders." Several years back administrators tried to hire a rabbi at New Folsom, yet the job search was called off when the Nazi Low Riders threatened to kill any Jew who walked onto the yard.

And here we have the riddle of radicalization: two failed prisons sitting side by side with religious cultures that are poles apart. One is organized and tolerant; the other is muddled and ruthless. What role do these cultures play in radicalization?

* * * * *

Chaplains agree that most inmates begin their incarceration with little or no religious background. Upon entering prison, they are suddenly cast into an environment where religious options abound. In just one Florida prison, for instance, chaplains recognize ninety-two different religions, ranging from Pentecostal, Wicca, and Sunni Islam to Rastafarian, Santeria, and Odinism/Asatru. Due to their inexperience with sacred texts, rituals, and the disciplinary practices of religion, some prisoners will struggle in their attempts to find a faith. They become searchers, defined by behavioral scientists as those who yearn "for some satisfactory system of religious meaning to interpret and resolve their discontent."[36] Some join a religion for protection, some join out of haste, some affiliate with a group out of peer pressure, and still others become serial joiners, bouncing from one religion to another. These inmates embark upon a "conversion career" whereby they are able to assume and subsequently abandon a succession of convert roles.[37] Conversion is therefore a process of trial and error where inmates seek religious meaning primarily through friends and family. This is especially so for nontraditional faiths. Research shows that social networks are very important in explaining how people are recruited into new religious movements and organizations.[38]

Chaplains also agree on another point: membership in a religious group does not necessarily equate with conversion. Inmates can be members of the same group in different ways and with varying degrees of commitment. It is possible to participate in religious groups and rituals either with, or without, assuming a new way of life. Historically, researchers have been interested in the authenticity of religious conversions. Authentic conversions involve radical personal change—a deep religious experience in which a person is "slain in the spirit" through reflection, study, and ritual. They become penitent and then attempt to redirect the focus of their lives. The word conversion comes from the Latin *convertere*, meaning to resolve, turn around, or head in the opposite direction. As the term implies, authentic conversions are genuine human transformations involving "the displacement of one universe of discourse by another or the ascendance of a formerly peripheral universe of discourse to the status of primary authority."[39] Authentic conversions are thought to occur more often in maximum-security prisons—with their stringent control mechanisms, scarce resources and programs, longer periods of idleness conducive to reflection, and a greater number of serious felons—than in lower-custody institutions with fewer controls, more leisure-time activities and fewer violent offenders.[40] The process of authentic conversion is succinctly captured by a Folsom chaplain:

After they are here for awhile, some inmates come to understand the need for a higher power. Some start studying and eventually they convert to a religion. You can see the difference almost immediately. You see the difference in their comportment, in their tolerance of others. The only place you can forget prison is the chapel. Those in administration don't understand how important religion is to rehabilitation. The recidivism rate for true conversions is 15 percent, compared to 70 percent for the general population.

Things are much different at New Folsom Prison. Due to the scarcity of chaplains, there is no overarching authority to ensure religious tolerance. This becomes especially important in the case of Islam. Because the religion has no central authority akin to the papacy or priesthood, matters of Koranic interpretation are left to the individual. All Muslims are therefore free to study and interpret the sacred text as a matter of personal prerogative. When questions of interpretation or doctrine do arise, Muslims turn to prayer leaders, or imams, who provide respected answers through teaching. In Islam, the believer's first loyalty is to a teacher, not a system. "Trust is more important than anything," said an imam about his work with Muslim extremists in prison. "Then you can provide them a context within which to reflect." When there are no imams or chaplains to assume this teaching role in prison, then religious searchers become susceptible to other inmates who operate on their own, some of whom hold radical views that may include the use of racial or political violence. Young searchers are especially vulnerable to these views. As Wiktorowicz found, people who lack a good grounding in religion are the most likely to be attracted to radical Islam.[41] Such is the condition at New Folsom. One inmate described the prison as a "refugee camp, a terrorist recruitment center for the dumb." A New Folsom chaplain pulls no punches in his rendering of the problem:

> Chaplains are too busy to help with serious conversions due to overcrowding. Chaplains are hired here simply for compliance and nobody's in charge. I've reported to five bosses in fifteen years. . . . There's an element of evil in this prison due to the stupid, brain-dead mentality of the [department]. The administration is in chaos, there's no stability. Inmates who come here are all pressed into a gang because there are no safety measures to avoid violence in the yards. Chapels are used by gangs mainly to do gang business. The inmate population is not computerized, so you can't even track religious affiliation or gang membership. Inmates will use any opportunity to lash out against society. There's no state-sponsored effort to save them. The recidivism rate is 70 percent and 40 percent have hepatitis C. Most inmates sit around making knives at night. This makes the prison a petri dish just waiting to foment terrorism. The same mentality that drives prisoners drives the suicide bombers in Iraq.

Evidence shows that some prison gangs are capable of using the same or similar tactics as terrorist groups against the prison communities in which they are confined, which itself can be considered a form of terrorism if it is committed for religious or political causes. Of primary concern to intelligence officials are improvised explosive devices, normally referred to as IEDs. (An estimated 70 percent of all terrorist attacks worldwide are carried out with IEDs.) The prison gangs most capable of using IEDs are the white supremacy organizations, including the Aryan Brotherhood and skinheads who claim religious affiliation with Druidism and Odinism/Asatru, especially if these inmates have access to a prison horticulture program that keeps fertilizers, heating oil, or various chemicals that can be rigged up to a "booster" capable of creating an electrical shock wave out of the material.[42] For example, investigators in the Virginia Department of Corrections recently interrogated a former Aryan Brotherhood member who served as sergeant-at-arms for the gang. "There's no crime you can't do in prison," he admitted. "I've made shanks and pipe bombs, spears and blow darts and zip guns. For fun, I used to kill birds with bombs made out of matches. Matches can be used to make a bomb that can blow a hole in a concrete wall."[43]

Three groups at New Folsom are on the intelligence radar for this sort of threat: skinheads, the Nazi Low Riders, and the Aryan Brotherhood. I interviewed two Aryan Brothers in protective custody (a prison within a prison) at New Folsom who posed a terrorist threat, as well as six in the general population at Folsom who did not. Several case studies drawn from the interviews are presented below, but first I must provide a caveat that applies to all of the prisoner interviews here. Because inmates self-selected themselves for the study, the life-story narratives concentrate on convicts who self-identified as "converts." However, I have no objective measure of authentic conversion to any religious faith. It is possible that inmates believed that they had converted as soon as they decided to do so, although they may not have achieved—and perhaps were not aware that they must enter—a state of inner worship. In short, I do not have a way to determine whether prisoners were radicalized through a process of profound spiritual discernment.

The cases show that institutional tradition plays a fundamental role in the radicalization process. At Folsom's Greystone Chapel, prisoners and chaplains have embraced a culture that respects its own house of worship. Based on its custom of tolerance, Folsom has maintained a religious authority steeped in humanist principles of American penology. Radicalization is checkmated before it is transformed into violence. New Folsom is the Wild West. It has no religious tradition or authority and radicalization thrives, now and again leading to terrorism. These dangers are illuminated in the first case.

* * *

Gus was born to an absentee father and an atheist mother in Long Beach, California, in 1977.[44] An average student, during his formative years Gus developed a love of the ocean and took up surfing with a passion. "I spent most of my time on the streets or at the beach," he says. "I always enjoyed nature more than anything." Also a voracious reader, by the time he was twelve Gus had read *Beyond Good and Evil* and *Thus Spoke Zarathustra* by Friedrich Nietzsche. "Probably not a good idea," he admits before expounding on Nietzsche's dictum, "God is dead. We have killed him you and I." Nietzsche caused Gus to challenge the premises of his beliefs at that point in life, leading him to break out of the box of social conformity and into the wild and woolly world of Southern California youth subculture.[45]

Gus became a punk and then drifted into the glam rock scene. From there he shaved his head, acquired a pair of Doc Marten boots, a flight jacket, and a set of brass knuckles—symbols of the international neo-Nazi skinhead movement. By the time he was seventeen Gus had become straight-up white power, covered with tattooed images of swastikas, Vikings, and Nordic symbols. Drinking heavily now, he began committing the odd hate crime: first he bashed gays along the ocean and then assaulted Asians and blacks on the streets. By twenty-one, Gus was a legend among Long Beach boneheads. Then the event occurred that would irrevocably change his life. In 1998, he committed a double homicide and was sentenced to life in prison without the possibility of parole.

Gus arrived at New Folsom the following year. Due to his neo-Nazi credentials he was quickly pressed into the Aryan Brotherhood where he was introduced to a plethora of white supremacy religions—Christian Identity, the World Church of the Creator, Odinism/Asatru, and Wicca. "I met this one guy on the yard," he recalls in reference to an Aryan Brotherhood leader. "[He was] a very strong character. He gave me some books to read." Included among them was Robert Greene's *48 Laws of Power*, which has been described as the heir to Machiavelli's *Prince*. Greene's basic premise is that learning one's emotions and the arts of deception are essential for survival. His laws include such principles as everyone wants more power; emotions, including love, are detrimental; and deceit and manipulation are life's paramount tools. Embracing power is a ruthless game, intended to give practitioners an advantage over their fellow man. Essentially, the book can be read as a how-to manual for surviving in a failed prison.

Working against this grim philosophical grain, ironically, was the Aryan Brotherhood, with its code of total domination over members. Deceit and manipulation of the Brotherhood and the withholding of fealty from its leaders are exploitative tactics worthy of the most awful sort of punishment. "The Aryan Brotherhood is all about control," says Gus. "You have no rights. Your ass is owned and operated by the AB." The inconsistency between philosophy and gang processes is a constant theme I hear among the searchers at New Folsom. Bob, a former Hell's Angel and veteran Aryan Nations member, said that when he arrived at New Folsom on a drug-related homicide charge in 1987, it was "really easy to get sucked into" the gang's religious aspects. "When I first came here I was handed a kite and a knife and told to do what I had to," he says. "All the cool guys talking about Nordic blood, passing around the Old Testament, Identity and Odinism: It never felt right. All it led to was hole time. Stuff I didn't believe in but I'm stabbin' people for it anyway. Instead I got active in the Native American community. I'm part Black Foot. I would have rather wrapped my hands around a flute than a knife. What drove me to it was I was so tired of being fake."

Also included among the books Gus was given on the yard that day were several tracts on Odinism/Asatru. "That's how I learned about [the Nordic

God] Thor," he says. "I'd always loved nature so Odinism was meant for people like me. I thought, 'This is what I've been looking for all my life.'" Gus converted to Odinism in 1999 at the age of twenty-two. From then on he practiced its ceremonies, followed its rituals, and gave up drinking and smoking. A ritual of Odinism is the selection of a "favorite God," so Gus chose a woman, Freyja, the goddess of Norse and German mythology associated with earth, fertility, and beauty, because "it fit [his] genetic makeup," he says. "It's old." Gus also became a fully constructed figure during this period. When I met him, Gus was a coiled knot of unfocused tension and fear, his skin was pale from too much cell time, his fingernails bitten to the quick, and his arms, neck and face were covered with a web of bad tattoos, giving him the look of sheer malevolence.

By the mid-2000s, Gus was a seasoned veteran of doing time the hard way. He was still practicing the *48 Laws*, and because of the "blood in and blood out" oath he was still an Aryan Brother. He had no choice in that matter—he was in for life. But choice was what Odinism and the *48 Laws* were all about. It was at this point that Gus could have used some counseling from a prison chaplain to resolve his dilemma, but that was not to be for the reasons already mentioned. Claiming what he called his "Odinic right" to self-determination, Gus began distancing himself from the white drama of yard politics. Such a decision implied a faltering resolve on his part and it set him on a collision course with the Brotherhood leadership.

Details of the plot are classified, yet intelligence officers were able to give a broad outline. In 2006—around the time that then-governor Arnold Schwarzenegger declared a state of emergency in California prisons due to the severe overcrowding problem—a conspiracy was forged inside "a major white supremacy gang" at New Folsom to overpower guards and execute a major crime. There is no graver breach to the staff/inmate code of conduct. Such an act provides the essential principle in the complex algorithm that permits the use of deadly force against a prisoner. Guards were able to thwart the takeover, however, based on information obtained from a confidential informant inside the plot. Officers were also willing to say this: that confidential informant was Gus.

Gus will possibly spend the rest of his life in protective custody, never again to walk the mainline because he is a "rat" marked for retribution by the Aryan Brotherhood. "I found out what was missing in my life," he concludes. "I don't have to be controlled anymore. Now I'm here to practice religion and nothing more."

This case demonstrates classic elements of prisoner radicalization and terrorism. Gus's extremism was based on a prison-gang model; that is, he

was radicalized in his early twenties through a process of one-on-one proselytizing by a charismatic gang leader. His involvement in the New Folsom
plot occurred around the age of thirty. The plan was inimically linked with
a prisoner subculture through religious extremism. A prison social network
mattered in Gus's case just as social networks matter to terrorists in the free
world. Equally important, Gus's case reveals something about the complexity of extremist groups in prison. In his classic sociological treatise on deviance, *Outsiders*, Howard Becker argues that people in any society will form
subcultures and that they will create their own set of subcultural rules and
norms.[46] This is what Gus tried to do: establish his own norms within the
Aryan Brotherhood, indicating that the gang is not a monolithic entity.

The Brotherhood is typically described as a racist organized-crime syn-
dicate focused on drug trafficking, extortion, inmate prostitution, and mur-
der-for-hire schemes. But this varies from prison to prison. In the Arizona
prison system where I worked for eleven years as a guard, teacher, and warden, the Brotherhood is known as the "kindred" who organize into "families." Their recruiting strategy is based on mentoring young inmates in the
maximum-security mix. They are aligned with the Mexican Mafia (also
known as La Eme). Once bitter rivals, the Brotherhood and La Eme now
share a common hatred of the Black Guerrilla Family, their chief competitor
in controlling the prison heroin trade. Other crimes may occur, but dealing heroin and, more recently, methamphetamine is their stock and trade.
There is some evidence that elements of the California Aryan Brotherhood
have moved in this direction, creating a set of unanticipated behaviors that
defy the gang's stereotypes.

The criminologist Rebecca Trammell interviewed California male prisoners involved in the drug trade, focusing on inmate leaders or "shot-callers."[47]
Included were shot-callers of two white supremacy gangs, both allies of the
Aryan Brotherhood and both enemies of the Crips, Bloods, and the Black
Guerrilla Family: the Nazi Low Riders and Public Enemy Number 1, a Southern California gang known on the outside for identity theft and contract hits
on the police. Trammell found that the shot-callers use violence primarily
against their own gangs in order to reduce the chance of riots. In short, these
white supremacy gangs value peace and profit above all else—they are not
the kind of group that would overpower guards and execute a major crime
worthy of getting shot and killed, as was the case with Gus at New Folsom.
The underground economy, moreover, relies on maintaining safety, a goal
consistent with the interests of prison administration.

Although my focus is on the religious aspects of the Aryan Brotherhood
rather than their drug trafficking, Trammell's findings are consistent with my

research on the Brotherhood at Folsom Prison, where chaplains and a charismatic inmate leader worked in harmony to maintain safety, thereby containing the terrorist threat. That case is considered next.

* * *

Next to Greystone Chapel is one of the most remarkable sights one is likely to behold in any prison. There sits the Wicca/Asatru Circle, an open-air cage about the size of three cells where pagans spend their yard time worshipping the sun, the sky, the wind, and the birds. I'm permitted to spend time at the Circle on my visit to Folsom, talking to inmates about their beliefs and customs. Generally, what I find is that these prisoners hate buildings and will do anything to avoid them—including behaving themselves so they can continue the privilege of visiting the Circle. Were it their choice, they would rather live out here in the open air than in the overcrowded cellblocks.

Most of them wear black-framed sunglasses and are shirtless, tanned and covered with Nazi and Celtic tattoos; they epitomize what the criminologist Jack Katz would call a "bad-ass presentation of self."[48] This is where I meet Jesse, their shot-caller. Having spent three decades behind the grey walls of Folsom Prison, he personifies the stereotype of an "Aryan warrior." I'm told that sometime during the 1990s Jesse organized a group of prisoners who petitioned the administration for their religious right to open and maintain the Circle. The pagans have been here ever since but their efforts have produced few tangible results. They have no outside sponsor and no resources beyond a few ragged paperbacks, a deck of Tarot cards, and the ground they stand on. As whites, they are a minority on the yard, constantly ridiculed by blacks and Mexicans. "This Circle makes me feel fulfilled," says Jesse. "Some guys come out here to start shit about my tattoos sometimes. Some think I'm a devil worshipper, but I just blow 'em off."

Later, inside Greystone Chapel, Jesse lays out his story. He was born in Simi Valley, California, in 1953 to a Catholic mother and Freemason father. Jesse was raised Catholic but generally, as he recalls, "I hated everything." His teenage years coincided with the peace and love era, though, and Jesse fell in with the California hippie movement where he saw a different side of life. LSD introduced him to the possibilities of expanded consciousness and flower power provided the social network to make those possibilities happen, or so he thought. Throughout the late sixties and early seventies he tripped, sold marijuana, grew his hair long, and moved from one commune to another. "Life was different then," he says without the faintest hint of sarcasm. During these years Jesse also did two terms in the California Youth

Authority on theft charges. He never went to school, never held a job, and by 1972 the nineteen-year-old was an acid casualty. As he says, "LSD fried my brain."

Jesse murdered someone in 1972—he does not offer details and I do not press for them—and was sentenced to life without parole. At first he did his time with the same abandon he displayed on the streets. He didn't work, didn't program, and had no use for religious groups because he thought they "were weak." Mainly he walked the yard and developed the reputation of a thug. In 1977 Jesse was transferred to Folsom where he joined the Aryan Brotherhood and began tattooing himself with symbols of the German Reich. Two years later, he reached a turning point:

> I went to the hole for stabbin' somebody in '79. There was a war between the Aryan Brotherhood and the Mexican Mafia. They [the Brotherhood] sent me down two books to read. One was on Odinism/Asatru. It didn't make any fuckin' sense. The other was on Teutonic Wicca. Wicca is a young religion. It's only fifty-four years old. I liked the stuff about Celtics. I think it was called *Solitary Practice for Wiccans*. It made things a lot simpler.

Jesse emerged from solitary confinement as a devotee of the Wiccan religion. Wicca's practices and rituals, focusing on the sanctity of nature, recalled for him the hippie communes with their psychedelics and back-to-the-land philosophy. Like Gus, the Aryan Brotherhood was directly responsible for Jesse's "spiritual awakening," as he calls it. And like Jesse, most of the Circle inmates came to paganism for personal reasons. Max, a forty-year-old lifer and Circle elder, arrived at Folsom when he was eighteen years old. Following a divorce and the loss of a child, Max fell into a deep depression. Eventually he began to claw his way out, first by attending AA/NA meetings and then by immersing himself in the self-help literature. After that he turned to Christianity but found it too dogmatic, so he tried Buddhism, then astrology, string theory, and the Hindu-influenced principles of Bo Lozoff's *We're All Doing Time*. "I was just searching," he says, "searching for something." In 1998 another prisoner introduced him to three books on Wicca: *Drawing down the Moon*, *The Spiral Dance*, and *Solitaire Practicing*. "Wicca made my life in prison easier," he explains. "It helped me deal with the environment. Before, I let the slightest things stress me out. I can only control what I do. I learned just to accept things and move on."

This issue of control over one's inner state under the worst of conditions is a common refrain I hear among the searchers at Folsom and elsewhere.

Jesse expressed it and found guidance not only in Wicca but also in the Bible and Lozoff's *We're All Doing Time*. Go into any prison chapel in the United States, in fact, and you are likely to find a copy of Lozoff's classic prisoner self-help book on the library shelf.[49] Recalling his days as an Aryan Brother at Folsom Prison, Kenneth Hartman writes, "Lozoff's work stands out as one of the first books to speak to me with clarity. I'm particularly moved by his simple lessons regarding meditation. Follow the breath, in and out, works for me more effectively than grand dissertations on the cosmic connections of Eastern mysticism."[50] As for Jesse, today he claims, "My white power days are gone. I'm not much of a hater anymore. Cops [guards] here call us a piece of shit. But if I'm tied to this patch of Earth, I can relax." At the end of the day, Jesse says that the opportunity to practice Wicca is the best thing that has happened to him during his long years of captivity. For proof, he pulls out a card with two stars on it, indicating that he has had no disciplinary infractions over the past two years. Chaplains and other prisoners are quick to speak of Jesse's talent for mentoring younger inmates in the Wicca/Asatru community. "Religion," he says, "that's what makes me feel good now."

What distinguishes Folsom Prison from New Folsom Prison, it becomes readily apparent to me, is religious agency. The pagan faiths at New Folsom are concealed, contradictory, and dangerous. At the Big House, paganism is freely available and aligned with the values of chaplains and inmate leaders, making it less likely to be dangerous. It is a partnership that works for both parties, and it works from the bottom up. In case I need evidence of this partnership, as he leaves the interview room Jesse calls for someone down the hall. "Here," he says a moment later. "See what you can do with this one," as if I'm there to do counseling.

In walks a traumatized young convict with one ear: the other has been hacked off in some gruesome affair that he does talk about and I do not ask. All of my interviews have been scheduled through the prison chaplains, except this one. It was arranged by Jesse, a confirmation of his trusted status as a leader within the inmate-chaplain partnership.

His name is Tim, a diminutive thirty-one-year-old white man serving life without parole for a hate crime murder. Raised by a Baptist family in Sacramento during the 1980s, religion meant nothing to Tim, so he turned to anarchy. After a flirtation with the punk scene he drifted into the skinhead movement, which led him to an unbridled anger at the "double standards" he saw in life. His religious search began with Nietzsche when he was a high school senior. From there he explored Carl Jung's societal archetype theory, which said that the Norse-Germanic people's archetypes could only be inherited, not culturally transmitted. And this set the stage for his involvement in the Church of the Creator, or Creativity, a religion founded by the racist Ben Klassen in 1973, which holds that whites are the sole creators of civilization and technology. Tim's hate crime was an act of Creativity.

He was brought to Folsom Prison in 2001. "I realized if I was going to survive in this place I'd have to do some soul searching," he says. Asked what he found by looking into himself, he replies, "Man left to himself is meaningless. We must find destiny's chain." This is a term he uses throughout our conversation. It seems to imply an ordained linearity in the religious search, with one turning point evolving into the next. It was "destiny's chain" that led Tim to the Circle and a conversion to Odinism at the age of twenty-seven. "I'm still a racist and still believe in the racial struggle," he says. "But now I'm into Odinism. I came to believe that Odinism was our natural religion. Odinists are in prehistory. Jung and Nietzsche provided the background for Odinism."

Asked how his life has changed, Tim says that the religion "gives me direction in life, a link in destiny's chain. It helps me keep away from drugs and gives meaning to my life. I've shed a lot of anger from my youth. It was a herd mentality that led me to the hatred that caused my crime. Hate made me self-destruct. Odinism made me more introspective."

If the riddle of radicalization for white pagans can be solved through a theory of collective action whereby chaplains and prisoners can organize themselves voluntarily to "retain the residuals of their own efforts," as the Nobel Prize–winning economist Elinor Ostrom would say, then an obvious question arises: does the same hold true for Black Muslims?[51] I address that issue in chapter 8. Presently, Gus's case begs an equally compelling question about the riddle of radicalization: if the absence of religious agency creates the necessary preconditions for terrorism on the part of white pagans, as it did at New Folsom Prison, does the same hold true for black Salafi-Jihadists? The short answer is yes. But it also involves an incredible amount of criminal cunning. It is to that story that we now turn.

7

Al-Qaeda of California

The rise of Islam in American prisons cannot be separated from the nation's experiment with mass incarceration. For the sociologist Loïc Wacquant, mass incarceration can be traced to delayed consequences of the civil rights movement, the burgeoning of Black Power activism, and the outbreak of urban riots that stormed across America during the mid-1960s.[1] According to Wacquant, black communities never recovered. The ghetto imploded. "It was left to crumble onto itself," Wacquant argues, "trapping lower-class African Americans in a vortex of unemployment, poverty, and crime abetted by the joint withdrawal of the wage-labor market and the welfare state."[2] As the ghetto lost its economic bearing and its inclusionary hold on young black men, the penal state was enlisted to contain a population widely viewed as destitute and dangerous.

Wacquant identifies two historical trajectories that fused the ghetto and the prison together in an iron cage entrapping lower-class blacks. In one direction, the *ghetto came to resemble the prison* as its residents became impoverished, its social fabric torn asunder by fear and cynicism, and its indigenous organizations (churches, schools, and civic groups) collapsed only to be replaced by social institutions of the state, primarily criminal justice in nature. In the other direction, the *prison came to resemble the ghetto* as severe racial divides pervaded custodial institutions and predatory street culture came to replace the "convict code" (expressed in the term "do your own time") that had traditionally maintained equilibrium within the inmate society. John Irwin noticed this shift as early as 1974 when observing the aggressiveness of black and Hispanic gangs at San Quentin.[3] By 1987, with California tilting toward its epic phase of warehousing prisoners, Irwin's observations had become more pointed. "Now, in addition to the indigenous prison gangs," he wrote, "numerous street gangs, such as the 'crips' and 'bloods' from Los Angeles . . . operate in many of the state prisons. There is no longer a single, overarching convict culture . . . as there tended to be twenty years ago."[4]

This *deadly symbiosis* of prison warehouse culture and ghetto culture, as Wacquant calls it, would play a vital role in the reemergence of Islam in U.S. prisons during the era of mass incarceration. A leading theory of prisoner radicalization asserts that disorderly, overcrowded and understaffed institutions breed a desire in convicts to defy the authorities. This creates a condition where "identities of resistance" are looked upon favorably by other prisoners.[5] Some scholars argue that Islam, or the "religion of the oppressed," is fast becoming prisoners' preferred ideology of resistance, playing the role that once belonged to Marxism.[6] Along with protection from victimization and the search for meaning and identity, this ideology of resistance has assumed its place as a primary catalyst for inmate conversions to a range of new religious faiths, including militant interpretations of Islam. Once radicalized by these extremist religions, prisoners become vulnerable to terrorist recruitment. "The most spectacular cases," argues the radicalization theorist Peter Neumann, "are those in which 'free world' terrorist plots had their origins in the prison environment. They include . . . the Assembly of Authentic Islam (JIS)."[7] My research bears this out. In fact, JIS represents the most spectacular case of all.

Prisoners—especially those in gangs—have long recruited other convicts to act as their collaborators upon release. Jam'iyyat Ul-Islam Is-Saheeh, however, was led by a gang member who radicalized other inmates into joining a gang with a terrorist agenda. Yet the case is important for another reason. The JIS plot was part of an international post-9/11 trend toward homegrown terrorist cells whose members tend to seek al-Qaeda's blessing.

* * *

The JIS story begins with Kevin James, born to African American parents in South Central Los Angeles in 1976. On the face of it, James's radical bona fides came naturally. His father was a Black Panther who came from the same L.A. streets as Eldridge Cleaver, Bunchy Carter, and George Jackson, who were all Black Panthers of the 1960s, of course, and prison radicals of the spectacular kind. But the fact of the matter is that Kevin James never knew his father.[8] Along with a brother, a sister, and a cousin, James was raised by his mother in a middle-class home on Hoover Boulevard. He came of age during the urban crack epidemic of the 1980s when the streets of South Central were ruled by gangs. As a boy, James was seen as an average student but an exceptional threat to school safety. He bounced from one elementary school to the next—from West L.A. to Beverly Hills and others—and was expelled from each of them for stealing supplies to support his artistic interest in hip-hop graffiti. Like Eldridge Cleaver, Kevin James had a strong interest in subculture. "I was fascinated by art and stealing for the party," James said to an investigative journalist, Eric Longabardi, in a videotaped interview at the Santa Ana Jail in Southern California. "I kept getting in trouble in school for graffiti. I liked to carry guns and steal. I didn't start out as a hard-core gang member, but a graffiti artist who hung around with gangs."[9]

James was arrested and sent to juvenile hall at the age of twelve, marking the end of his formal education. Between stints in juvenile custody James was slowly drawn into the gang life. He found a surrogate family in the Hoover Criminals, one of the city's numerous Crip factions, and he claimed affiliation with the 76th Street set. Distinguished by their orange do-rags, the 76th Street division was at perpetual war against the Hoovers' arch enemy, the Rollin' 60s Crips. Over the next several years James was incarcerated numerous times for theft. He went from reform school to juvenile camp to the California Youth Authority. James was released from CYA custody on September 27, 1995, and returned to South Central where he took a bride and a menial job in El Segundo. James was not destined for civilian life, however, and three months later he was convicted of robbery and sentenced to ten years.[10]

He began his sentence at the Centinella State Prison near Imperial Valley, soon to be the most overcrowded prison in California with more than five thousand inmates warehoused in spaces designed to hold fewer than half as many.[11] Shortly after his arrival, James experienced a turning point. On the yard one day, to his surprise James ran into his brother, who had recently joined the Nation of Islam. The James brothers were celled together and over the next several months Kevin James adopted the Nation's beliefs as well. "I met my brother in state prison," James recalled. "I bunked with him and turned to Islam by my brother's influence. . . . I decided to take my life seriously then. The Muslims were the only ones on the yard who [had] achieved a sense of peace out of chaos."[12]

In 1997, Kevin James—then twenty-one—was transferred to the California State Prison at Tehachapi, another massively overcrowded maximum-security institution, where he continued to follow the Nation's teachings. Yet Tehachapi was a different ballgame. "There was lots of gang activity there," said a former Tehachapi inmate and Nation of Islam member in my interview with him at New Folsom. "You had to be in a gang to survive. That's when I turned [from the Nation] to Sunni Islam in a serious way. We had to have our services on the yard because the guards wouldn't let us have chapel. I recall a confrontation behind that." Bonded across gang lines for protection and deprived of chaplaincy services that might have assisted them in their spiritual searching, the Sunnis of Tehachapi began to congregate under a Muslim banner of their own creation. James also found something missing in the Nation of Islam at Tehachapi, and he drifted toward these Sunnis as well. According to the FBI, it was at this point that James founded the radical prison religion Jam'iyyat Ul-Islam Is-Saheeh based on his idiosyncratic interpretation of Sunni/Salafi texts. James has repeatedly denied this charge. In a letter to PBS's *Frontline*, James wrote, "I didn't found any radical Islamic group; J.I.S. is a name used by prison Sunnis to distinguish themselves from the N.O.I. [Nation of Islam], Shiites and other sects."[13] To the journalist Eric Longabardi, James described JIS as simply a group of "like-minded Muslims." Although JIS had a spiritual leader on each yard at Tehachapi, said James, these inmate imams did not communicate with each other and there was neither organized leadership nor hierarchical structure to JIS.

Not in dispute is the fact that, after meeting the Sunnis of Tehachapi, Kevin James underwent a religious transformation to the Salafi-Jihadist tradition, leading him to a nihilistic worldview that went far beyond norms and customs common to the Nation of Islam. Historians argue that Salafists are much more willing than the traditional Islamic schools to declare other Muslims to be unbelievers and to wage jihad against them.[14] James's ire would therefore be directed not only against those outside the Muslim faith but also against those whom he saw as betraying and degrading Islam from within. In addition to waging a holy war against the U.S. government, James would also soon call for attacks against fellow prisoners who belonged to the Nation of Islam, as well as Shiites and Muslim prison guards.[15]

This constituted the most significant turning point of James's life. Using a variety of aliases, including "Shahaab James" and "Ash Shakyh Sudani," James began proselytizing recently arrived inmates at Tehachapi, preaching that it was the duty of Muslims to target enemies of Islam, including the U.S. government and supporters of Israel, for violent attacks. Claiming to have spent time with jihadists in Sudan (an apocryphal story that well served James's mythmaking) James recruited fellow prisoners by secretly distributing a handwritten document entitled "JIS Protocol," which described James's religious beliefs, including his justification for killing "lawful targets," including non-Muslims. In the document, James supported the establishment of an Islamic Caliphate in the United States and described jihad as "the only true 'anti-terrorist action' . . . a defensive battle against the aggression of theological imposters led by Zionism."

Throughout the late 1990s and into the early 2000s, up to and beyond 9/11, James spread his Protocol (updated in 2002 to more than one hundred pages) to other California prisoners by using bundled kites—long strips of thin paper tightly rolled into round packages and distributed prisoner-to-prisoner. He also used the U.S. mail by sending letters to third parties in the community (perhaps the Hoover Criminals) who then forwarded the letters to designated prisoners. Prisoner radicalization was not a security issue in California during these years. "Terrorist screening, investigation and assessment did not exist in the California Department of Corrections and Rehabilitation at the time," admitted the department's security chief.[16] Neither was prisoner radicalization an issue for the FBI. As a result, James's communications went unmonitored. It was not until late 2002 that officials caught wind of James's agitation and began to develop intelligence on JIS. In early 2003, some two dozen JIS members were identified, rounded up, and transferred to other institutions. In short, the JIS membership was spread around the California prison system in an attempt to squelch the movement.

New Folsom Prison was built specifically for such purposes. James arrived at New Folsom—"a petri dish just waiting to foment terrorism," as its chaplain would later call it—in mid-2003 where he was celled up with a thirty-four-year-old Hispanic named Peter Martinez, who was doing time for second-degree murder. James brought Martinez into the fold and Martinez began his own recruitment campaign. By this time, James had become a prisoner of considerable charismatic bearing. "The only thing I can say about Kevin James," said a New Folsom employee who knew him, "is that he's all man. Guys in prison are under a lot of pressure and he never appeared to buckle."[17] Longabardi described James as "articulate, calm, sedate, and well read in the Koran. Quite honestly, I was impressed by him." James is remembered at New Folsom as a slight, soft-spoken inmate with large cornrows running back from his forehead, an untrimmed goatee, and tattoos of crescents on his neck and of "Allah" (in Arabic) covering "7" and "6" tattoos on his forearms (for 76th Street Hoover Criminals). Yet what was most striking about James's appearance was a prayer bump, a *zabidah* (Arabic for raisin) in the middle of his forehead, the sign of dedication and piety caused by grinding one's forehead into the ground during Muslim prayers. James's raisin actually protruded from his forehead, a mark of the most pious, which would first be seen on the forehead of Ayman al-Zawahiri in 2006.[18]

In 2004, James wrote a second call to jihad called "Blue Print 2005." The Blue Print was modeled after a training manual for al-Qaeda, also known as the Manchester document (publicly available on the Internet, though James did not have Internet access himself), which instructs al-Qaeda operatives to set up "an Islamic program for themselves" if they are incarcerated and to try to recruit "brothers" who are "disenchanted with their country's policies." James's recruitment strategy would follow the Manchester document to a tee. The document instructs Muslim inmates "to communicate with brothers outside prison and exchange information that may be helpful to them in their work outside prison," further noting that "mastering the art of hiding messages is self-evident here." In terms of leadership qualities, the document says, "The brother in prison should be a role model in selflessness. Brothers should also pay attention to each others [sic] needs." The brothers "have to be treated gently," it instructs, "and should be offered good advice, good treatment, and pray that God may guide them."[19]

"Al-Qaeda can't get their militants to the places they want to hit," observed the terrorism expert Brian Levin of the recruitment strategy, "so they rely on an ideology to gain converts who do it for them."[20] James's Blue Print represented a significant tactical advancement in prisoner radicalization. Going beyond the Manchester document in order to incorporate American gang tactics, it required that prospective JIS members take an oath of obedience to James, swear not to disclose the existence of JIS, and swear to obey a "90-day rule," whereby members were required to communicate with James at least once every three months. The secret manuscript also detailed plans for producing and distributing a propaganda CD to facilitate recruiting, and the Blue Print gave instructions on how parolees can "blend into society" to establish JIS cells once they were released to the community. Blue Print 2005 instructed parolees to get married, dress casually, study Arabic, acquire two pistols with silencers, and learn how to make bombs. James would later claim that the Blue Print was never meant for "the real world." Rather, it was intended for consumption only among people of his world—the prisoners of California.

As expected, James's recruitment strategy focused on black convicts with backgrounds similar to his own. California prisons are full of such inmates. I interviewed a prisoner involved with JIS at New Folsom during the height of James's recruiting campaign. Like James, he was a Crip from South Central L.A. who was sentenced to prison as a teenager. After converting to the Nation of Islam at the California State Prison-Calipatria in 2001, he fell in with a group of Sunni Muslims, making him a prime candidate for JIS recruitment once he was transferred to New Folsom two years later. Yet his radicalization was also clearly tied to the harsh conditions of imprisonment at New Folsom. "People should be worried about us," he said.

> People in this prison feel there is no way out. It's all about winning and losing. I'm lookin' for justice. That's the difference between me and these other niggers up in this bitch. When our back is against the wall we [JIS] will seek justice. This prison is a cauldron of the realities [we face]. Prison is big business in California and we're its slaves. This is not so much about Islam. I'm radical. Radical means you're holding to foundation. That's what the suicide bombers do. There's nothing but God left, so let's go find a bomb.

As James's writings circulated, JIS's reputation for militancy became well known on the yard at New Folsom. "People should be concerned with JIS," said the leader of a Hindu group of prisoners at the facility. "There's a fundamental brokenness about Islam in this place. You hear it mainly in the chow halls. Muslims talk about decidedly antagonistic things. In prison, Islam tends to reinforce a negative vibration centered on pride and ego. Many of my people are completely terrorized by this." James used his reputation to expand JIS's recruitment program by introducing opportunities for inmates to undergo guerrilla training while inside prison. James's violent discourse was conducted, in part, under the guise of religious worship, such as it existed at New Folsom. A gang intelligence officer, who used to shake down James and his JIS companions for weapons as they entered the chapel for Jumna services, recalled walking into a service one Friday evening to discover JIS engaged in martial arts practice. "At that time, the JIS was about fifteen large. They would do all this radical stuff," he said, "even while the imam [a state chaplain] was there. Once he [the imam] even brought in razor blades and handed them out to inmates. He's *still* working here!"

In early November 2004, James met an inmate who perfectly fit al-Qaeda's profile for terrorist recruitment. Levar Washington was a twenty-five-year-old African American from South Central doing a three-year bit for robbery. "I met him four weeks before he paroled in the yard," James recalled, describing Washington as a member of an "enemy" gang who had recently converted to Islam.[21] Washington had done time in four California prisons and was a member of the Rollin' 60s Crips—a rolling dice tattoo covered part of his forehead. According to key documents in the JIS case, shortly before Washington's parole on November 29, James instructed Washington to recruit five people from the L.A. community without felony records to train in covert operations, acquire firearms with silencers, and find contacts with explosives expertise to make bombs that could be detonated from a distance. In response, Washington pledged his loyalty to James "until death by martyrdom."

* * *

Six months later, in May 2005, Washington walked into the Jamat-e-Masjidul mosque in Inglewood, California, wearing an improvised headdress intended to conceal the gang tattoo on his forehead.[22] There he met twenty-one-year-old Gregory Patterson, the son of two black educators from Gardena—his father was a college professor; his mother, a university administrator. Patterson, who had no criminal background, was described by a former teacher as "an overachieving nerd." He attended classes at both El Camino College in Torrance and Cal State in Northridge. Patterson also worked part-time at a duty-free shop at Los Angeles International Airport. But more important for the moment, like Washington, Patterson was newly converted to Islam.[23] He had begun attending the Inglewood mosque the previous March, enrolling in a one-on-one Arabic class taught by twenty-one-year-old Hammad Samana, a Muslim born and raised near Karachi, Pakistan, but now living as a permanent U.S. resident with his parents in an apartment across the street from the Inglewood mosque, which served mainly South Asian Muslims. Also something of a nerd, Samana had worked at a Barnes & Noble bookstore to support his family and had attended Santa Monica College where he was on the dean's list. Described by the president of the Inglewood mosque as "gracious and respectful toward others," Samana had no known criminal history or connections to overseas extremists.[24]

Like the other major terrorist events since 9/11—the 2003 suicide bombings in Casablanca, the 2004 Madrid train bombings, and the London subway bombings of 2005—the JIS plot was inspired by George W. Bush's military adventure in Iraq.[25] By seeking revenge against the United States for invading Iraq, JIS would express its collective aspiration to gain the approval of Osama bin Laden. Just as the Madrid train bombers referred to themselves as "Al-Qaeda of Europe," JIS became "Al-Qaeda of California."[26]

In late May, Patterson and Washington rented an apartment on West 27th Street in South Central where, with Samana, they held intense discussions about the Iraq War and the treatment of Muslim detainees at Abu Ghraib and Guantanamo. At the time, the news was dominated by stories about ongoing criticisms of America's role in Iraq and its mistreatment of detainees. A June *Washington Post*/ABC poll found that almost 60 percent of Americans considered the war a mistake.[27] A June Gallup poll showed that only one in three Americans believed the United States was winning the war. In July, the National Council on Churches officially took a stand against the war, calling it dishonorable and urging a change in U.S. policy.[28] George Bush confronted the growing pessimism in a televised speech from Fort Bragg, North Carolina, on June 28, 2005, urging Americans not to forget the lessons of 9/11 and pointing to links between bin Laden and Abu Musab al-Zarqawi.[29] On June 24, Dick Cheney had defended the treatment of prisoners by the U.S. military at Guantanamo, telling a CNN reporter, "They're living in the tropics. They're well fed. They've got everything they could possibly want."[30] Days later the Guantanamo detainees launched their first hunger strike, calling for "starvation until death."[31]

According to the FBI, Levar Washington believed that something "had to be done to punish the United States" for Iraq and detainee abuse and "Samana agreed."[32] "Washington really believed that the Muslim world is majorly oppressed right now," said an individual Washington had attempted to recruit, "and their only way out is to fight jihad by harming innocent people."[33] Therefore, Samana and Patterson swore allegiance to Washington and his jihad mission, vowing to serve as JIS mujahedeen in the greater Los Angeles area—information that Washington passed on to Kevin James. James, in turn, gave Washington advice about his recruiting efforts. "Be careful (brother)," James warned, "there are agents everywhere looking for al-Qaeda recruiters or any other threat to national security."[34] James also informed Washington that he had added Gregory Patterson's name to his list of approved visitors at New Folsom. As for Samana, James said he was a "beautiful addition" to the gang. Although Kevin James was locked up in a maximum-security prison, he was still the shot-caller.

Similar to the other homegrown terrorist attacks since 9/11, the JIS plot was based on precursor crimes that financed the conspiracy. The Casablanca bombers sold hashish to fund their operation; the Madrid bombers stole explosives and peddled drugs; the Bali bombers robbed a jewelry store. Moreover, precursor crimes have an indomitable history in terrorism. Carlos the Jackal raised an astounding $50 million by taking hostages in his deadly 1975 raid on the OPEC conference in Vienna; the Irish Republican Army raised millions by robbing banks and running protection and extortion rackets and underground brothels; the Order generated more than $4 million from armored-truck heists.[35] JIS was in a different league and it was the minor league at best. Members would rob gas stations, stealing no more than $3,000.

Acquiring firearms was the group's first order of business. Investigators believe that Washington did so by relying on either his prior contacts with the Rollin' 60s or his newly established relationship with the Hoover Criminals (arranged by Kevin James). Either way, finding guns in South Central was no great achievement. On May 30, 2005, Gregory Patterson—who had never committed a crime in his life, who had been a Muslim for less than six months, and who had known the ex-con Levar Washington for only a few weeks—donned a black ski mask, armed himself with a shotgun, and robbed a Los Angeles gas station. Thus began an armed robbery spree that Patterson would later describe as "part of a jihad against the U.S., particularly against American oil companies who are stealing from our countries [Muslim countries]."[36]

On June 6, Patterson robbed another gas station in Torrance. A week later, Patterson and Samana stuck up a station in Playa Del Ray. Patterson hit a second gas station in Torrance on June 16, then another in Bellflower on June 18. On June 20, Patterson was back in L.A. where he attempted another robbery but failed. JIS had better luck the next day, June 21, when Patterson robbed stations in Pico Rivera and Walnut, while Samana robbed one in Orange County. The next day, June 22, Patterson sent James an update on the gang's activities.

The missive to James was followed by a flurry of activity. On June 29, Patterson bought a .223 caliber rifle and ordered an AR-15 rifle from a sporting goods store. On July 2, Samana conducted Internet searches on the Israeli Consulate in Los Angeles, including the identity of specific Israeli officials, and three U.S. Army recruiting centers (in Long Beach, Torrance, and Harbor City)—thereby identifying the first set of targets for the upcoming strike. Samana and Patterson downloaded computer images depicting overhead and street-level views of the target locations. On July 3, Patterson used the .223 rifle to rob a gas station in Playa Vista, and he then returned to the apartment where he ran an Internet search on Jewish holiday events in the city, focusing on Yom Kippur, the most solemn of Jewish holidays, thereby identifying a second set of targets. On July 4, Samana took part in martial arts practice in an L.A. park.

For all intents and purposes, by this time the gang's South Central apartment represented an activated al-Qaeda sleeper cell. Shotguns and shotgun shells were stored there, along with reloading equipment, knives, bulletproof vests, camouflaged battle fatigues, ski masks, and jihadist literature (printed in English). On the wall was a poster of Osama bin Laden. Washington was the undisputed leader of what he called his "council of Muslims who had planned to carry out two operations in the Los Angeles area as part of jihad against the United States."[37] To drive home the point, the date of the attack was scheduled for September 11, 2005.

The first attack would be on an Army recruiting office, a potent symbol of U.S. involvement in Iraq. The plan called for two JIS men to enter the office wearing ski masks and armed with rifles. Then they would open fire and kill everyone in sight. They would flee in a getaway car driven by a third man and return to the apartment where planning for the second attack would begin. Ultimately, the goal of JIS was "to die for Allah in a jihad," as Patterson put it. But the law enforcement whip was about to come down. Though long on ideology, JIS was short on criminal skill. In fact, the gang was made of rank amateurs.

On July 5, James telephoned Washington to discuss details of the plot and Washington responded with concern about Samana's suitability for the task ahead. Gang intelligence officials now believe that this and other calls were made by James from New Folsom Prison with a smuggled cellphone. Technology was omnipresent in the conspiracy. That same day Patterson conducted an Internet search on El Al (the national airline of Israel) at L.A. International, thus identifying still another target for terrorism, while Samana drafted a computer document listing the addresses of the Army recruiting offices and of the Israeli Consulate.

That evening, robbery investigators from the Torrance Police Department spotted two black males parked near a gas station, observing the flow of customer traffic. Earlier, the investigators had received a tip concerning a string of gas-station robberies in the area. That tip dealt with a remarkable case of criminal stupidity. In a previous robbery, Patterson had left his cellphone at the scene. Therefore, investigators put a tail on the two men, believing one of them to be Gregory Patterson, identified as the owner of the recovered cellphone. At 11:00 p.m., the same two men, wearing ski masks and armed with shotguns, robbed a Chevron station on Crenshaw Boulevard in Fullerton, making off with $252. As they were leaving the station, police pulled the car over and arrested the two men without incident. They identified themselves as Gregory Patterson and Levar Washington.

* * *

When police searched the South Central apartment they found the JIS documents, attack plans complete with geospatial photographs, and the poster of bin Laden. More than anyone, the evidence implicated Hammad Samana, who was arrested at his parents' home on July 7 after confessing to two of the robberies. By then, some five hundred law enforcement officers from the federal, state, and local levels had joined the investigation, dubbed "Torrential Rain" due to the Torrance connection. More than one hundred officers came from the L.A. Police Department alone. Evidence found in the apartment led investigators to New Folsom Prison and Kevin James. Discovered among James's possessions was a document entitled "Notoriety Moves," which appeared to be a press release that James wanted wrapped in a turban and sent "to *all* news stations" after the attack of September 11. Also included was a list of JIS enemies. Topping the list were Louis Farrakhan, followers of the Nation of Islam, and Shiite Muslims, including inmates and guards. In early September, all four JIS members were indicted on federal charges of conspiring to wage war against the U.S. government through terrorism by killing armed service members and foreign officials.

The indictments led to a combined state and federal investigation of radical Islamist prison gangs in California, which determined that JIS still had about a dozen hard-core members inside the system. This created serious concerns at the FBI that disaffected inmates were being drawn to radical Islam as a source of terrorist activity across the country. "Gangs have long recruited in prisons for people to act as their supplicants once they got out," said a high-ranking FBI official at the time. "What is new here is the focus on radicalizing people in prisons."[38]

* * *

What, then, are the implications of the JIS case for terrorist recruitment in prison? The figure below presents a way of thinking about the problem. It is important to understand where criminological problems originate. The JIS recruitment strategy began with Kevin James's conversion to the Nation of Islam, which occurred through James's kinship network. This traditional form of Islam within the United States was used as a foundation for embracing an alternative religious vision: Jam'iyyat Ul-Islam Is-Saheeh, a form of Salafi-inspired Prison Islam. Like a prison gang (and despite what James would say about it), JIS not only had its own hierarchical structure, code

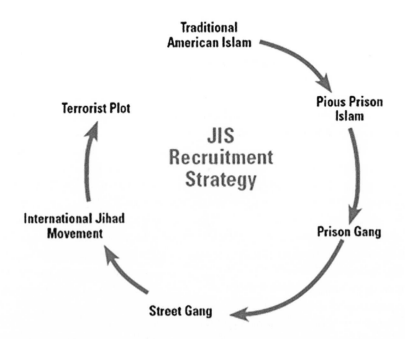

JIS recruitment strategy.

of conduct, and clandestine communication system—including built-in mechanisms to maintain fealty and secrecy—but it also had its own collective identity. This identity provided JIS members with sources of meaning that became internalized, leading to resistance against the otherwise intolerable conditions of their confinement. Just as Erving Goffman noted that religious conversions insulate true believers against psychological assaults of the total institution, JIS sheltered its converts from the dangers of mass incarceration, thus redeeming them from the humiliation of what Goffman called the *spoiled identity*.[39]

Because its numbers paled in comparison with other prison gangs, JIS operated below the security radar, often under the pretext of constitutionally protected rights to religious worship. Facilitating this bottom-up criminality was the total absence of computerized intelligence gathering by California prison authorities. Twenty-first-century ideology was fought with 20th-century technology. Asked if a computerized management information system would have made a difference, the department's security chief replied, "Yes. If we had intelligence capabilities across institutional lines back then we could have monitored James's phone calls and mail. This would have led us to the plot."[40]

But more than anything, JIS was distinguished by its leadership. According to Sageman, JIS is the sort of group that is not supposed to have a formal leadership. He argues that a loosely structured group based on the affinity of members for one another ("just a bunch of guys") is the defining characteristic of post-9/11 jihad in the Western world.[41] Not only was James a formidable leader, but he was also full of his own self-constructed piety. James's oversized raisin in the middle of his forehead created a powerful mode of symbolic interaction between leader and convert. If Islam is the new language of resistance for black convicts, taking the place of Marxist ideology once championed by the Black Panthers, then pious forms of Prison Islam are successful when they offer inmates the most radical form of resistance possible: devotion to Osama bin Laden and the Salafi-Jihadist tradition of Sunni Islam.

In the JIS case, radical resistance was encapsulated in prison-gang culture. So powerful was the attachment to JIS that devotees (one deeply devout and the other freshly converted) were able to overcome past grievances against one another. In the world of extremists, it is often said that "the enemy of my enemy is my friend." That precept played out in the JIS case over the bonding between two fierce rivals: James of the Hoover Criminals and Washington who banged Rollin' 60s. This approach to fusing JIS's spiritual identity onto its gang history played a significant role in creating a support system capable of fostering the transition to terrorism. The spiritual and strategic basis for launching a violent attack against "infidels" of the U.S. government was now in place.

The plan was then taken to the streets by the parolee Levar Washington, demonstrating a long-overlooked facet of prisoner subcultures. Irwin argued that prisoner behavior, roles, and identity do not arise exclusively from prison conditions but to some degree are determined by the culture inmates bring with them into prison. Irwin called this importation theory.[42] JIS did just the opposite: it *exported* convict beliefs and behaviors from the prison to the community. For logistical support, Washington turned to a street gang to provide firearms for a series of precursor crimes intended to raise funds for the operation. For foot soldiers, he relied on the impulse of the international jihad movement inspired by the war in Iraq. Potential members were easily found at a neighborhood mosque in the persons of a brand-new convert to Islam and his teacher, neither of whom had a criminal record. All the while, the cell continued to take its marching orders from a charismatic convict walking the mainline more than three hundred miles away. Al-Qaeda of California was now ideologically, strategically, and logistically complete. The next step was terrorism.

And that is where the conspiracy went off the rails. The JIS plot was toppled not by intelligence-led police work or the successful cooperation between different branches of the counterterrorism community, but by its own criminal incompetence, something that is not uncommon among terrorists.[43] The moment that Gregory Patterson left his cellphone behind at the scene of an armed robbery was the moment JIS was done with. Law enforcement only had to clean up the pieces. This does not mean, however, that everyone in JIS was just as witless.

With respect to tactics, most terrorist groups assume a conservative posture, rarely attempting anything new.[44] In this sense, Kevin James was a terrorist entrepreneur who advanced several innovations unique to the United States. His recruitment system was especially sophisticated. By keeping JIS small in numbers, James successfully operated below the radar for years without detection. The recruitment by a prison convict of community collaborators with clean criminal records into a fully operational terrorist plan was another innovation. James's secret communication system—his use of kites, third-party mailing, and a smuggled cellphone as early as 2005—was another.[45] Mobilizing the gang cultures of prisons and the streets into a unified terrorist cell organized at a local mosque was yet another. Although its take was small, the gang pulled off ten successful armed robberies relying mainly on inexperienced gunmen, keeping its leadership out of harm's way.

The JIS case led to an FBI investigation of prisoner radicalization involving oversight inspections of some two thousand U.S. correctional facilities.
Among its findings the FBI determined that there was *not* a JIS-like pattern
of terrorist recruitment in U.S. prisons.[46] In fact, the FBI could find no pattern of terrorist recruitment whatsoever, indicating just how difficult it is to
identify and predict the spectacular few. The JIS case demonstrates, moreover, that terrorist recruitment is a problem so atypical of everyday prison
life that it defies prediction. In 2004, there were some 2.3 million inmates
in U.S. prisons. More than one hundred thousand of them had converted to
Islam since the 9/11 attacks.[47] Exactly one of them—Levar Washington—was
recruited into an actual terrorist plot. Identifying one person out of a population of one hundred thousand is statistically impossible. The lesson of the JIS
case, then, is that it is not the sheer number of prisoners following extremist interpretations of religious doctrines that poses a threat; rather, it is the
potential for charismatic leaders to radicalize small groups of prisoners into
support networks for terrorist goals upon release.

The JIS case also led to a large-scale investigation by California law
enforcement, which uncovered several homegrown terrorist plots in the Los
Angeles area. The JIS case has been the subject of news documentaries and
countless media reports and is widely used in law-enforcement training on
prisoner radicalization. JIS is cited by researchers worldwide as an instance
where a free-world terrorist plot was hatched in prison. In 2011, the JIS case
became the focal point of a congressional hearing on prisoner radicalization.
And Kevin James himself has done much to bring the issue of charismatic
leadership to the table.

But perhaps the enduring legacy of JIS is that the terrorist plot even happened at all. Orchestrating a terrorist conspiracy involves a lot of moving
parts under the "best" of circumstances. That James was able to manage
such a multifaceted plot while locked up in maximum-security custody is
unprecedented. No other U.S. case in the database evidences anything close
to this level of criminal proficiency. That is why, as I've written elsewhere,
years from now when criminologists write their textbooks on American terrorism, alongside such infamous figures as Osama bin Laden, Ramzi Yousef,
and Timothy McVeigh may appear the name Kevin James.[48]

Postscript

James and Washington pled guilty to terrorism charges on December
14, 2007. "This is a case in which a terrorist cell grew out of a prison cell,"
announced the FBI director, Robert Mueller. "Despite the fact that they had

no connection to al-Qaeda leaders, they had adopted their cause."[49] Levar Washington was sentenced to twenty-two years in federal prison and Kevin James was given a twenty-year federal sentence. Gregory Patterson received a federal sentence of 151 months. Hammad Samana was found unfit to stand trial and was sent to a federal medical facility for psychiatric care.

Yet there is a lingering mystery about the JIS case. When Kevin James was taken into federal custody in July 2005 for his role in organizing the JIS plot, he was only five months away from completing his ten-year sentence for robbery. After that, he would have been a free man. If James was really the brains behind the operation, and his plea agreement indicates that he was, then why didn't James simply wait a few months and carry out the attack himself? Perhaps James realized that there is no better place to organize a terrorist cell than from within a failed prison.

8

The New Barbarians

The JIS case confirms the breakdown theory of prisoner radicalization. Confined to a mismanaged and overcrowded maximum-security prison, a small group of inmates sought protection, meaning, and identity through an ideology of resistance. Once radicalized by that ideology, JIS initiated a terrorist plot against the United States. Yet it would be impulsive to think of these influences as a definitive explanation of prisoner radicalization. In the JIS case, a host of other factors came into play: the rift between Prison Islam and traditional Islam, the mobilization of prison-gang culture to the streets, the international jihad movement inspired by the Iraq War, a sophisticated prisoner communication system, and charismatic leadership—all overlooked in the breakdown theory. A closer inspection of the breakdown's consequences reveals something else that has been overlooked: a flicker of light shining from the positive side of radicalization's double-edged sword. The best way to see this light is by concentrating on prisoners who rise to leadership positions within the inmate society. As it turns out, these inmate leaders—who make the "same noise" as terrorists but offer constructive solutions—also emerge from broken-down prisons with their own ideology of resistance, religious rifts, and grievances over U.S.-led wars in Muslim lands. They, too, are extremely charismatic.

Inmate leadership is a central part of prisoner subcultures. The subject has intrigued scholars since penology's beginnings as a field of study.[1] Penologists have historically organized their thinking on this matter along two theoretical lines. Functional theorists argue that leaders arise from the collective adaptation of inmates to the prison environment. This begins with the process of *prisonization*, or "the taking on in greater or less degree the folkways, mores, and customs, and general culture of the penitentiary."[2] Prisonization reinforces the inmate's criminal status as a social "outlaw," further deepening his commitment to the convict code, traditionally expressed as "do your own time." The convict code represents a set of values and beliefs distinct to prisons; it has no applicability to leading a successful crime-free life in the free world. The convict code is the unofficial rule book of behavior for prisoners. It holds that prison is a predatory jungle where only the strong survive. A more elaborate version of the code is "Don't gamble, don't mess with drugs, don't mess with homosexuals, and don't steal, don't borrow or lend, and you might survive."[3]

Those most committed to the convict code, the ones who actively celebrate it, are known in prison argot as "right guys." Right guys remain loyal to fellow inmates and never let others down, no matter how rough things get. Right guys are dependable and always keep their promises. As such, right guys often become leaders within the inmate society.[4] Right guys are hard-core cons. They typically serve sentences of many years, often exhibit unstable personalities, have few or no positive relations with people on the outside, are able to integrate easily into their chosen prisoner subculture, display an almost blind acceptance of the dogmas and norms of that subculture, and never snitch.[5] These leaders typically emerge in maximum-security institutions and are known for displaying hostile, antisocial attitudes toward the prison staff.[6]

The second theory does not take issue with the right guy stereotype of the inmate leader, and it does not reject the notion that such leaders typically emerge from maximum-security prisons. But it does dispel certain assumptions about prisonization. This model is couched in John Irwin's importation theory, which asserts that what is understood as prisonization resulting from deprivation is actually a form of antisocial behavior that is deeply rooted in a prisoner's criminal history. In other words, inmate subculture stems from beliefs, attitudes, and lifestyles imported from the free world.[7] Penologists have supported this theory by revealing the process through which gangs import their organizational roles and ideologies from the streets into the penitentiary. In fact, the prison environment often serves to strengthen the subcultural identity of inmates, making gang members more respected by fellow inmates than they were by gang members on the streets.[8] According to importation theory, these inmates are most likely to become leaders.

However, these theories are largely the creation of research conducted prior to the prisoners' rights movement. Since then, the factors associated with confinement in U.S. prisons have changed dramatically—sharp increases in the number of minority prisoners in custody, massive overcrowding, the ascendancy of prison gangs, and the rise of non-Judeo-Christian religions behind bars, including the various schools of Islam. As the following analysis shows, these factors require a new way of thinking about inmate leadership.

* * *

To begin with, the intelligence officials and chaplains I interviewed were unanimous in their view that most black inmates join religious groups in order to gain protection. "When a young black man comes to prison," said one official, "he is introduced to all these new religions. Technically, he's lost. But everyone tells him, 'Don't mess with the Muslims. They got their stuff together.' Muslims got their own protectors. The Nation of Islam, they police their own. They are very well groomed and have an inner strength. You rarely see Muslims involved in a fight." Officials also agree that there is growing hostility between Prison Islam and traditional Islam. "It's the fringe element we worry about most," said another intelligence official. "The Muslims who practice Prison Islam, they look down on traditional Islam. So inmates who hold to the traditional practices and teachings have to stand up and show they're strong."

The influence of Prison Islam cannot be overstated. Not only does it co-opt and beat down the efforts of inmates who follow traditional Islamic teachings, but Prison Islam provides a safe haven for gang members who have absolutely no interest in the faith. There is one "jacket" that today's prisoners try their best to avoid: being classified as an affiliate of a security threat group, that is, a known gang member. Gang membership can result in reassignment to a closed custody unit, fewer privileges, and an unshakable stigma at parole board hearings. So they become "Muslims" instead. A veteran imam explains the subterfuge: "Major Black gangs—like the Gangster Disciples and the Crips—hide themselves under a religious banner. Religion is a protected class. Religion offers these gang members an opportunity to meet. Islam has nothing to do with it."

Given these problems, I found that many Muslim groups are now facing a leadership void. This is due primarily to black inmates' changing value systems and their acute lack of knowledge about African American history. "The inmates have changed over the years," said the intelligence chief for the Florida Department of Corrections. "Today inmates have no values. Most of them can't even tell you who Martin Luther King was. Most of them never heard of the civil rights movement. They have no history of the struggle black people went through here in the South. They're all about the money, the clothes and the gold chains." Other officials attribute the leadership void to pervasive mental deficiencies within radical Muslim groups. The administrative chaplain for a large Midwestern state remarked, "Our prisoners are thugs. Tossing around names like 'al-Qaeda' and 'Jihad' is simply opportunistic. Those who say they're connected to al-Qaeda are psychotic or suffer from varying degrees of ambulatory psychosis and are housed in a closed wing of the State mental hospital."[9]

Moreover, during the era of mass incarceration, religion has emerged as the most important prisoner subculture of all and as the starting point for understanding inmate leadership. In my study, African Americans who emerged as inmate leaders were distinguished by the sincerity of their religious quest. Those who appeared to be on a genuine spiritual search were most likely to end up as leaders of Sunni, Shiite and American Black Muslim groups, as well as groups of Black Hebrew Israelites.[10] They were better educated, better read, and more articulate than those who joined these groups solely for protection. Inmate leaders were also more likely to cross racial boundaries in the maximum-security mix, were more familiar with world events, and were more confident in expressing their political views. A veteran prison chaplain from Florida described the complex social milieu in which inmate leaders arise, conditions not unlike those that inspired JIS and other prison-based terrorists of the post-9/11 era.

> Today's inmates are more dissatisfied with the government than they were ten years ago or even twenty years ago. The seeds of dissatisfaction are everywhere. Inmates display more aggressive posturing. They cluster on the yard by religion. More aggressive people are doing the evangelizing. Racism is rampant. Most of these men grew up in an evangelical home and became alienated by religion. Now they are open to anything. They find a new religion in prison which reinforces their opposition to authority. Serious offenders are showing up in these groups. Some of these inmates are a very fertile ground for jihad. . . . It may be time to take another look at America's rich religious heritage and be more discriminate when religious liberty becomes a shank in the back.

Among the black inmate religious leaders I interviewed, none were prepared to put a "shank in the back" of anyone. For the most part, they were openly repentant for their crimes. They typically supported politically conservative views and revealed an astonishing aversion to popular culture, particularly black ghetto realism with its expressions of misogyny, outrage and urgency, and its fascination for crass materialism. "I hate hip-hop music," said the leader of a Black Hebrew group. "Hate it. Hip-hop has been the worst influence on our people, puttin' down a generation gap through our people. Negativity has no place among us." Essentially, black leaders had experienced enough violence and destruction in their own lives to have any truck with a media abstraction. What they wanted was a history that gave them spiritual succor, not gold chains and gangster rap. They despised television as well, save the news, and because they were forbidden access to the Internet (most are therefore computer illiterate), for entertainment and enlightenment they turned to sacred texts, history and philosophy books, videos, and folk knowledge. A Black Hebrew elder said he experienced a turning point after seeing Alex Haley's well-known docu-drama *Roots*. Another Hebrew elder claimed to have been transformed by Yahweh Ben Yahweh's *You Are Not a Nigger! Our True History, the World's Best-kept Secret*.[11] Rejecting the dogmatic bonds of Black Nationalism, this inmate leader preached that prison was actually a gift from God because it was part of the black man's cultural heritage. Once understood, this insight promised to set black convicts on a "revolutionary path to self-betterment." He further explained: "I learned that eight out of ten of the biblical prophets had a spiritual awakening while in prison. I saw that the blacks were like that, too. We didn't have time to study in the free world. Now in prison we do. There's no mistake about it: prison is the best thing that ever happened to me and it's the best thing that ever happened to lots of black men."

A black Shiite leader at Folsom Prison followed a similar pathway. A former big-time crack dealer for the Bloods in Los Angeles, he said, "I hated what I was doing. God answered my prayers by locking me up for good." His Islamic conversion was precipitated by a five-year study of philosophy, history, and religion. "I read everything I could find about people being in harmony with other people," he explained. These works included such literary masterpieces as James Allen's essays on thought and consciousness, *As a Man Thinketh*; *Complete Poetry and Prose of William Blake*; and *Essays* by Francis Bacon—works that spoke eloquently to the hell of tortured isolation and were once on Gandhi's prison reading list.

* * *

These examples provide an instructive contrast to JIS because they identify individual-level differences between black inmates who do *not* support terrorism and those who do. I found that inmates joined JIS mainly for protection. Their politics were shaped by the charismatic leader Kevin James and the nihilism of his JIS Protocol and Blue Print 2005. Other than references to suicide bombers in Iraq, JIS members were not particularly conversant in international affairs and spoke little beyond catchphrases about injustices against Muslims around the world. None, that I could tell, were repentant for their crimes. They were not able to recall any books they had read while undergoing their conversions. When asked to explain the influences that motivated his conversion to JIS, one member cited *Enter the Wu-Tang Clan (36 Chambers)*, a classic 1993 hip-hop album blending the banal mentality of kung-fu movies with Nation of Islam preaching and comic-book characters (Ghostface Killah and Ol' Dirty Bastard) for just the right touch of levity. This is a far cry from the intellectual ground laid by his Muslim forbearers.

"No university would ask any student to devour literature as I did," wrote Malcolm X after his prison conversion to the Nation of Islam, "of being able to read and *understand*."[12] Devouring literature was certainly not something Kevin James was known for.

In the hundreds of pages James wrote and distributed over the years, there is no mention of classic literature, current events, ghetto realism, prison, or Islamic scholarship beyond the Koran and the *Sunnah* (the practices of the Prophet Mohammed), and the sacred texts were then interpreted by James only to repeat the worldview espoused by Osama bin Laden and the Salafi-Jihadists. It is little wonder, then, that James's followers at New Folsom Prison spoke candidly of their moral outrage against the United States for its role in Iraq, openly praised bin Laden, and glorified suicide bombers. It is little wonder that they became Al-Qaeda of California.

Yet the riddle of radicalization thrives in California prisons. From the same conditions that created the nihilism of JIS also came a religious program of profound sociological depth grounded in human suffering. Given alarmist fears about Western prisons becoming "incubators" for terrorist ideology, the simple appearance of Islam in prison is often viewed as evidence of radicalization, rather than as an authentic expression of faith. Nothing could be further from the truth. While all members of the IRA were Irish Catholics, not all Irish Catholics were terrorists. The final case shows the unforeseen potential for counter-radicalization (or counter-jihad) intrinsic to the coalition between black Islamic leaders and supportive chaplains found at Folsom Prison. The case shows that they cannot meet a challenge as complex as violent extremism alone but with cooperation only.

* * *

The story centers on Akeem, born in Richmond, California, in 1970. His father was a black Baptist preacher and Akeem had a strict upbringing within a tightly knit family. Accordingly, his grades were excellent and he avoided the allure of drugs and gangs. Akeem graduated at the top of his high school class in 1988 and joined the Army, serving in various capacities in the United States and abroad until 1992. He began questioning his Christian faith during these years and developed an interest in Eastern religions, first studying Buddhism, then Taoism and finally Confucianism. Yet things were far from righteous in his life.

Akeem returned to Richmond in 1993. One night, he got into an argument with an acquaintance over an unpaid debt. The situation escalated, a fight ensued, and Akeem beat the man into a coma. "Unfortunately," says Akeem, "the guy died and I got life without parole."

Irwin reasoned that inmates serving life sentences (or lifers) are a sustainable resource of the prison community. "Short termers come and go," he argued, "lifers accumulate."[13] Lifers know more about the prison and prisoner subcultures than short-termers and often more than staff. They are frequently willing to engage in prolonged study, taking advantage of every available resource the prison has to offer in an attempt to, in Irwin's words, "seek atonement and, perhaps, even redemption through a multitude of programs, most of which they, the prisoners themselves, create."[14] Redemption takes shape over decades as lifers scrupulously work through psychological problems that led them to commit the most serious of crimes—homicide—until they one day arrive at an awakening. The awakening originates, said Irwin, "with a religious conversion, most often to Christianity or Islam."[15]

Akeem arrived at Folsom Prison in June 1994 where he was celled up with an L.A. Crip who had recently converted to Sunni Islam. During his processing Akeem was given an intelligence test showing that he had an IQ of 140. His spiritual searching was accelerated by this high intelligence level. "My cellie had taught himself to read Arabic," he says. "And he taught me Arabic in two days. After that I read the entire Koran from cover to cover." Once the reading was complete, Akeem began attending services at Greystone Chapel where chaplains counseled him on the Sunni faith. A short time later, Akeem converted. "Islam helped me set boundaries," he says. "It taught me to have respect for others. It taught me to understand the true nature of humanity. It keeps me from doing the bad things of my past." Yet this was not the end of Akeem's searching. Sometime around 2000 he embarked on a mission to read voluminous writings of the eminent Arab scholar Ibn Khaldun, leading him to a turning point.

* * *

Understanding Akeem's turning point and the benefit it would bring to Folsom Prison requires a brief background on this towering figure of Islamic scholarship. Ibn Khaldun was born to a family of professional politicians in Tunis, on the Mediterranean coast of North Africa, in 1332.[16] Sincere in his reverence for traditional Islam and the dogmas and practices it had produced, Ibn Khaldun eventually became a high-ranking government official, holding jurist posts in Granada, Morocco, Algeria, Tunisia, and Egypt. He spent a number of years among the Bedouins and in 1363 negotiated their case in the Spanish court of Pedro the Cruel (so-named for perpetrating a series of ruthless murders). Each of Ibn Khaldun's postings ended in acrimony, however, and he was eventually exiled to a fortress in Algeria where he began thinking about the bases of political power, concentrating on the rise and fall of empires. Ibn Khaldun's theoretical conclusions became the basis of his most famous book, the *Muqaddimah* (*Introduction to Universal History*, translated into English by Franz Rosenthal and published by Princeton University Press in 1981). More than five centuries after Ibn Khaldun's death in Cairo in 1406, the British historian Arnold Toynbee described the *Muqaddimah* as "undoubtedly the greatest work of its kind that has ever yet been created by any mind in any time or place."[17]

Ibn Khaldun contended that the history of the Arab world revolved around the Bedouins, who were nomadic tribes perpetually locked in conflict with settled agricultural societies over the issue of mobility. Bedouins, who lived off grazing and hunting, had to be peripatetic, and this prevented them from constructing a specialized economy. Mobility also created among the Bedouins a tribal ethic known as *asabiya* (meaning kinship or tribal solidarity based on the innate psychological need to belong and give support to one or more leading personalities of a group) and the subsequent militarization of the tribes. When asabiya was reinforced by Islam, its power to bond men to one another was multiplied. As the tribes grew, so did their military might, eventually outperforming the military strength of armies hired to defend agricultural societies and the cities they served. As the Bedouins conquered agricultural societies, they appropriated their means of production. The key to this conquest was asabiya—hence, tribal solidarity had the power to transform a society's culture, ethics, and economics. For Ibn Khaldun, asabiya was the decisive element in the formation of empires in Islam. As the Bedouins became settled through the specialization of labor, however, the asabiya ethic deteriorated. Once tribal solidarity was broken, the society became vulnerable to raids from the Bedouins who still roamed the desert.

According to Ibn Khaldun, these social laws had universal validity. Historical processes are defined by cyclical change brought on by the interaction of nomads and townspeople. Nomads were tough, savage, and uncultured. Although they were inimical to civilization, nomads were also hardy, frugal, morally incorruptible, freedom-loving, and self-reliant. Conversely, because towns were centers of commerce, science, arts, and culture, these luxuries corrupted its inhabitants and made them a liability to the state.

Four centuries before Marx published his theory of class struggle (*The Communist Manifesto*, 1848), Ibn Khaldun had advanced a theoretical model of social conflict that went something like this. Social cohesion arises spontaneously in tribes and other small kinship networks due to the existence of prophets, a succession of chosen humans who are transmitters of a divine message. Cohesion is then enlarged and intensified by the religious convictions of tribesmen. Yet group cohesion contains within it the seeds of the group's destruction. When a society becomes a great civilization, its high point will be followed by a period of social decay. Social decay diminishes the civilization, of course, and in time it will be conquered by new barbarians. Once the new barbarians solidify their control over the conquered society, they, too, become attracted to its more refined aspects (literacy, the arts, and the acquisition of wealth). Solidarity is then compromised, and the arts of defending oneself and of attacking the enemy are forgotten. And within a period of three generations (or about 120 years) the former barbarians will be conquered by new barbarians who will then repeat the process. "States are like men," argued Ibn Khaldun. "You cannot revitalize them when they begin to die."[18] In this way, the *Muqqadimah* can be read as a general philosophy applicable to any series of historical events at different times or in different places.

* * *

Since converting to Islam, Akeem has been a model prisoner. Chaplains extol his virtues and fellow inmates speak openly of his sway. This is due in no small measure to the way that Akeem presents himself. He is a slender six-footer dressed in neatly pressed denims and horn-rimmed glasses, giving him the appearance of a scholar. He has no visible tattoos and no raisin in the middle of his forehead. He greets others with a smile, exuding optimism. As far as I can tell, Akeem is a charismatic genius—a Malcolm X, if you will, minus the goatee and attitude. Accordingly, Akeem now leads the Islamic Studies Program (ISP) at Folsom. In this capacity, Akeem trains other prisoners as teachers based upon what he calls the "Three R's"—rehabilitation, repentance, and reform. The ISP not only provides prisoners with a viable treatment program, but, as I will demonstrate below, it also serves as a mitigating force against the spread of Islamic extremism.

In 2007 there was one chaplain for every two thousand inmates at Folsom Prison. One part-time cleric was assigned to the Muslims and he was responsible for about 10 percent of Islamic instructional duties at the institution. Akeem and his team of inmate teachers were responsible for the other 90 percent. "We can't rely on the prison to rehabilitate us," says Akeem. "So we have to do it ourselves. I get help with my self-help groups because I have the foundation."

MH: Can you explain that foundation?
AKEEM: The *Muqaddimah*. Everything we need is in the *Muqaddimah*.

The *Muqaddimah* concentrates on asabiya, the spirit of cohesion that allowed generations of barbarians to conquer civilized societies. Akeem and his cohorts see themselves as the new barbarians in this epic struggle. No one is more inimical to civilization than they—poor black men who will spend the rest of their lives in prison. In order to survive, they have become hard, lean, and pious. Like Gandhi, they are closer to God precisely because of their suffering. It is not hard to appreciate their veneration of the *Muqqaddimah*, particularly given the desperate conditions of their confinement. Ibn Khaldun defined government as "an institution which prevents injustice other than such as it commits itself."[19] Statements such as this caused Toynbee to reason that Ibn Khaldun had become an "immortal philosopher whose thought still lives in the mind of every reader of the *Muqqaddima*."[20] Or, as Ibn Khaldun put it, history is "eagerly sought after. The men in the street aspire to know it. Kings and leaders vie for it."[21] Ibn Khaldun lived in an age when Arab civilizations were struggling to bring order out of the chaos of failed states. This led Toynbee to invoke Hobbes's famous dictum when he wrote that Ibn Khaldun was "the one outstanding personality in the history of a civilization whose social life on the whole was 'solitary, poor, nasty, brutish, and short.' "[22] From Ibn Khaldun's perspective, asabiya offered the only hope for transcending this existential agony.

Akeem's group is trying to transcend human depravations every bit as cruel as those experienced by Ibn Khaldun. Like David versus Goliath, they are pitted against the civilized and powerful: namely, representatives of a law-and-order bureaucracy who function on the left-over scraps of wealth, culture, technology, and reason generated by the State of California. Californians spend more than $1 billion each year on plastic surgery; legions of newly minted tech millionaires and billionaires make Silicon Valley their home, while thousands of California teachers have been laid off due to budget woes, dozens of hospitals and emergency rooms have been shut down, and thousands of young black men can't find jobs so they end up selling crack and terrorizing entire neighborhoods. California raises millions of dollars in yacht taxes, while schoolchildren get shot because of the color of their headbands. This is a weak civilization: one that has subverted God's will and lost its moral fiber through decadence and conspicuous consumption; its agents have become sedentary and weak, tyrannical and corrupt. "Dynasties," wrote Ibn Khaldun, "have a natural lifespan like individuals."[23] And now California has reached its end. But more to the point of Akeem's struggle, it is a state that has failed to live up to its moral obligation to provide transgressors with the opportunity for reformation. Max Weber reasoned that the success of capitalism rested in the Protestant ability to transform religion from its ecclesiastical base to one of worldly material wealth garnered through hard and honest work.[24] Because there is no "hard and honest work" at Folsom Prison anymore (it vanished in the dust of warehousing inmates), Akeem and his group represent something akin to 21st-century wheelbarrow men, without even the dignity of wheelbarrows. This inability to reckon with the physical and spiritual lives of inmates is the hallmark of a failed prison. Toynbee argued that the failure of a civilization to survive is the result of its inability to respond to such moral and religious challenges.

"Overcrowding is the main problem here," says Folsom's head chaplain. "It affects everything we do, foremost among them the way we deliver services to the Muslims. . . . The Nation of Islam is the biggest problem. They pressure inmates to convert. Their preachers encourage inmates to overthrow the government." Another chaplain adds, "We are called on by the administration to monitor Muslim preachers who come into the prison. The problem is that many of these volunteers go over our heads to get credentials. We are left out of the loop when it comes to selecting and approving volunteers. Also, we get no gang intelligence down here [in the chapel]. There is no officer presence in the chapel. Yet we have to abide by the chaplain's code: We won't permit one religious group to speak negatively about another."

These chaplains face enormous obstacles: the burden of overcrowding, the strident voices coming out of the Nation of Islam, gang politics and Prison Islam, security lapses, rampant hepatitis C and drug abuse, and, on top of it all, role conflicts between chaplains and intelligence officers. These challenges have led the chaplains to believe that the only way of providing Islamic services is by turning to Akeem and his Muslim teachers. "In the JIS case," says the chaplain, "inmates were disenchanted with the religious offerings they received from the institution. To avoid that problem again, we must offer inmates something they are *not* disenchanted with." Volunteer clergy are not the answer to this problem because they are beyond the chaplains' control. But Akeem and his teachers will control themselves if they are allowed to be active and authentic representatives of inmate concerns about Islam. There is the added benefit that Akeem's people have credibility among the Muslim population and are not seen as "sellouts." Therefore, in the Islamic tradition of honoring loyalty to teachers above loyalty to systems, Akeem's group is able to effectively challenge extremist ideas held by young searchers.

* * *

Scholars such as Christian Parenti and Noam Chomsky identify several crucial elements of a failed state, one being the ascension of religious millenarianism. Such was the case with the two failed prisons at Represa. Whereas JIS was a form of 7th-century Salafi-inspired Prison Islam led by a charismatic convict who adopted the beliefs and then innovated on the terrorist tactics of al-Qaeda, the ISP was a form of traditional Sunni Islam led by a charismatic prisoner who adopted the cause of counter-radicalization. While Kevin James and JIS rejected medieval interpretations of Islam, thereby directing their wrath not only against apostates but also those they saw as betraying Islam from within, Akeem and the ISP immersed themselves in the reckonings of a 14th-century sociologist (arguably the world's first sociologist), thereby embracing medieval explanations of Islam stressing the social perspective rather than the theological, especially the reciprocal relationships between group solidarity and religion, human labor and socioeconomic stratification. JIS was a secret organization that was intolerant of religious pluralism, thus confirming the alarmist view that prisons are incubators for radical Islam and terrorist ideology. The ISP was a civic organization, one that exemplifies the reassuring view that Islamic groups can offer their adherents a sense of social solidarity and higher purpose without it leading to violence against innocents. This can only happen in pluralistic prison environments, like Greystone Chapel, where Salafi-Jihadist teachings are deemed too narrow-minded and sectarian to appeal to large numbers of inmates. As such, the ISP at Folsom Prison demonstrates that prisoners themselves—if they are on a path of authentic transformation and are supported by chaplains—can do more than the state to prevent the spread of radicalization. More broadly, by increasing opportunities for Muslim prisoners to play a full part in a new form of rehabilitation being created from their own hands, the ISP provides a built-in control mechanism against terrorist recruitment that is evocative of a wider movement in the Muslim world—revealed in the more egalitarian features of the Arab Spring—which is increasingly rejecting various forms of extremism, including the ideology of al-Qaeda.[25] For that reason alone it should be replicated far and wide.

Finally, the Folsom cases reveal a vital lesson about inmate leadership. In every sense of the term, Kevin James was a "right guy." Within JIS, he was trustworthy, showed respect for his followers, and adhered to the convict code. James had adopted these characteristics through years of incarceration, allowing him to easily integrate into various extremist sects in prison. Though moderate in his personal affairs, when it came to religion James was a fanatic. Fanatical dedication to a cause is a necessary precondition for terrorism. James had no positive (pro-social) relations with people on the outside; he blindly accepted the dogmas and norms of JIS (in fact, he created them); and he was the shot-caller for a range of prison rule violations, from conducting martial arts training and smuggling contraband to instigating intimidation and violence against other inmates. Not only was James known for his antisocial attitude toward guards, but he also designed a plan to kill them. James's activities on behalf of JIS represented both an *importation* of gang customs and roles into the prison and an *exportation* of convict roles and behaviors from the prison to gangs in the community. James was a terrorist, one of the spectacular few.

Akeem represents the opposite. Rather than importing gang customs and roles into the prison, he imported a program intended to support prisoner reformation through the restorative power of religion. Significantly, he did so by drawing on the teachings of a bona fide prison radical. We should not flinch from this fact: the *Muqaddimah* was conceived by Ibn Khaldun during his incarceration at that Algerian fortress centuries ago, a biographical fact that gives his writings enormous credibility among some Islamic prisoners today. This is important because a growing body of research shows that effective Islamic counter-radicalization policies typically share general premises with the overall extremist worldview (such as opposition to Western wars in Muslim countries), while differing from it on the essential issue of violence.[26] Akeem was known not for antisocial attitudes toward guards but for cooperation with them. He did not carry the reputation of a rule violator; rather, his program was considered essential for institutional stability. Akeem was recognized for his moderation in all affairs and fanaticism in none. In every way, Akeem breaks the classic mold, suggesting the basis for a new paradigm of inmate leadership: the *righteous guy*. The righteous guy is devoted to rehabilitation, not the convict code.

Because he has earned the administration's respect for his service to Folsom Prison, Akeem has appeared on CNN, PBS's *Frontline*, and the National Geographic Channel, sharing his views on inmate Islam with worldwide audiences. This would have never been possible without the tradition of religious tolerance at Greystone Chapel, the dauntless work of chaplains, and the endorsement of the warden. Reflecting the positive side of radicalization's double-edged sword, Akeem's program reveals elements of an indigenous Arabian sociology, one preceding modern European thought by epochs, where Islam creates a worldly social network and individual sense of purpose equal to that of asabiya, as he explains:

> The potential for radicalization is there, no doubt. But there is no one from the outside who will radicalize us. That can only happen from the inside. Maximum-security is more likely to produce radical prisoners because there is more violence in this environment. Yards are so politically charged these days, so guys who teach Islam teach from that perspective. They have to in order to maintain their credibility with inmates. . . . The potential for radicalization must be understood on a one-to-one basis, because nobody's going to risk going radical in a public place! You must remember: Islam has always been shaped by the environment in which it is practiced. Prison is no different. As long as you can keep the environment right, you can avoid having radical Muslims.

So, how do you "keep the environment right" to avoid having radical Muslims? That question is at the center of one of the most hotly contested debates of the post-9/11 era.

9

Terrorist Kingpins and the De-Radicalization Movement

On March 6, 2011, some sixty days before American forces killed Osama bin Laden in Pakistan, the Obama administration issued a warning that al-Qaeda is "increasingly attempting to recruit and radicalize people to terrorism here in the United States. . . . The threat is real and it is rising. [Al-Qaeda] is trying to convince Muslim Americans to reject their country and attack their fellow Americans."[1] Based on this assessment, in June the House Committee on Homeland Security held hearings on the threat of Islamic radicalization in U.S. prisons. "The Obama administration recognizes prison radicalization is a serious threat and that prisons are a fertile ground for recruitment," said the committee's controversial chairman, Peter King (R.-N.Y.), in his opening remarks. "A number of cases since 9/11 have involved terrorists who converted to Islam or were radicalized to Islamism in American prisons then subsequently attempted to launch terror strikes here in the U.S. upon their release from custody."[2] What happens inside American prisons had become a matter of national security.

The hearings focused mainly on Kevin James and JIS, though no mention was made of the dangerous conditions of confinement at New Folsom that led to the terrorist plot. The committee also heard testimony on the importance of vetting prison chaplains because, in King's words, "too many prison chaplains [have] radical and/or serious criminal backgrounds."[3] This claim had been floating around Washington for some time. Back in 2006, the Senate Committee on Homeland Security heard testimony from an FBI official who attributed the radicalization problem to "anti-U.S. sermons provided by contract, volunteer or staff imams."[4] Testifying in support of the threat this time around was Patrick Dunleavy, a former Deputy Inspector General of the Criminal Intelligence Division in the New York State prison system. Dunleavy, however, provided evidence of only one prison chaplain who had a "radical and/or serious criminal background": Warith Deen Umar (Wallace Gene Marks), a former Nation of Islam prisoner who went on to become the head of Ministerial Services for the New York Department of Corrections. In 2003, Umar gained notoriety when he told a reporter from the *Wall Street Journal* that the 9/11 hijackers should be considered martyred heroes. Umar was banned from entering New York prisons for life and the U.S. Justice

Department launched an investigation into the in the Federal Bureau of Prisons' hiring of Muslim clergy. In its final report issued in 2004, the Justice
Department recommended the founding of a verifiable religious body that
would certify Islamic clergy prior to hiring. But the recommendation failed
to gain traction. "To this date no Islamic organization has been appointed to
fulfill this role," Dunleavy concluded.[5] Moreover, the committee was given
little proof that prison chaplains were routinely recruiting inmates into radical Islamic thought and practice; indeed, the 2004 Justice Department report
found that staff chaplains "were *not* the cause of inmate radicalization."[6] Neither was the committee given any evidence linking chaplains to actual cases
of prison-based terrorism.

Essentially, for the American public these events raised more questions
than answers. Neither the White House nor Congress provided specific
details about the evolving threat from al-Qaeda. What kinds of terrorist
attacks were being planned? If threats were evolving from prisons, which
prisons presented the greatest danger and which prisoners were most vulnerable to terrorist recruitment? And if prison chaplains weren't radicalizing
inmates, then who was?

* * *

Several years earlier, similar charges were leveled against Muslim clerics
from Saudi Arabia. According to this line of thought, Western prisons were
becoming incubators for terrorist ideology due primarily to the Saudi government, which spends billions of dollars promoting Wahhabi Islam.[7] In
intelligence terms, the threat was based on a complex organizational model
of terrorist recruitment involving foreign powers. The fear is that while visiting a prison or preaching in one, a Saudi-backed Wahhabi imam will notice a
pious convert to Islam, and refer his name to a mosque or nonprofit government organization (NGO), who, in turn, would speak of him to al-Qaeda.
This is a classic "spot, assess, develop, and handle" mode of terrorist recruitment. The Wahhabi threat, however, never reached this level of sophistication. Nor was the threat based on evidence about the organizational factors
supporting prisoner radicalization.

Testifying before a Senate committee on the influence of Saudi-backed
Wahhabi groups on U.S. prison populations in 2003, Senator Charles
Schumer (D-NY) declared that "these organizations have succeeded in
ensuring that militant Wahhabism is the only form of Islam that is preached
to the twelve thousand Muslims in federal prisons. The imams flood the
prisons with antigovernment, pro-bin Laden videos, literature, and sermon

tapes."[8] Yet the senator failed to identify who was doing the radical preaching. Was it prison chaplains, religious volunteers, or prisoners? Nor did Schumer explore the possibility that inmate communication systems were used to distribute the extremist materials or that there was a countervailing effort being led by prison chaplains and inmate leaders, as surely there was.

Confirming the assessment on Wahhabi clerics was the security expert Michael Waller who testified that "Radical Islamist groups, mostly tied to Saudi-sponsored Wahhabi organizations suspected by the U.S. government of being closely linked to terror financing activities, dominate Muslim prison recruitment in the U.S. and seek to create a radicalized cadre of felons who will support anti-American efforts."[9] But Waller also failed to identify precisely how this radicalization was being conducted and which prisoners were most likely to join the "radicalized cadre." One analyst told Congress that the Saudis were supplying "money that has been spent on funding leading terrorist and other extremist organizations that disseminate hatred in 'education centers,' charities, mosques, and even prisons—including many here in the United States."[10] Another expert claimed that nearly ten thousand copies of the Wahhabi Koran had been distributed to American prisoners.[11] Once again, these experts could not identify who was disseminating the materials and how. Echoing the alarmist view of prisoner radicalization, the Washington-based Center for Security Policy went so far as to charge the Saudi government with "efforts to recruit convicted felons in the U.S. prison system as cannon-fodder for the Wahhabist jihad."[12] The goal here, so went the argument, was the conversion of large numbers of African American prisoners to Wahhabism and its radical Islamist agenda.[13] When released back into the community, it was predicted that these Black Muslims would support terrorist goals, "murdering their own countrymen in a kind of 'payback' for perceived injustices done to them by 'white America.'"[14] This was perhaps the wildest assertion because it ignored the well-researched facts that terrorist groups seek a small number of recruits and that only a minuscule fraction of prisoners turn radical beliefs into terrorist action.

Paralleling the case against prison chaplains in the King hearings, these earlier specialists did not provide any evidence linking Saudi-backed clerics to actual cases of prison-based terrorism. Their claims would be refuted, in fact, by the FBI's post-JIS investigation showing that most cases of prisoner radicalization in the United States are instigated by domestic extremists with few or no foreign connections.[15] As such, the threat posed by Wahhabi clerics would also fail to gain traction as a public policy to fight terrorism. In fact, the threat turned out to be a fraud.

Making claims in the absence of supporting evidence is a common rhetorical device used by experts to introduce their various worldviews into the debate on counterterrorism policy. Abraham Miller once made the sobering observation that "the literature on the subject of terrorism has become part of a propaganda war where objectivity has been unabashedly replaced by advocacy."[16] Much the same can be said for expert opinions on prisoner radicalization. They are often based on reasoning by analogy (e.g., one untrustworthy chaplain in New York indicates that all chaplains are untrustworthy) rather than on findings from empirically based fieldwork. That research shows that Islam in prison poses a security threat only under certain conditions of confinement: in mismanaged understaffed and overcrowded maximum-security prisons where offenders are radicalized through a process of one-on-one proselytizing by charismatic leaders. Otherwise, Islam has a moderating effect on prisoners, which plays an important role in prison security and rehabilitation.

Another tactic used in the propaganda war is the counterfactual argument, exemplified by the sociologist Bert Useem's testimony at the King hearings. In support of research claiming to show that U.S. prisons are not at risk for Islamic radicalization, Useem argued that Kevin James's prison experience was inconsequential. That is, he said that the trajectory of James's pre-prison life—growing up without a father, his involvement with the Hoover Criminals, and the stints in juvenile lockup—destined him to become a terrorist no matter what while James's actual prison experiences—conversions to the Nation of Islam and JIS, his introduction to Salafism and the Manchester document, and his role as a major player in the gangs of New Folsom—were all somehow irrelevant. In Useem's words, "The difficult judgment to make is whether Kevin James, had he been on the streets rather than behind bars, would have been equally inclined toward violence and more capable of leading a terrorist strike."[17] A counterfactual argument is a theory about what might have happened, not a theory about what did happen. Due to their speculative nature, counterfactual arguments are usually dismissed by historians because they do not meet the standards of mainstream historical research.[18] Counterfactual arguments are routinely rejected by the intelligence community if not treated with a sense of amusement. In other words, it is fruitless to second-guess history.

Likewise, criminologists have long pointed to the dangers of overstating a case. Doing so may lead to what police call a "tunnel investigation syndrome," where experts are steered toward a predetermined conclusion. The obsession with impending perils posed by radical chaplains and Saudi-backed Muslim clerics, along with useless historiographies, represents such a danger. For in advancing unfounded conclusions about prisoner radicalization, analysts obscure a potentially far more serious threat operating beyond the orbit of public scrutiny: the imprisonment of al-Qaeda terrorists.

Like an army, al-Qaeda is an entitative group, meaning that it is a pure entity that is embedded in a clear, rigid, and absolute belief system; rules and regulations; and organizational command structure. It is this clarity, simplicity, and distinctiveness (entitativity) that makes al-Qaeda so attractive to others, especially when the appeal was communicated through its charismatic leader, Osama bin Laden. The U.S. government enables this appeal by framing terrorists as warriors subject to imprisonment without charges. As such, al-Qaeda foot soldiers do not stop being terrorists simply because they are in prison. They continue to view themselves as foot soldiers in a sacred war and look upon guards as soldiers in an opposing army. Even more important, imprisoned al-Qaeda terrorists have been known to conduct extensive outreach to other inmates and free-world extremists as well, instigating fear by claiming that anti-American terrorists, including the 9/11 hijackers, should be remembered as martyrs and heroes.[19] Every resource wasted on groundless assumptions about prisoner radicalization is a resource that could have been wisely used to train prison staff in the verifiable indicators of al-Qaeda radicalization and organizing behind bars, thereby identifying warning signs of an impending terrorist attack.

* * *

Today, there are an estimated one hundred thousand suspected terrorists in custody around the world.[20] Some of the most influential Islamic terrorists are locked up in Western prisons. A notable example is Omar Abdel Rahman, a blind sheikh who has been in U.S. custody since 1993 for his role in the New York City Landmarks plot—a plan to bomb the United Nations Building, along with the New York office of the FBI as well as the Lincoln and Holland tunnels. Years ago the sheikh issued a fatwa, calling on al-Qaeda to attack the United States should he die in an American prison, which is most likely inevitable. Not only has the sheikh's fatwa reached worldwide audiences via the Internet and satellite television, but from federal custody he has sent similar communiqués to the Egyptian terrorist organization Al-Gama al-Islamiyya.

Yet when it comes to the mythopoeia of modern terrorism—an essential element in understanding how extremists from different cultures create violence in similar ways—no one is more important than Ilich Ramírez Sánchez, better known as Carlos the Jackal. The first terrorist to achieve universal media fame for organizing a series of outstanding European and Middle Eastern terrorist strikes during the 1970s, Carlos played a definitive role in turning the terrorist into an incandescent celebrity, paving the way for Osama bin Laden's enlargement as a living myth at the turn of the millennium. Today, Carlos the Jackal is serving a life sentence in France's Le Sante prison, where he periodically issues press releases praising al-Qaeda.[21]

The imprisonment of terrorist kingpins therefore raises an important question for Western nations: what is the best practice for incarcerating terrorists? As it turns out, there are at least three models to consider: the *total segregation* model used by the United States, the *partial segregation* model used by Israel, and the *dispersal* model employed by Great Britain. An analysis of these three models is undertaken in the concluding pages.

The challenges of doing comparative criminology are well known. Cross-cultural comparisons are subject to the vagaries of language and customs, politics, penal law, and criminal subcultures. Yet at the end of the day, the United States, Israel, and Great Britain share a common dilemma: each country is struggling in its own way to work out the institutional methods and conceptual frameworks for controlling the threat of radicalization brought on by the long-term imprisonment of Islamic terrorists.

* * *

A total of 362 federal prisoners were serving lengthy sentences on terrorism-related charges in the continental United States at the end of 2011 (out of a combined state and federal prison population of 2.3 million). Most (269 inmates) were involved in international terrorism with another 93 inmates locked up for domestic terrorism.[22] Another 172 suspected terrorists were being detained without trial, "for the duration of hostilities" against al-Qaeda, by the U.S. military at Guantanamo, including five al-Qaeda operatives charged in connection with the 9/11 attacks.[23] A reported ninety-six of the Guantanamo detainees were Yemeni.

Among the 269 international terrorists in the Bureau of Prisons (BOP) were about two dozen al-Qaeda terrorists, some of whom were trained in bin Laden's camps. They included men involved in the 1993 World Trade Center bombing, the 1998 East African embassy bombings, the 1999 millennial plot to bomb the Los Angeles International Airport, and the 2000 bombing of the USS *Cole*. New York's BOP detention centers in Manhattan and Brooklyn held another dozen or so al-Qaeda members awaiting trial, including one high-ranking jihadist who was once bin Laden's bodyguard. Yet this may represent only the initial phase of incarcerating terrorists as federal prisons are experiencing what an official report called "a constant population of new inmates arrested on terrorism-related charges."[24]

Die-hard extremists, these imprisoned terrorists need little proselytizing from off-the-reservation chaplains or Wahhabi clerics in Saudi Arabia. They are already religious militants, many of whom are fully capable of radicalizing other prisoners on their own. The danger to U.S. security, then, is not the sheer number of Muslims in prison; rather, it is the potential for small networks of true believers to instigate terrorist acts, either by other radicalized prisoners once released or by existing support structures in the community. Or they can integrate all of these resources and wage a terrorist plot from behind bars under the auspices of a charismatic leader, as JIS did.

The kingpin threat first surfaced several years after 9/11 when an MSNBC news correspondent, Lisa Myers, reported that three federal prisoners— Mohammed Salameh, Mahmud Abouhalima, and Nidal Ayyad—incarcerated at the BOP's Administrative Maximum security facility (Supermax) in Florence, Colorado, for the 1993 World Trade Center bombing, had written more than ninety letters to Islamic militants outside the prison between 2002 and 2004. Fourteen of these letters were sent to Spanish prisoners who had links to the terrorist cell behind the Madrid train bombings. There could not have been a more serious breach of prison security in the early post-9/11 years. Yet Mohammed Salameh had also managed to smuggle several letters in which he praised bin Laden as a hero to Arabic newspapers. The government's after-action report condemned the BOP in the strongest of terms, charging that it had failed to monitor terrorists' communications, including mail, phone calls, visits with family and friends, and cellblock conversations, resulting in "little or no proactive" intelligence on the activities of terrorist inmates in custody. "Consequently," the report concluded, "the threat remains that terrorist . . . inmates can use mail and verbal communications to conduct terrorist activities while incarcerated."[25] Thus was born the total segregation model.

Between 2006 and 2008 the Justice Department transferred all but the most highly secured terrorist inmates (e.g., Theodore Kaczynski, Ramzi Yousef, Terry Nichols, and Richard Reid) to two newly established maximum-security Communication Management Units (CMUs) within the federal system. One unit was the former death row at the U.S. Penitentiary in Terre Haute, Indiana, and the other was at the U.S. Penitentiary in Marion, Illinois, a prison with an extensive history of human rights violations, including a permanent lockdown from 1983 to 2006 following a series of high-profile escapes.

The little that is known about these prisoners and their conditions of confinement is primarily due to the investigative reporting of National Public Radio's Carrie Johnson. According to her reporting, prisoners are under twenty-four-hour surveillance in the CMUs. Guards and cameras record their every move and hidden microphones pick up every word they speak—a snooping operation that costs U.S. taxpayers more than $14 million a year.[26] Such information—along with data gleaned from monitoring phone calls, mail, and visits—is routinely gathered by prison intelligence officers who share their findings with counterterrorism analysts in Washington.

The CMUs prohibit group prayer beyond the hour-long services on Fridays and restrict inmate visitation to lawyers and immediate family members. Visits from journalists, human rights experts, and volunteers are off limits. As are researchers, who are denied access to the CMUs; hence, there is no primary criminological research on the incarceration of terrorists in the United States. Inmates are required to hold all conversations in English. Using open sources, Johnson determined that most of the CMU prisoners are Arab Muslims, though the units also hold some African American Muslims charged with radicalizing other inmates. Several environmental and animal rights activists are also locked up in the CMUs, along with at least one neo-Nazi, a tax resister, a Palestinian terrorist, a member of the Japanese Red Army, and several prisoners who had threatened officials while in custody or had ordered murders while using cellphones.

In addition to virtually banning the prisoners' contact with the outside world, the objective of the CMUs is to fully segregate terrorist inmates from the general populations to prevent them from both converting other convicts to radical Islam and plotting terrorist acts behind bars. By fully segregating terrorists, the BOP argues that it can better concentrate its resources on language translation, content analysis of letters and phone calls, and intelligence sharing. Despite repeated media requests, authorities have refused to release a full list of the CMU inmates, though Johnson has compiled a partial list based on open sources. Among them are three felons who have previously waged terrorist attacks while confined to maximum-security prisons. One is the Egyptian El Sayyid Nosair; while serving time at Attica in connection with the assassination of the ultra-nationalist Rabbi Meyer Kahane, Nosair conspired with Mohammad Salameh and others to bomb the World Trade Center in 1993. The other two are the JIS members Kevin James and Levar Washington.

Nothing is known of the prisoners' psychological status, the criteria by which they have been chosen for incarceration in the CMUs, or their conflicts with guards and other inmates. Nor is anything known about their rehabilitation, their preparation for community reentry, or their recidivism. Yet many of the CMU prisoners will one day finish their sentences and return to society (some three hundred terrorist-related prisoners have completed their sentences and been set free since 2001). Civil rights attorneys have filed lawsuits contending that CMU inmates are denied the rights both to review the evidence that sent them there and to challenge that evidence. There is some evidence that the CMUs are counterproductive. Johnson's investigation found two "law-enforcement sensitive" reports describing religious tensions among the different Muslim groups in the special units. In its inspection of America's secret prisons, the New York Times argued that by creating Muslim-dominated control units, the BOP has inadvertently fostered solidarity and defiance among the CMU prisoners, thereby increasing levels of radicalization.[27] Adding to these risks, the BOP has failed to institute de-radicalization programs, which are common in other countries. Beyond that, the creation of secret facilities to primarily house Muslim inmates marks a radical expansion of the all-but-forgotten Bush-era war on terrorism, which has increased anti-U.S. sentiment within Muslim and Arab communities around the world. Because of the legal complaints, combined with the atmosphere of secrecy and suspicion surrounding the disproportionate placement of Muslim prisoners in the CMUs, Terre Haute and Marion have become known internationally as "Guantanamo North."

* * *

The effectiveness of the U.S. total segregation model for incarcerating Islamic terrorists can be best understood by contrasting it with other methods. Israel has a more flexible approach. Yet the outstanding feature of the Israeli experiment with locking up terrorists—at least from an American perspective—is its emphasis on rehabilitation. In 2009, I was invited by Retired General Orit Adato, a former Commissioner of the Israel Prison Service, to present my research on prisoner radicalization at the World Summit on Counter-Terrorism in Herzliya, Israel. There I met with counterterrorism officials affiliated with the Prison Service, including a former chief of investigations. The following description is based on those encounters, official documents, and academic research.

The first thing one discovers about Israel's prisons is the contentions of language. In official reports, people who commit violence for political causes are alternatively referred to as "terrorists" or "security prisoners." Inmates reject these terms and call themselves POWs. The most recent figures indicate that Israel has approximately 10,000 terrorists in custody (out of a total prison population of 25,000), representing a spectacular 1,200 percent increase over the 802 terrorists held in 2000.[28] Security prisoners are divided into two categories: those in administrative detention without formal charges, and those with "blood on their hands"—including convicted terrorists who have killed Israeli citizens; terrorists who were en route to a suicide bombing mission but changed their minds; suicide dispatchers; masterminds of the attacks; those responsible for making the explosives; and senior members of terrorist groups. Seven out of ten security prisoners belong to this category. Roughly seven hundred of them are serving life sentences (like most of the world, Israel does not have the death penalty) that are often "stacked" upon one another. It is not uncommon to find security prisoners serving multiple life sentences. Nearly all of them are Islamic militants from the Palestinian territories. A reported 44 percent are members of Fatah (which governs the West Bank), 26 percent are members of Hamas (which rules in Gaza), and 14 percent belong to Islamic Jihad (active in both Gaza and the West Bank). They are spread out among thirty-two prison facilities and three detention centers in Israel proper. About 140 of the security prisoners are juveniles (some as young as fourteen) who are held at two separate facilities.

Terrorists are physically segregated from the general prison populations, yet their confinement is not secret and they are not totally segregated from other prisoners or the outside world. Security prisoners have been able to cooperate with criminal inmates inside Israel's prisons, pursuing various goals, both illegal and mundane. They are also allowed to receive food from family and militant groups during Muslim holidays. Journalists, documentary filmmakers, legal aid groups, the International Red Cross, and human rights advocates are all permitted access to these inmates, as are researchers. Between 2002 and 2009, for instance, Ariel Merari conducted a series of important psychological studies on Palestinian would-be suicide bombers and their commanders inside Israeli prisons.[29] Among his findings, Merari determined that more than half of the suicide bombers had already spent time in Israeli prisons. He also found that commanders were uniformly charismatic. The suicide bombers, fittingly, exhibited dependent-avoidant personality characteristics: such people find it hard to say no to authority figures and are likely to carry out tasks against their better judgment. Another research team led by the criminologist Edna Erez conducted interviews with Arab and Palestinian women locked up in Israeli prisons on terrorism offenses, exploring their motivations for attempted suicide bombings.[30] The study found that women terrorists differ from common female offenders in terms of important background characteristics and the manner in which their crimes were influenced by the Israeli-Palestinian conflict.

Terrorists are confined to large dormitory-style units—cultural communes holding as many as forty inmates—where they manage a common money pool and keep personal decorations, books, magazines, electrical appliances, radios, televisions, food, soft drinks, and cooking utensils. (There is no documented evidence on the electronic surveillance of these prisoners, though one can assume such measures are taken.) The inmates wear street clothes; women wear *hijabs*, or headscarves, as part of their traditional Muslim dress. The security prisoners are allowed to pray together in special areas. They are housed by militant faction; a good number of them were senior leaders of these factions prior to incarceration. Their declared purpose, with firm support from the outside, is to continue the Israeli/Palestinian conflict within the prison system.

According to prison rules, each political faction appoints an inmate leadership council that negotiates with the guards for prisoners' rights. Each faction is organized hierarchically in accordance with the structure of the organizations on the Palestinian street. The prisoners present themselves in a clean and orderly fashion, yet there are distinct differences between the factions. Hamas is organized like an army while the more moderate Fatah reflects the looseness of a Middle Eastern bazaar. There is also conflict between Hamas and Fatah, which has become a security concern for guards. Each faction is afforded extensive rehabilitation.

Security prisoners are offered a fourteen-point rehabilitation program, beginning with religious rehabilitation, where Muslim clerics offer Koranic lessons on reversing radical beliefs. Point 2 involves educational, vocational, and occupational training; Point 3 emphasizes psychological treatment designed to "heal the anger" from years of living under Israeli occupation. Point 4 involves social and family intervention, including flexible mail and visitation rights for Palestinian families. Families from Gaza are currently forbidden from making these visits, however, due to military restrictions on border crossings into Israel. In those cases, photographs of prisoners are sent to family members twice a year in an effort to show that they are being humanely treated. Other modes of rehabilitation include the creative arts and prison coping skills. But the crown jewel of the treatment program is its mandated practice of holding congenial interactions between prisoners and guards. According to one prison commander, these interactions give Palestinians a chance for perhaps the first time to see Israelis as people "rather than through their gun sights." Another commander said that prison is the first time Palestinians have seen Israelis "without the horns of a devil."

Such an ambitious rehabilitation program promises an effective counterweight against Islamic radicalization. But the interventions are impeded by a labeling process wherein imprisonment bestows a hero status on terrorists. Security prisoners have immense prestige in the occupied territories; some have been elected to the Palestinian legislature while in custody. Reinforcing this status is a formidable ideology of resistance. Prisoners blatantly refuse to take part in the occupational programs afforded them by the Prison Service. Instead they spend time educating themselves in political science, international politics, and Israeli politics—often under the auspices of the Open University. They also study terrorism tactics, demolition, and other subjects relevant to their struggle. In so doing, they have turned Israeli prisons into de facto universities of Palestinian nationalism. On the complexity of the Israeli prison system, the scholar Leslie Fishbein observes, "On one level it seeks to be humane and provide education for the inmates, and you see some possibility of political harmony. On the second level, you have prisoners who remain committed to the Palestinian cause and terrorism, and the prison system seems to foster that."[31] Put another way, the effectiveness of Israel's partial segregation model is being compromised by the Israeli/Palestinian conflict. Due to the conflict, there is a total lack of buy-in from those whom the model purports to help. Beyond that, of course, the unsettled Palestinian question contributes to the legitimacy of jihad in the eyes of many Muslims in the Middle East and beyond.

Contraband smuggling is a significant problem in Israel. Though forbidden by Fatah and Hamas leadership, heroin and alcohol are recognized problems among their members, as is the smuggling of cellphones, which can sell on the prison black market for as much as $10,000 (US) per phone. Yet their primary mode of communication is the *ashgarim*—crimped notes written on thin transparent paper rolled into bindles ("kites" in the United States or "stiffs" in Britain). Weapons—in the form of shanks, blow darts, and all manner of improvised explosive devices—present a major problem in the hands of security prisoners. As does smuggled intelligence on the security arrangements of the prisons, which is often furnished to prisoners by visiting family members and Palestinian lawyers acting as "mailmen" for Hamas and Fatah. Inmate leaders use this intelligence not only to advance militant goals but also to ensure internal security by interrogating fellow prisoners and punishing those who deviate from the party line.

Officials agree that the security situation inside Israeli prisons began to take a turn for the worse in 2002 following the 9/11 attacks and the renewal of terrorist strikes by Hezbollah in Lebanon. The trend reached a tipping point in 2006—a year marked by Hamas's landslide victory in the Palestinian legislative election followed by Hamas's decision to call off its truce with Israel and begin attacking the South with rockets, eventuating in Hamas's

June 25 kidnapping of the twenty-five-year-old Israeli soldier Gilad Shalit, prompting severe military reprisals by Israel. Amid these tumultuous events, a United Nations study declared the humanitarian situation in Gaza "intolerable," with 75 percent of its 1.6 million residents dependent on food and aid.

Since then a new generation of terrorists has flooded the prisons of Israel. They are younger than those who came before, more daring, belligerent, and proficient in the use of explosives. They are also more politically extreme and reject all dialogue with the Prison Service. This generational shift has led to an increase in hunger strikes, disturbances, and security breaches involving violence. Since 2006, security prisoners have directed terrorist activities in the streets using ashgarims and cellphones. (Cellphones are used in nearly all Palestinian suicide bombings. In 2007 guards confiscated over a thousand cellphones from security prisoners.) They have been involved in a range of attacks on staff, including stabbings, beatings, attempted murders and kidnappings, and throwing boiling oil into the faces of guards. Security prisoners have attempted to blow up a van carrying guards en route to Jerusalem. Suicide bombing plots have been uncovered inside prisons. Some of these carry the mark of extraordinary criminal ingenuity. In one case, pigeons trained by Hamas flew from the Gaza Strip to the yard of an Israeli prison carrying explosives and cellphones strapped to their talons. In effect, prisons have become the center for terrorist planning and coordination with one goal in mind: destroying the State of Israel and replacing it with an independent Palestinian state. "Everyone is a target," said a prison commander of his staff. "Fighting terrorism in Israel is like emptying the ocean with a tea spoon." As a result, most prison guards are now recruited from combat units within the Israeli military.

Still, there may be hope. Some argue that the best chance for the long-suffering peace process may actually rest in the hands of the fifty-three-year-old terrorist kingpin Marwan Barghouti, currently serving five life sentences in an Israeli prison on murder charges. General Adato refers to Barghouti as the "Nelson Mandela of the Palestinians." (Mandela, recall, was a political prisoner for over a quarter of a century before he was elected the president of South Africa.) No less a figure than Jimmy Carter has described Barghouti as a "revered prisoner . . . [whose] influence is enormous."[32] Barghouti is a member of the Palestinian legislature and a Fatah leader who has been locked up since 2002. Fluent in Hebrew, English, and Arabic, Barghouti has strong grassroots support among Palestinians of various political stripes and has spoken out against both Islamic fundamentalism and suicide bombing attacks on Israelis. From prison, he helped negotiate the unilateral truce declared by Fatah and Hamas in 2003 and has subsequently declared his willingness to negotiate with Israel in order to achieve lasting peace. In 2011, the Israelis released 1,027 Palestinian prisoners in exchange for the soldier Gilad Shalit. Due to internal political disputes of the Palestinian Authority, however, Marwan Barghouti was not among them.

This does not mean that the goal of partial segregation is misguided. Extensive rehabilitative efforts, including de-radicalization, along with man-dated civility between inmates and guards, public transparency and open access to prisons for families, lawyers, politicians, human rights experts, journalists, and researchers have all been carefully designed by the Israelis to counteract radicalization. Such a model is, according to any theory of penol-ogy, far superior to the secret and hugely unpopular total segregation model used in America. Yet at the end of the day, conditions outside Israel's prisons will dictate what happens inside. Hanging in the balance are some exception-ally rich policies to promote humane treatment and political harmony.

* * *

While the Israeli model is compromised by factors external to the prison, the U.S. model suffers from a problem of penal pragmatism. Failing to appreci-ate the implications of the George Jackson incident at San Quentin in 1971, U.S. prison authorities have over the years increasingly used total segrega-tion as a discipline and management tool for common criminals. For these prisoners, segregation is essentially a second sentence imposed by prison security officers—one that is typically unrelated to the conviction for which the inmate is incarcerated. Studies show a number of adverse effects result-ing from segregation. Inmates held under these conditions experience new or exacerbated mental-health disturbances, assaultive and other antisocial behaviors, and chronic health problems. Other research shows that prisoners who are released from segregation directly to the community recidivate at a higher rate than prisoners released from general populations.[33] Few Western nations, including the United States, have heeded this advice in their incar-ceration policies for terrorists. Britain is the exception.

Between 2009 and 2011, I made four trips to the United Kingdom in an effort to understand its experiences with prisoner radicalization. Included was an invitation by Scotland Yard to give the plenary address at its 2011 National Prisons Intelligence Unit conference in Manchester, England. Attending the conference were eighty-five police detectives assigned to the nation's prisons. In addition to meeting with a number of these officers, I conferred with the chief of the Extremism Unit at Manchester Prison (for-merly known as Strangeways Prison, the site of the most violent prison riot in British history in 1990) and a Ministry of Justice official who over-saw prisoner radicalization issues. In London, I consulted with officials in the Extremism and Radicalization Unit at Her Majesty's Prison Service and met with two of Britain's leading gang scholars. The following description is based on that fieldwork, along with official reports and recent research.

The British are very precise with their numbers and definitions. A total of 150 terrorists are currently locked up in U.K. prisons (out of a total prison population of 95,000, roughly equivalent to one-half of California's prison population). Eighty-nine of them are al-Qaeda-inspired extremists "who jus-tify violence through distorted interpretations of Islamic texts."[34] These ter-rorists are unknown to most Americans but their deeds are not. Included among them is Abu Doha, once al-Qaeda's main European recruiter and a central figure in the millennium plot to bomb the Los Angeles International Airport, along with Sajid Badaat and Nizar ben Trabelsi, the accomplices to Richard Reid in a second bombing attempt on a U.S.-bound aircraft in 2001. These cases, among others, prompted FBI Director Mueller to warn the U.S. Senate in 2007 that "al-Qaeda's strategy for attacking the U.S. homeland includes using the U.K. as a stepping stone for al-Qaeda operatives to enter the United States."[35]

While the Israelis deal specifically with incarcerating Palestinian terrorists and the United States deals primarily with the imprisonment of Arab Mus-lims, the British lock up a relatively broader spectrum of political criminals. Also in their prisons are Irish Republicans who reject the 1989 Belfast Agree-ment and who seek to continue terrorist campaigns against British interests; Ulster Loyalists, the violent manifestation of opposition to a unified Ireland; animal rights extremists who commit violence motivated by the perceived exploitation of animals; anarchists who use violence in pursuit of overthrow-ing democracies or the global economy; and a growing number of far right activists whose crimes were motivated by neo-Nazism.

There are 140 prisons in the United Kingdom, designated by security classification. Category A is the top classification (with three designations: standard, high, and exceptional risk). Any escape by Category A offenders, according to the Prison Service, "would be highly dangerous to national security." There are eight high-security (or maximum-security) prisons deemed "suitable to hold Category A prisoners." Al-Qaeda terrorists are housed in these prisons, usually in single-occupancy cells. Most of them are British-born ethnic minorities. Their primary grievance is British and Amer-ican foreign policy in Muslim lands.[36] For the most part, they are model prisoners: quiet, polite, clean, and often university-educated. They are also known for their charismatic demeanor. Yet unlike in the United States and

Israel, in Britain terrorists are not segregated from the general populations. Rather, they are "dispersed" within those populations. Dispersal is also used to mix Category A and B prisoners. During my tour of Manchester Prison, Britain's largest high-security facility, I saw bearded al-Qaeda terrorists walking the cellblocks alongside murderers, rapists, drug dealers, skinheads, and old-school IRA members.

Al-Qaeda prisoners are subject to strict security precautions, including restricted movement, pat-down searches, daily strip searches, cell searches (called "spins"), and round-the clock camera coverage. Guards, or "personal officers," are assigned to individual terrorists and are required to monitor them for intelligence, which is shared with Scotland Yard detectives apportioned to the facilities. To prevent them from building power bases, terrorists are required to change cells every twenty-eight days. They are offered a full complement of rehabilitative services. Programs include education, involving opportunities to discuss current affairs, politics, and world history in multiethnic groups; a library, inmate tutoring, and recreation; multifaith worship allowing for group prayer and counseling by Muslim chaplains; and psychological treatment and creative workshops as well as visitation privileges, including the opportunity to meet with selected researchers from the Home Office. Terrorist prisoners appear to be treated civilly by guards and treatment staff.

The British dispersal model has three objectives. The first is to promote a sense of inclusiveness common to civil society. One facet of this mission is finding ways to enhance mutual accommodation between Western values and respect for the peaceful traditions of Islam. This has been an enduring goal of multicultural Britain, as exemplified in this excerpt from a 1993 Oxford speech by Prince Charles:

> We fall into a trap of dreadful arrogance if we confuse "modernity" in other countries with their becoming more like us. The fact is that our form of materialism . . . television, fast-food, and the electronic gadgets of our everyday life . . . can be offensive to devout Muslims—and I do not mean [only] the extremists among them. . . . Western civilization has become increasingly acquisitive and exploitative in defiance of our environmental responsibilities. This crucial sense of oneness and trusteeship of the vital sacramental and spiritual character of the world about us is surely something important we can re-learn from Islam.[37]

The second objective is to de-radicalize terrorist inmates through rehabilitation. The primary focus here is on what prisoners do (behavior) not on what they think (ideology). The idea is that attitude changes will follow from behavior. Through the various educational, psychological, and religious programs, the Prison Service attempts to destabilize behavioral areas around terrorism. In so doing, prison authorities are prepared to negotiate and accommodate the views and identities of terrorist prisoners, with the expectation that they will be inclined to put more trust in the government and therefore moderate their grievances.

The third objective is more practical, reflecting Britain's historical shift to criminal justice "managerialism" in the early 1980s. As a security matter, the dispersal model is intended to prevent the clustering of terrorists in cellblocks, thereby preventing them from forming paramilitary gangs. The model has its roots in the Irish "Troubles," which began in 1969 as incarcerated members of the Irish Republican Army became the central focus of the decades-long conflict. IRA prisoners embarked on a campaign to challenge their status as ordinary criminals, seeking instead to be classified as political prisoners, through organized resistance against British prison authorities. The movement eventually erupted in rioting, arson, and the taking of prison staff and volunteers as hostages, as well as a number of prominent escapes. By 1972, IRA prisoners at Belfast's Maze Prison were running their own paramilitary training and indoctrination programs. The campaign reached a tipping point with the 1981 Maze hunger strikes.[38] When Prime Minister Margaret Thatcher refused to give in to IRA demands, she became the person most responsible for the painful deaths of Bobby Sands and nine other hunger strikers. As a result, the IRA decided to kill Margaret Thatcher, leading to the spectacular 1984 assassination attempt against her at the Grand Hotel in Brighton, England, killing five and injuring more than thirty others. Known in England as "the bomb that changed politics," the Brighton attack also changed the way Britons viewed the incarceration of terrorists. When the terrorist convicted of the bombing, Patrick Magee, was released after serving only fourteen of his thirty-five-year sentence, terrorist classifications became less important than the certainty of their confinement. "The main lesson from Northern Ireland regarding prisons," argues the terrorism scholar Richard English of the Brighton bombing legacy "is that it matters less how one designates terrorist prisoners once they have been incarcerated, than that large numbers of people engaged in terrorism should be credibly imprisoned for lengthy terms as part of a containment strategy."[39] Meanwhile, violence between different dissident groups also spilled over beyond the prison walls, with twenty-nine prison officers being killed on the streets of the United Kingdom during the Troubles.[40] The goal of the dispersal model is to prevent this violence from reoccurring with al-Qaeda.

In general terms, the British dispersal model has rendered a split decision. On one hand, prisoners charged with al-Qaeda-related offenses have been spread out over a number of institutions, undermining their concentration of power. Incarcerating individual terrorists within general populations limits their influence as long as they remain a sufficient minority.[41] The dispersal model has also yielded increased intelligence, low recidivism rates, and thus far no repeat of the violence against prison officers witnessed during the Troubles. But on the other hand, officials still worry about the long-term radicalization effect that these terrorist kingpins are having on other prisoners. For example, while locked up at Maghaberry Prison in 2006 for possessing information about the bombing of passenger aircraft, Abbas Boutrab was caught with a smuggled laptop computer with downloaded al-Qaeda materials on how to manufacture explosives.[42] Al-Qaeda prisoners have also found ways of recruiting followers beyond the walls. Abdel Abdel Bary, the leader of the U.K. branch of Egyptian Islamic Jihad, has smuggled a series of fatwas out of prison, calling for attacks by al-Qaeda and for the murder of moderate Muslims.[43] In 2006, a Libyan detainee wanted in Italy on terrorism charges used a public telephone at Long Lartin Prison to speak live on a popular Middle Eastern television program, comparing British prisons with Guantanamo and Abu Ghraib.[44] In 2007, guards confiscated a laptop computer from an al-Qaeda prisoner, Tariq al-Dour, who had used a smuggled cellphone to connect to the Internet. From his high-security cell, Dour was operating a website sympathetic to al-Qaeda.[45] When he refused to hand over his laptop, a riot ensued as guards clashed with al-Qaeda sympathizers.[46]

Despite the best of intentions, al-Qaeda terrorists have been able to skirt security regulations and establish themselves as de facto gang leaders who use forced conversions and other forms of coercion (theft and intimidation) to recruit vulnerable prisoners into the mix. This has occurred with a rise in minority religious groups in British prisons and fears of Islamic radicalization in the wake of the 2005 terrorist attacks on London's transportation system (the 7/7 bombings and the 7/21 follow-on attempt). Systemwide, prisoners identifying themselves as Muslim rose 141 percent between 1997 and 2007.[47] The Ministry of Justice estimates that there are about ten thousand Muslim inmates in British prisons.[48] This growth was due mainly to the appearance of a younger, more ethnically diverse generation of convicts who have formed a new gang culture in British prisons—a culture that not only has imported the values and behaviors of street life to prisons but also has glorified Islamic terrorists and their extremist ideologies.

Most notably, Alison Liebling inspected records on sixty-one assaults at the high-security Whitemoor Prison between 2009 and 2010—including stabbings, throat slashings, and beatings with dumbbells—and found that the most serious cases were tied to Muslim influence. Several guards were reportedly threatened with beheading. As a guard told Liebling, "You've got your proper al-Qaeda members. They're the top dogs, they are the recruiters. . . . They don't do the dirty work, they don't do the assaults. They will get people below them and they're so adored because they're so high up, they're so dangerous."[49] Reflecting on the changes at Whitemoor since the late 1990s, Liebling concluded that for some prisoners being a Muslim had become "an act or mode of resistance to the prison system and to staff," adding,

> The new world was different. Muslim prisoners had accumulated power in numbers, but the power of some of the heavier "players" wielded was hidden, and difficult to describe or evidence. Some of the prisoners in this group were powerful and "untouchable." The rules were different; their code was more "us and them"—they wanted no relationship with authority. . . . The new formation was less consensual and more forced. Loyalties were linked by fear as well as shared interests.[50]

Liebling's report came on the heels of an influential investigation by Britain's Chief Inspector of Prisons, warning of "a rising problem of prisoner radicalization and an increase in Muslim conversions" at Whitemoor, noting that Muslim prisoners "operated as a gang and put pressure on non-Muslims to convert [and] conform to a strict and extreme interpretation of Islamic practice."[51] The gang's victims were reportedly slashed with razor blades and scalded with boiling oil. All of this prompted a Prison Service official to proclaim in 2009 that Britain's high-security prisons were becoming "incubators of extremism."[52]

* * *

The confinement of al-Qaeda terrorists alongside Muslim gang members has presented significant challenges to high-security prison administrators in Great Britain. Most dauntingly, the dispersal model has led to increased levels of prisoner radicalization that, some say, now rivals the challenges once posed by the IRA. As with most U.S. wardens today, Britain's prison governors belong to a generation trained in what the criminologists Malcolm Feeley and Jonathon Simon termed the "new penology."[53] Whereas traditional penology stemmed from criminal law and criminology with an emphasis on punishing and rehabilitating individual prisoners, the new penology is based on a management style in which "specialists" think about criminal subpopulations as "aggregates" that need to be "herded" through "actuarial" risk assessments of danger. For Feeley and Simon, the new penologists provide an important "waste management" function for the state. Liebling aptly describes the challenges facing the new penologists:

> Al-Qaeda prisoners became a source of spiritual or scriptural guidance (and distortion) behind the scenes. Much of their power was intellectual, or in discourse. Meanwhile, front-stage physically powerful Muslim "players" used faith as a shield behind which they could carry out acts of violence and intimidation. These two key groups were not in a direct hierarchical relationship to each other, but reinforced each other's power, making life for other prisoners [and staff] uncomfortable and risky.[54]

Therefore, the primary focus of the dispersal model is on intelligence gathering and risk assessment of Islamic radicals. Prison officers and police detectives rely on a set of radicalization risk factors that manifest themselves in prison behavior and communication. Of key concern are overt "feelings of anger, grievance, and injustice." In this regard, intelligence is gathered on dialogue and actions of prisoners that reflect a preoccupation with the injustices or the corruptness of the Prison Service and/or the British government—particularly with the British-supported wars in Afghanistan and Iraq. Although some Muslim prisoners "use prison to politicize everything," efforts are made to distinguish normal prison behavior from a larger grievance against Islam. For instance, a Muslim prisoner who bangs on his cell door because he is upset about a broken toilet is one thing; complaining that the broken toilet is evidence of Western imperialism and hatred of Islam is quite another.

Many risk factors involving dominance and control are also used in intelligence collecting (e.g., appointing oneself as a leader or group spokesman; manipulating and controlling other inmates). Risk factors associated with correspondence and telephone calls include such things as giving commands and counsel to other prisoners, especially if the prisoner is ill-qualified to do so, and receiving requests for instructions from other prisoners. Intelligence is also assembled on susceptibility to indoctrination and groupthink. Here, officials are on the lookout for sudden behavioral changes among prisoners after these prisoners come into contact with charismatic leaders. The primary concern is with young minority prisoners who appear to be lost in the mix or are seeking a transformative experience. They are the prisoners considered most vulnerable to radicalization. As this study has shown, prison-based terrorists are usually radicalized behind bars when they are in their early twenties.

An innovative component of the control strategy is the identification of what the British call *jail craft*, or an inmate's show of personal skills necessary to survive in prison.[55] Those with immature jail craft—prisoners who have not yet learned how to "play the game"—are deemed especially susceptible to radicalization. The concept is also used as an anchor for counseling sessions intended to emphasize incongruities between an imagined jihad and actual life in Western prisons. The Manchester document offers several incongruities. For example, the Qaeda document has this stipulation: "Inside the prison, the brother should not accept any work that may belittle or demean him or his brothers, such as the cleaning of the prison bathrooms or hallways."[56] However, as anyone who has ever worked in a maximum-security prison knows, one of the most coveted jobs among prisoners is that of a janitor or custodian—it is the one assignment that affords inmates the freedom to move around the cellblocks and often to enter security offices.

Finally, for a host of practical and political reasons the dispersal model has become the subject of controversy. Guards who are required to be on "red alert" for signs of Islamic radicalization run the risk of alienating ordinary Muslims. The rise in Muslim extremism has created a power imbalance that leaves other prisoner groups in a state of anxiety. Increased tensions between staff and prisoners, combined with growing competition for state resources and official charges that high-security prisons have become "incubators of extremism," have led some governors and private prison companies to push for a specialized high-security unit for al-Qaeda terrorists and other extremists. Essentially, there is mounting concern in Great Britain that it may be time to cast aside the dispersal model in favor of the total segregation model employed by the Americans.

* * *

Yet the read-across from America to Great Britain may not be as obvious as some think. America's secret prisons of the post-9/11 era are hardly a model for forward-looking counterterrorism policy. By associating with the stain of Guantanamo, and by implication Abu Ghraib, the British could attract recruits into radical Islamic networks by making the terrorist's cause appear as a just response to an unjust enemy. It could also wreak havoc closer to home. Across Europe, Guantanamo has become a symbol of what many see as America's dangerous drift away from the ideals that made it a moral beacon in the post–World War II era.[57] Other nations have found that physically separating terrorist prisoners from the larger prison population can actually intensify radicalization. When the Sri Lankans isolated imprisoned terrorists of the Tamil Tigers during the 1990s, it strengthened their internal ties and increased their criminal skills. When the Saudis isolated al-Qaeda terrorists following their 2003 emergence in the Kingdom, they failed to adopt statehood loyalties.[58] The British may want to reconsider the new penology first.

An often-overlooked aspect of the new penology is Feeley and Simon's argument that it is not the new penology that has failed: instead, administrators have failed to go beyond the new penology "to a new way of narrating the power to punish that can help shape the public and political" discourse.[59] Understanding the possibilities of de-radicalization as a "soft" weapon in the fight against Islamic extremism may be such a narrative. It is a way to scale responses to a level appropriate to the real threat of radicalization without doing more damage militarily. This is not easy. Even in countries like Indonesia where de-radicalization programs are routinely offered to Islamic terrorists, recidivism is a genuine concern as are the radicalization of criminal offenders and even Muslim prison officers who watch over them. As one Indonesian terrorist recently told a researcher after completing his de-radicalization program, if he was released from prison today, he would bomb the U.S. embassy tomorrow.[60]

Decades of criminology show that rehabilitation lowers recidivism rates when cognitive behavioral treatments target known predictors of crime.[61] Although much work remains to be done, a handful of studies indicate that the predictors of prisoner radicalization are gang affiliations around Salafi-inspired Prison Islam and one-on-one proselytizing by charismatic leaders with a violent agenda. The British already employ treatment strategies targeting these predictors. Counter-radicalization typically involves law enforcement outreach to Muslim communities, but programs reaching out to Muslim prisoners are rare in many parts of the world, including the United States. Again, Britain is an exception. Its counseling policy aimed at minority prisoners with underdeveloped jail craft is one way of targeting the predictors of radicalization. Inverting the Manchester document by using it as a teaching tool to highlight incongruities between the jihadist dream and the reality of life in a maximum-security prison, is certainly another. In fact, it is a brilliant example of undermining al-Qaeda's appeal among the young without tackling ideology head-on, one that would make Churchill proud because of the promise he saw in inverting prison customs for a greater good. De-radicalizing older jihadists is about as easy as convincing Winston Churchill that he should have taken up arms against the British in South Africa, or asking Gandhi and Mandela to lick the boots of their captors. One reason for this is that Islam's sacred law, the *shariah*, is almost silent on the subject of incarceration as a rehabilitative venue.[62] The crucial step in de-radicalization, then, is getting to young offenders near the time of their conversion when they are not yet settled into their commitment to jihad.

In this regard there are also important lessons to be learned from Israel. Its elaborate rehabilitation program for terrorists will not work until the peace process is settled. But that does not mean that these strategies won't work with at-risk inmates in other countries. Employing Muslim clerics to challenge the tenets of Islamic radicalization has the potential to broaden transcendent horizons among the vulnerable to the point where serious discussions can be held about the meaning of such loaded concepts as *jihad* (struggle), *takfir* (blasphemy), *shahada* (martyrdom), and the establishment of the *caliphate* (Islamic State).[63] But perhaps most important, discussions can be held about al-Qaeda's long-term future in the post–bin Laden era, thereby addressing al-Qaeda's failure to offer any positive vision for building a society imagined by activists of the Arab Spring. Psychological interventions intended to "heal the anger" of prior victimization has the potential to reverse rigid antiauthoritarian views held by convicts at risk for radicalization, especially when tied to meaningful educational and occupational training. Research examining de-radicalization programs in eight Muslim-majority countries shows that religious dialogue alone does not eliminate violent extremism. Effective programs must also include the social, economic, and political factors that contribute to radicalization.[64] And the mandated practice of forming congenial relationships between prisoners and guards can potentially take the air out of moral panics about the transgressive other.

If these are international standards by which a new de-radicalization movement is to be judged, the United States has little to offer. Its practice of incarcerating terrorists is secret. It is not only secret but appears to be void of any operating penal philosophy concerning the rehabilitation of anti-Western jihadists. Consequently, most of these prisoners see their incarceration not as justice but as U.S. revenge against *all* Muslims for the attacks of 9/11. Beyond that, the total segregation model is counterproductive. One lesson of Guantanamo—in addition to the crucial point that it may produce terrorists rather than reform them—is that by severely restricting the circumstances in which prisoners are placed, the more this can be represented by their supporters as victimization, thus raising support for the extremist cause. Accordingly, prison becomes the grist for grievance. This will not change until the emblems of American injustice and abuse—Guantanamo and now "Guantanamo North"—are abolished and replaced with prisons that uphold America's core values. Researchers speak with one voice on this matter: Mr. Obama, tear down those walls.

Yet something might be learned from the troubled cellblocks of Folsom Prison. The best hedge against radicalization may be prisoners themselves, especially those serving life sentences. Stopping radicalization is no longer a job for psychologists only: some analysts argue that the messenger of the de-radicalization narrative is essential and that state actors should not be too visible in formulating and executing the narrative.[65] If the stories of Akeem and Jesse have any lesson at all, it is that lifers and righteous guys—with the support of chaplains—are capable of mounting de-radicalization programs from the same prison conditions that cause terrorism. These charismatic leaders had no interest in cherry-picking verses of sacred texts to justify violence, in gangbanging, in recruiting followers through intimidation, or in pitting believers of different faith groups against one another. They were beyond that. Their efforts reflect a growing trend, again evocative of the Arab Spring. One survey shows that more than half of all U.S. prison wardens acknowledge permitting inmates to serve as spiritual leaders.[66] The U.S. Justice Department found that the lack of Muslim chaplains, contractors, and volunteers makes inmate-led services a necessity in federal prisons.[67] Research conducted in Europe, the Middle East, Singapore, and the Philippines indicates that successful prisoner de-radicalization programs are often designed and carried out by inmates themselves. There is even a contagion effect at work here. Saudi Arabia's much-touted de-radicalization program—involving education, religious counseling, assistance with marriage and employment, and financial support to families of released detainees—has prompted al-Qaeda-affiliated prisoners in Jordan to request religious counseling and opportunities to de-radicalize on their own, further illustrating the global appeal of the de-radicalization movement.[68] As Scott Atran observes, "De-radicalization, like radicalization, engages mainly from the bottom up, not from the top down."[69] Other work shows that some individuals who start down the path of radicalization are dissuaded from proceeding by family and friends, underscoring the importance of community and kinship networks in reversing the commitment to terrorist violence.[70] Even President Obama has weighed in on this issue, arguing that the best expertise and solutions for a community's fight against violent extremism will be found in that community itself.[71]

Lifers can serve this cause in prison due to their influence over younger inmates at a time in their lives when they are undergoing a crisis that can produce a "cognitive opening" that shakes certainty in previously accepted beliefs, rendering these prisoners more receptive to the possibility of alternative views and perspectives.[72] Young cons are called "jitterbugs" and "fish" for a reason. They are usually incapable of creating their own lives from the bottom up. As John Irwin put it in his final book, no one is more adept at assisting young convicts with indecision and anxiety than lifers because they have lived through it themselves. Lifers, Irwin concluded, "demonstrate, to the extreme, the fulfillment of rehabilitation."[73]

The growth of Islam in Western prisons is taking place against the backdrop of a global economic crisis and a rise in religious extremism and ethnic conflict; changes in prisoners' class and race compositions; a declining interest among prisoners in Christianity; new developments in youth subcultures; increased access to smuggled cellphone technology; and shifting power dynamics of long-term maximum-security confinement—all situated within the framework of post-9/11 fear. Radicalization is an issue of such profound sociopolitical complexity that it is poorly understood even by those who run our prisons. Radicalization cannot be dealt with through normal techniques of prison administration. Yet if there is an answer, perhaps it lies in reversing the gaze of the new penology—away from the management of groups and toward the reformation of humans.

The Prisoner Radicalization/Terrorism Database

Part I

Case #	Prisoner Name	Year of Attack/Plan	Age at Attack/Plan
1	Cleaver, Eldridge (1935–1998), U.S. Black Panther	1968	33
2	Jackson, George (1941–1971), U.S. Black Panther	1971	30
3	DeFreeze, Donald "Cinque" (1943–1974), U.S. Symbionese Liberation Army	1973–1974	31
4	Yarbrough, Gary (1955–), U.S. The Order	1983–1984	26
5	Fort, Jeff (1947–), U.S. El Rukn	1986	39
6	Guthrie, Richard (1958–1996), U.S. Aryan Republic Army	1992–1995	32
7	Langan, Peter (1958–), U.S. Aryan Republic Army	1992–1995	32
8	Collins, Aqil (1974–), U.S.	1994	20
9	Vallat, David (1971–), France Algerian Armed Islamic Group (GIA)	1994–1995	22
10	Kelkal, Khaled (1972–1995), France (GIA)	1995	24
11	Raime, Joseph (unknown), France GIA	1995	Unknown
12	Bourada, Safe (1970–) (plus other prisoners), France Partisans of Victory	(1995) 2003–2008	33
13	Brewer, Lawrence (1967–), U.S. Confederate Knights	1998	32

Prison Religious Conversion	Age at Conversion (approx.)	Place of Conversion/ Incarceration	Lag between Release and Violence
Nation of Islam	23	San Quentin, California	2 yrs.
No (Marxism)		San Quentin, California	0*
No (Marxism)	30	Soledad, California	7 months
Christian Identity	24	Arizona State prison	4 yrs.
Moorish Science Temple	28 (1975)	Leavenworth, Kansas	0* (reincarnated, 1983) FCC-Bastrop, Texas
Christian Identity/Phineas Priesthood	25	Navy, Brig (unknown location)	8 yrs.
Christian Identity/Phineas Priesthood	19	Raiford Prison, Florida	13 yrs.
Sunni Islam	18	Juvenile boot camp, California	2 yrs.
Salafi-Jihadism	22	French prison	1 yr.
Salafi-Jihadism	22	French prison	2 yrs.
Salafi-Jihadism	Unknown	French prison	Unknown
No (already Salafi Jihadist)		French prison	0
Christian Identity	27	Beto One, Texas	9 months

(* Plot waged from prison)

Case #	Prisoner Name	Year of Attack/Plan	Age at Attack/Plan
14	King, John (1975–), U.S. Confederate Knights	1998	23
15	al-Zawahiri, Ayman (1951–), Egypt al-Qaeda	1998–2009	47 (at first attack)
16	Reid, Richard (1973–), Britain al-Qaeda	2001	28
17	Mubanga, Martin (1972–), Britain Taliban	2001	28
18	Felton, Leo (1970–), U.S. Skinhead	2001	30
19	al-Zarqawi, Abu-Musab (1966–2006), Jordan al-Qaeda in Iraq	2003–2006	37
20	Achraf, Mohammed (1973–) (plus four ex-prisoners), Spain Martyrs for Morocco	2004	30
21	Ahmidan, Jamal (1970–2004), Spain	2004	34
22	Bensmail, Abdel (unknown), Spain Martyrs for Morocco	2004	Unknown
23	Lamari, Allekema (unknown), Spain GIA	2004	Unknown
24	Trashorras, Jose (1976–), Spain	2004	28
25	Mehsud, Abdullah (1974–2007), U.S. Taliban	2004–2007	30
26	Ibrahim, Muktar (1976–), Britain	2005	29
27	James, Kevin (1976–), U.S. Jam'iyyat Ul-Islam Is-Saheed (JIS)	2005	29
28	Washington, Levar (1980–), U.S. JIS	2005	25
29	al-Fiqari, Mohammad (1964–), Britain	2006	42
30	Clem, Dennis (1983–2007), U.S. Aryan Circle	2007	24
31	Rasoul, Abdullah (1973–), U.S. Taliban	2007	34

Prison Religious Conversion	Age at Conversion (approx.)	Place of Conversion/ Incarceration	Lag between Release and Violence
Christian Identity	19	Beto One, Texas	2 months
No (already Wahhabist)		Egyptian prison	24 yrs.
Sunni Islam	22	Feltham Young Offenders Institution, Britain	6 yrs.
Islam	19	Feltham Young Offenders Institution, Britain	6 yrs.
White Order of Thule	28	Northern State Prison, New Jersey	1 month
Salafi-Jihad	33	Suwaqah, Jordan	4 yrs.
No (already Sunni Muslim)		Topas Prison, Salamanca, Spain	2 yrs.
Sunni Islam	31	Spanish detention	3 yrs.
No (already Sunni Muslim)		Topas Prison, Salamanca, Spain	2 yrs.
No (already Sunni Muslim)		French prison	2 yrs.
Sunni Islam	25	Spanish detention	3 yrs.
No (Guantanamo detainee, 2002–2003)		Guantanamo	6 months
Sunni Islam	21	Woodhill Prison, Britain	7 yrs.
JIS (Prison Islam)	21	State Prison, Tahachapi, California	0*
JIS (Prison Islam)	25	New Folsom Prison, California	2 months
Sunni Islam Salafi-Jihad	33	Wandsworth Prison, Britain	4 yrs.
Odin	Unknown	Texas prison	Unknown
No (Guantanamo detainee, 2001–2007)		Guantanamo	2 months

(* Plot waged from prison)

Case #	Prisoner Name	Year of Attack/Plan	Age at Attack/Plan
32	Shumpert, Rueben (1977–2009), U.S. al-Shabaab	2007	30
33	Smith, Tonya (1984–), U.S. Aryan Circle	2007	23
34	Adolf, Shawn (1974–), U.S. Aryan Nations	2008	34
35	al-Shihri, Said Ali (1973–), U.S. al-Qaeda in Yemen	2008	35
36	Cain, Howard (1975–2008), U.S.	2008	33
37	Floyd, Eric (1975–), U.S.	2008	33
38	Ramsey, Marc (1969–), U.S.	2008	39
39	Warner, Levon (1972–), U.S.	2008	38
40	Keeler, Sulayman (1972–), Britain al-Muhajiroun	2008	35
41	Abdullah, Luqman Ameen (Christopher Thomas) (1956–2009), U.S. Ummah	2009	53
42	Bassir, Mohammad (Franklin Williams) (1951–), U.S. Ummah	2009	50
43	Cromitie, James (1964–), U.S.	2009	45
44	Finton, Michael (1980–), U.S.	2009	29
45	Payen, Laguerre (1981–), U.S.	2009	28
46	Scruggs, Rasheed (1975–), U.S.	2009	33
47	Williams, Onta (1976–), U.S.	2009	33
48	Gardner, Kevin (1986–), Britain	2009	23
49	Bledsoe, Carlos (Abdulhakim Mujahid Muhammad) (1985–), U.S.	2009	24

Prison Religious Conversion	Age at Conversion (approx.)	Place of Conversion/ Incarceration	Lag between Release and Violence
Sunni Islam	25	Monroe State Prison, Washington	2 yrs.
Odin	Unknown	Texas prison	Unknown
Wicca/Odin	22	Colorado prison	11 yrs.
No (Guantanamo detainee, 2001–2007)			1 yr.
Prison Islam	29	Pennsylvania State prison	2 yrs.
Prison Islam	Unknown	Pennsylvania State prison	0* (halfway house resident)
Moorish Science Temple	Unknown	Indiana prison	0*
Prison Islam	Unknown	Pennsylvania State prison	Unknown
Islam	24	Young offenders institution, Britain	12 yrs.
Sunni Islam	29	Michigan prison	Unknown
Sunni Islam	Unknown	Michigan prison	0*
Islam	39	Fishkill, New York	5 yrs.
Islam	25	Illinois prison	4 yrs.
Islam	23	New York prison	5 yrs.
Prison Islam	Unknown	Pennsylvania State prison	Unknown
Islam	19	Bureau of Prisons, New York	2 yrs.
Islam	20	Stoke Heath Young Offenders Institution, Britain	2 yrs.
No (already Muslim convert) Radicalized Jihad		Yemen prison	0.5 mos.

(* Plot waged from prison)

Case #	Prisoner Name	Year of Attack/Plan	Age at Attack/Plan
50	Farah Mohamed Beledi (1984–2011), U.S. al-Shabaab	2011	27
51	Davis, Joseph (Abu Khalid Abdul-Latif) (1978–), U.S.	2011	33

Prison Religious Conversion	Age at Conversion (approx.)	Place of Conversion/ Incarceration	Lag between Release and Violence
No (already Muslim)		Minnesota prison	2 yrs.
Islam	24	Washington State prison	9 yrs.

(* Plot waged from prison)

Part II

Case #	Name	Nature of Offense
1	Cleaver, Eldridge	Attempted murder of police officers
2	Jackson, George	Murder of prison guards/inmates
3	DeFreeze, Donald	Assassination, kidnapping, bank robbery, bombing, murder
4	Yarbrough, Gary	Counterfeiting, murder, bank robbery
5	Fort, Jeff	Attempted bombing with Libyans
6	Guthrie, Richard	Attempted assassination of George H. W. Bush, bank robbery, bombing
7	Langan, Peter	Attempted assassination of George H. W. Bush, bank robbery, bombing
8	Collins, Aqil	Trained with al-Qaeda (1994); Islamic Chechen
9	Vallat, David	Trained with al-Qaeda (1994); French bombing (1995)
10	Kelkal, Khaled	Assassination, bombing campaign in France
11	Raime, Joseph	French bombing campaign
12	Bourada, Safe	Plotting terrorist attacks in France, Iraq; Paris Metro bombing
13	Brewer, Lawrence	Murder, hate crime in Jasper, Texas
14	King, John	Murder, hate crime in Jasper, Texas
15	al-Zawahiri, Ayman	East African bombings; 9/11 attacks, and so on
16	Reid, Richard	Trained with al-Qaeda; 2001 shoe-bomb plot
17	Mubanga, Martin	Terrorist-related activity
18	Felton, Leo	Counterfeiting, bank robbery, attempt to bomb the U.S. Holocaust Museum
19	al-Zarqawi, Abu-Musab	Multiple terrorist attacks; beheading of Nicholas Berg
20	Achraf, Mohammed	Plot to bomb Spain's National Court
21	Ahmidan, Jamal	Madrid train bombing (2004)
22	Bensmail, Abdel	Plot to bomb Spain's National Court
23	Lamari, Allekema	Madrid train bombing (2004)
24	Trashorras, Jose	Madrid train bombing (2004)
25	Mehsud, Abdullah	Kidnapping; mass murder; Coalition attacks
26	Ibrahim, Muktar	London subway bomb plot (2005)
27	James, Kevin	Plot to attack Army recruiting offices, L.A. (2005)

Nature of Plots	International/ Homegrown	Ethnicity / Nationality	Source
Executed	Homegrown	African American	Cleaver, 1975
Executed	Homegrown	African American	Cummins, 1994
Executed	Homegrown	African American	McLellan & Avery, 1977
Executed	Homegrown	Caucasian	Smith, 1994; Flynn and Gerhardt, 1989
Operational	International	African American	Schmidt, 1987
Executed	Homegrown	Caucasian	Hamm, 2002
Executed	Homegrown	Caucasian	Hamm, 2002
Executed	International	Caucasian	CNN.com, 2002
Executed	International	African (Algerian)	Mili, 2006
Executed	International	African (Algerian)	Mili, 2006
Executed	International	African (Algerian)	Mili, 2006
Operational	International	North African (Algerian)	Global Jihad, 2008
Executed	Homegrown	Caucasian	Blazak, 2009; Texas DCJ Records, n.d.-b
Executed	Homegrown	Caucasian	Blazak, 2009; Texas DCJ Records, n.d.-a
Executed	International	Arab	Wright, 2006; Brandon, 2009
Operational	International	African-Caribbean	Brandon, 2009; Elliott, 2002
		African (Zambia)	Brandon, 2009
Executed	Homegrown	Jewish/African American	Tough, 2003
Executed	International	Arab	Brandon, 2009; Brisard, 2005
Aspirational	International	North African (Algerian)	Associated Press, 2004; Haahr, 2004
Executed	International	North African	Rotella, 2004
Aspirational	International	North African (Algerian)	Bakker, 2006
Executed	International	North African (Algerian)	History Commons, 2004
Executed	International	Hispanic	Cuthbertson, 2004
Executed	International	Arab	Masood, 2007
Operational	International	African (Eritrea)	Brandon, 2009; Lyall, 2007
Operational	Homegrown	African American	Hamm, 2007

(* Plot waged from prison)

Case #	Name	Nature of Offense
28	Washington, Levar	Plot to attack Army recruiting offices, L.A. (2005)
29	al-Fiqari, Mohammad	Attending terrorist camps, U.K.
30	Clem, Dennis	Homicide of two police officers (2007)
31	Rasoul, Abdullah	Bombing Coalition forces in Afghanistan
32	Shumpert, Rueben	Counterfeiting; weapons; joined Somali network
33	Smith, Tonya	Homicide of two police officers (2007)
34	Adolf, Shawn	Attempted assassination of Barack Obama
35	al-Shihri, Said Ali	Bombing of U.S. Embassy, Yemen (2008)
36	Cain, Howard	Bank robbery; murder of police officer
37	Floyd, Eric	Bank robbery; murder of police officer
38	Ramsey, Marc	Attempted anthrax attack on John McCain
39	Warner, Levon	Bank robbery; murder of police officer
40	Keeler, Sulayman	Supporting terrorism
41	Abdullah, Luqman Ameen (Christopher Thomas)	Multiple felonies; shooting at FBI; plot to bomb Super Bowl
42	Bassir, Mohammad (Franklin Williams)	Multiple felonies; shooting at FBI; plot to bomb Super Bowl
43	Cromitie, James	Plot to bomb synagogues and military
44	Finton, Michael	Plot to bomb federal building
45	Payen, Laguerre	Plot to bomb synagogues and military
46	Scruggs, Rasheed	Murder of police officer
47	Williams, Onta	Plot to bomb synagogues and military
48	Gardner, Kevin	Bomb plot of U.K. military
49	Bledsoe, Carlos (Abdulhakim Mujahid Muhammad)	Murder/wounding
50	Farah Mohamed Beledi	Suicide bombing, Somalia
51	Davis, Joseph (Abu Khalid Abdul-Latif)	Attack on U.S. military base

Nature of Plots	International/ Homegrown	Ethnicity / Nationality	Source
Operational	Homegrown	African American	Hamm, 2007
Aspirational	Homegrown	African (Trinidad)	Brandon, 2009
Executed	Homegrown	Caucasian	ADL, 2008
Executed	International	Arab	Evans, 2009
Executed	International	Hispanic/African American	Shumpert 2006; NEA, 2008
Executed	Homegrown	Caucasian	ADL, 2008
Operational	Homegrown	Caucasian	Cardona, 2009
Executed	International	Arab	Worth, 2009
Executed	Homegrown	African American	Schilling, 2009
Executed	Homegrown	African American	Teague, 2008
Executed	Homegrown	African American	Associated Press, 2008
Executed	Homegrown	African American	Schilling, 2009
Operational	International	Caucasian	Brandon, 2009
Aspirational	Homegrown	African American	USA v. Luqman Ameen Abdullah
Aspirational	Homegrown	African American	USA v. Luqman Ameen Abdullah
Aspirational	Homegrown	African American	Wakin, 2009
Aspirational	Homegrown	Caucasian	Robinson, 2009
Aspirational	Homegrown	African (Haiti)	Wakin, 2009
Executed	Homegrown	African American	Schilling, 2009
Aspirational	Homegrown	African American	Wakin, 2009
Operational	Homegrown	Caucasian	Brandon, 2009
Executed	Homegrown	African American	Goetz, 2010
Executed	International	African	Yuen, 2011
Aspirational	Homegrown	African American	Esposito & Ryan, 2011

(* Plot waged from prison)

APPENDIX 2

DATABASE SOURCES

ADL. (2008, November 5). *Extremism in the News.* Washington, D.C.: Anti-Defamation League.

Associated Press. (2004, October 20). "Spain Says Terrorist Plotted 'Big Blow.' "

Associated Press. (2008, August 22). "Officials: Threat Sent to McCain Colorado Office."

Bakker, E. (2006). *Jihadi Terrorists in Europe, Their Characteristics and the Circumstances in Which They Joined the Jihad: An Exploratory Study.* The Hague: Clingendael Institute.

Blazak, R. (2009). "The Prison Hate Machine." *Criminology & Public Policy, 8,* 633-640.

Brandon, J. (2009). *Unlocking Al-Qaeda: Islamist Extremism in British Prisons.* London: Quilliam.

Brisard, J. (2005). *Zarqawi: The New Face of Al-Qaeda.* New York: Other Press.

Cardona, F. (2009, January 30). "Obama-Plot Figure Sentenced." *Denver Post.*

Cleaver, E. (1975). Excerpt from *Soul on Ice.* In J. Trupin (Ed.), *In Prison: Writings and Poems about the Prison Experience* (pp. 174-182). New York: New American Library.

CNN.com. (2002, July 3). *Insight.* (Transcript).

Cummins, E. (1994). *The Rise and Fall of California's Radical Prison Movement.* Stanford, Calif.: Stanford University Press.

Cuthbertson, I. (2004). "Prisons and the Education of Terrorists." *World Policy Journal, 21,* 15-22.

Elliott, M. (2002, February 16). "The Shoe Bomber's World." *Time.*

Esposito, R., and Ryan, J. (2011, June 23). "Feds: Converts to Islam Planned Ft. Hood-Style Assault in Seattle." *ABC News.*

Evans, M. (2009, March 13). "Afghans Pressed to Explain Release of Abdullah Ghulam Rasoul." *The Times* (London).

Flynn, K., and Garhardt, G. (1989). *The Silent Brotherhood: Inside America's Terrorist Underground.* New York: Free Press.

Global Jihad. (2008). "Safe Bourada," accessed at http://www.globaljihad.net/view_page. asp?id=904.

Goetz, K. (2010, November 14). "When Carlos Bledsoe Became Abdulhakim Jujahid Muhammad." *Memphis Commercial Appeal.*

Haahr, K. (2002). "Algerian Salafists and the New Face of Terrorism in Spain." *Terrorism Monitor 2,* online version.

Hamm, M. (2002). *In Bad Company: America's Terrorist Underground.* Boston: Northeastern University Press.

Hamm, M. (2007). *Terrorist Recruitment in American Correctional Institutions: An Exploratory Study of Non-traditional Faith Groups.* Washington, D.C.: National Institute of Justice.

History Commons. (2004). "Allekema Lamari," accessed at http://www.historycommons. org/entity.jsp?entity=rachid_oulad_akcha_1.

Lyall, S. (2007, July 6). "Britain Convicts 4 in Separate Terrorism Trials." *New York Times.*

Masood, S. (2007, July 25). "Taliban Leader Is Said to Evade Capture by Blowing Himself Up." *New York Times.*

McLellan, V., & Avery, P. (1977). *The Voices of Guns; the Definitive and Dramatic Story of the Twenty-Two-Month Career of the Symbionese Liberation Army, One of the Most Bizarre Chapters in the History of the American Left.* New York: Putnam.

Mili, H. (2006). "Al-Qaeda's Caucasian Foot Soldiers." *Terrorism Monitor 4*, online version.

NEA. (2008). "Al-Shabaab Stories from the Muhajireen: Ruben Shumpert," accessed at http://revolution.thabaat.net/?p=741.

Robinson, M. (2009, September 24). "Michael Finton Charged by FBI for Attempting to Bomb the Springfield Federal Courthouse." Associated Press.

Rotella, S. (2004, February 23). "Holy Water, Hashish and Jihad." *Los Angeles Times.*

Schilling, C. (2009, February 17). " 'Jailhouse Islam' Converts Gun Down U.S. Cops." *WorldNetDaily.*

Schmidt, W. (1987, November 5). "U.S. Squares Off against Tough Gang." *New York Times.*

Shumpert, R. (2006, June 5). Letter transmitted from Amir Abdul Muhaimeen to U.S. District Judge Marsha J. Pechman.

Smith, B. (1994). *Terrorism in America: Pipe Bombs and Pipe Dreams.* State University of New York Press.

Teague, M. (2008). "The Radicals among Us." *Militant Islam Monitor.org*, accessed at http://www.militantislammonitor.org/article/id/3877.

Texas DCJ Records. (n.d.). "John King," accessed at http://www.tdcj.state.tx.us/stat/offendersondrow.htm.

Texas DCJ Records. (n.d.). "Lawrence Brewer," accessed at http://www.tdcj.state.tx.us/stat/brewerlawrence.htm.

Tough, P. (2003, May 25). "The Black Supremacist." *New York Times.*

Wakin, D. (2009, May 23). "Imams Reject Talk That Islam Radicalizes Inmates." *New York Times.*

Worth, R. (2009, January 23). "Guantanamo Detainee Resurfaces in Terrorist Group." *International Herald Tribune.*

Wright, L. (2006). *The Looming Tower: Al-Qaeda and the Road to 9/11.* New York: Knopf.

Yuen, L. (2011, June 7). "Family IDs Minn. Man Allegedly behind Somali Suicide Bombing." Minnesota Public Radio.

LEGAL CASES

USA v. Luqman Ameen Abdullah. Case: 2:09-mj-30436.

NOTES

NOTES TO PREFACE

1. The White House, Office of Press Secretary, remarks by the president on strengthening intelligence and aviation security, January 7, 2010.
2. Karen DeYoung and Michael A. Fletcher, "Attempt to Bomb Airliner Could Have Been Prevented, Obama Says," *Washington Post*, January 6, 2010.
3. "Profile: Al-Qaeda in the Arabian Peninsula," BBC News, January 3, 2010.
4. Brian Ross, Joseph Rhee, and Rehab El-Buri, "Al Qaeda Leader behind Northwest Flight 253 Was Released by U.S," ABC News, December 28, 2009, http://abcnews.go.com.
5. Pierre Thomas, Jason Ryan, and Theresa Cook, "Holder: Homegrown Terror Threat Increasing," ABCNews.com, July 2009, http://abcnews.go.com.
6. Robert Mueller, "Remarks for Delivery by FBI Director Robert Mueller at City Club," Cleveland, Ohio, June 27, 2006.
7. Eric Cummins, *The Rise and Fall of California's Radical Prison Movement* (Stanford: Stanford University Press, 1994); Marie Gottschalk, *The Prison and the Gallows: The Politics of Mass Incarceration in America* (New York: Cambridge University Press, 2006).
8. Michael Hall, "Homeland Security Team to Focus on American Terrorists," *USA Today*, March 15, 2007.
9. Charles Allen, "Threat of Islamic Radicalization to the Homeland," U.S. Senate, Subcommittee on Homeland Security and Governmental Affairs, March 14, 2007.
10. *Al Qaeda in Yemen and Somalia: A Ticking Time Bomb*, a report to the Committee on Foreign Relations, U.S. Senate, January 21, 2010.
11. Mona El-Nagger and Jack Healy, "Saudis Say They Have Arrested 113 Militants with Qaeda Ties," *New York Times*, March 25, 2010.
12. Homeland Security News Wire, "Gitmo Repeat Offender Rate Rises Sharply," December 9, 2010.
13. Bin Laden's message was broadcast in Arabic on al-Jazeera Television on January 24, 2010.
14. J. M. Berger, *Jihad Joe: Americans Who Go to War in the Name of Islam* (Washington, D.C.: Potomac Books, 2011).
15. Catherine Herridge, *The Next Wave: On the Hunt for Al Qaeda's American Recruits* (New York: Crown Forum, 2011).
16. Nick Bunkley, "Would-Be Plane Bomber Is Sentenced to Life in Prison," *New York Times*, February 17, 2012.
17. Barack Obama, introduction to *National Strategy for Counterterrorism*, The White House, June 2011.
18. Gottschalk, *Prison and the Gallows*.
19. "Seven Inmates Hospitalized after Riot at Folsom Prison," *MSNBC*, August 28, 2010, accessed at http://www.msnbc.msn.com/id/38890984/ns/us_news-crime_and_courts/.
20. Gregg Barak (ed.), *Crimes by the Capitalist State: An Introduction to State Criminality* (Albany: State University of New York Press, 1991).

21. Diana B. Henriques, *The Wizard of Lies: Bernie Madoff and the Death of Trust* (New York: Henry Holt, 2011).

NOTES TO CHAPTER 1

1. The Rt. Hon. Winston S. Churchill, *A Roving Commission: My Early Life* (New York: Chas. Scribner's Sons, 1939), p. 261.
2. Ibid.
3. Ibid., p. 276.
4. Ibid., p. 291.
5. Ibid., p. 297.
6. Roy Jenkins, *Churchill: A Biography* (London: Plume, 2002).
7. Victor Baily, "Churchill as Home Secretary: Prison Reform," *History Today* 35 (1985): 10.
8. For example, see David Ramsbotham, *The Shocking State of British Prisons and the Need for Visionary Change* (London: Simon & Schuster, 2005).
9. Churchill, *A Roving Commission*, p. 259.
10. C. B. Dalal, *Gandhi: 1915–1948 A Detailed Chronology* (New Delhi: Gandhi Peace Foundation, 1971).
11. Robert Payne, *The Life and Death of Mahatma Gandhi* (New York: Dutton, 1969), p. 507.
12. Nelson Mandela, "Gandhi the Prisoner: A Comparison of Prison Experiences of Mahatma Gandhi and Nelson Mandela," in B. R. Nanda (ed.), *Mahatma Gandhi: 125 Years* (New Delhi: Indian Council for Relations, 1995).
13. Payne, *Life and Death of Mahatma Gandhi*.
14. B. R. Nada, *Mahatma Gandhi: A Biography* (Boston: Beacon, 1958).
15. Payne, *Life and Death of Mahatma Gandhi*.
16. Dennis Dalton, *Gandhi: Non-Violent Power in Action* (New York: Columbia University Press, 1993).
17. Payne, *Life and Death of Mahatma Gandhi*.
18. Quoted in Yogesh Chada, *Gandhi: A Life* (New York: John Wiley, 1997), p. 326.
19. Payne, *Life and Death of Mahatma Gandhi*, p. 446.
20. Chada, *Gandhi*.
21. Payne, *Life and Death of Mahatma Gandhi*, p. 450.
22. "India: Unto Death," *Time*, March 13, 1939, accessed at http://www.time.com/time/magazine/article/0,9171,760919,00.html#ixzz0hEzqfSYY.
23. Albert Einstein, *Out of My Later Years* (New York: Wings Books, 1956), p. 240.
24. Mandela, "Gandhi the Prisoner."
25. Ibid.
26. Mac Maharaj, "Where Thought Remained Unprisoned," in Mac Maharaj (ed.), *Reflections in Prison: Voices from the South African Liberation Struggle* (Amherst: University of Massachusetts Press, 2001), pp. ix–xvii.
27. Nelson Mandela, *Long Walk to Freedom* (Boston: Little Brown, 1995).
28. Richard Stengel, "Prison Was Mandela's Greatest Teacher," MSNBC.com, March 30, 2010.
29. Mandela, *Long Walk to Freedom*, p. 361.
30. Fran Lisa Buntman, *Robben Island and Prisoner Resistance to Apartheid* (Cambridge: Cambridge University Press, 2003).
31. Mandela, *Long Walk to Freedom*.
32. Ibid., p. 415.

33. Nelson Mandela, "Whither the Black Consciousness Movement? An Assessment," in Maharaj, *Reflections in Prison*, pp. 36–37.

34. "The Big Read: Nelson Mandela: A Living Legend," *Daily Observer*, July 25, 2008.

35. Larry Rohter, "The Long Story of a Long Revolution," *New York Times*, April 13, 2010.

36. Walter C. Langer, *The Mind of Adolf Hitler: The Secret Wartime Report* (New York: Basic Books, 1972).

37. Emil Lengyel, *Hitler* (New York: Dial, 1932).

38. Ian Kershaw, *Hitler 1889–1936: Hubris* (New York: W. W. Norton, 1998).

39. Joachim C. Fest, *Hitler* (New York: Harcourt Brace Jovanovich, 1973).

40. Ibid.

41. Photograph of Hitler's cell, accessed at http://www.uncp.edu/home/rwb/hitler_cell_landsberg.jpg.

42. Anthony Read, *The Devil's Disciples: Hitler's Inner Circle* (New York: W. W. Norton, 2004); Fest, *Hitler*.

43. Fest, *Hitler*, p. 199.

44. Kershaw, *Hitler 1889–1936*, p. 283.

45. Ibid. For a discussion of Rosenberg's influence on Hitler during this period, see Robert Cecil, *The Myth of the Master Race: Alfred Rosenberg and Nazi Ideology* (New York: Dodd Mead, 1972).

46. Michael Burleigh, *Sacred Causes: Religion and Politics from the European Dictators to Al Qaeda* (New York: Harper Perennial, 2006).

47. Zeev Sternhell, "Fascist Ideology," in Walter Laqueur (ed.), *Fascism: A Reader's Guide* (Aldershot, U.K.: Wildwood House, 1976), pp. 315–378.

48. Alvin Rosenfeld, *Imaging Hitler* (Bloomington: Indiana University Press, 1985), p. 90.

49. "Churchman to Hitler," *Time*, August 10, 1936, accessed at http://www.time.com/time/magazine/article/0,9171,762289,00.html.

50. Read, *Devil's Disciples*.

51. Langer, *Mind of Adolf Hitler*.

52. Fest, *Hitler*.

53. More than one historian has observed that *Mein Kampf* had nothing to say that had not already been said by ranking European intellectuals of the day. See Sternhell, "Fascist Ideology."

54. James J. Barns and Patience P. Barns, *Hitler: Mein Kampf in Britain and America* (Cambridge: Cambridge University Press, 1980).

55. Kershaw, *Hitler 1889–1936*.

56. Langer, *Mind of Adolf Hitler*, p. 198.

57. Landsberg Citizens Association, "Landsberg: 'City of the Youth,' " accessed at http://www.buergervereinigung-landsberg.org/english/press/buergervereinigung/chronic.htm.

58. Barns and Barns, *Hitler*.

59. Dennis Mack Smith, *Mussolini: A Biography* (New York: Vintage, 1983), p. 172.

60. Winston Churchill, *The Second World War, Volume 1* (New York: Houghton Mifflin, 1986), p. 50.

61. Quoted in Fest, *Hitler*, p. 206.

62. Barns and Barns, *Hitler*.

63. Max Weber, *The Theory of Social and Economic Organization*, trans. A. M. Henderson and Talcott Parsons (New York: Free Press, 1947), p. 390.

64. "Gandhi Enters Prison Walls," accessed at http://citizencentre.virtualpune.com/html/mahatma-gandhi.shtml.

65. Burleigh, *Sacred Causes*, p. 403.
66. David Beresford, *Ten Men Dead* (New York: Atlantic, 1987); Bill Rolston, " 'Trying to Reach the Future through the Past': Murals and Memory in Northern Ireland," *Crime, Media, Culture*, 6 (2010): 1–23; Kevin Toolis, *Rebel Hearts* (New York: St. Martin's, 1995).
67. Owen Bowcott, "Hope Dies in Turkish Prison Hunger Strike," *The Guardian*, January 18, 2002.
68. Laird Harrison, "Anti-Wall Street Protestors Rally against Prison Conditions," Reuters, February 20, 2012.
69. Tim Golden, "Tough U.S. Steps in Hunger Strike at Camp in Cuba," *New York Times*, February 9, 2006.
70. Jane Mayer, *The Dark Side: The Inside Story of How the War on Terror Turned into a War on American Ideals* (New York: Anchor, 2009).
71. Evan F. Kohlmann, " 'The Eleven': Saudi Guantanamo Veterans Returning to the Fight," NEA Foundation, February 2009.
72. Audrey K. Cronin, *How Terrorism Ends: Understanding the Decline and Demise of Terrorist Campaigns* (Princeton: Princeton University Press, 2009).
73. They include Farah Mohamed Beledi, Carlos Bledsoe, Michael Finton, and Ruben Shumpert.
74. Ronald L. Akers, "Religion and Crime," *The Criminologist* 35 (November/December) (2010): 1–6.
75. Todd Clear, "Politicization of Prisoners Is an Old and Contemporary Story," in Richard Rosenfeld, Kenna Quinet, and Crystal Garcia (eds.), *Contemporary Issues in Criminological Theory and Research: The Role of Social Institutions* (Belmont, Calif.: Wadsworth, 2012), p. 206, emphasis in original.
76. Dan Berger, *Outlaws of America: The Weather Underground and the Politics of Solidarity* (Oakland, Calif.: AK Press, 2006).
77. "Brian Michael Jenkins," accessed at http://en.wikipedia.org/wiki/Brian_Michael_Jenkins.
78. George McMillan, *The Making of an Assassin: The Life of James Earl Ray* (Boston: Little, Brown, 1976); Gerald Posner, *Killing the Dream: James Earl Ray and the Assassination of Martin Luther King, Jr.* (New York: Random House, 1998).

NOTES TO CHAPTER 2
1. David Freeman Hawke, *Benjamin Rush: Revolutionary Gadfly* (Indianapolis: Bobbs-Merrill, 1971).
2. Ibid., p. 364.
3. Benjamin Rush, *Essays: Literary, Moral, and Philosophical* (Schenectady, N.Y.: Union College Press, 1988), p. 90.
4. Negley K. Teeters and John D. Shearer, *The Prison at Philadelphia: Cherry Hill* (New York: Columbia University Press), 1957.
5. Walter Isaacson, *Benjamin Franklin: An American Life* (New York: Simon & Schuster, 2003).
6. Chai Woodham, "Eastern State Penitentiary: A Prison with a Past," Smithsonian.com, October 1, 2008.
7. Michael A. Gomez, *Black Crescent: The Experience and Legacy of African Muslims in the Americas* (New York: Cambridge University Press, 2005).
8. Amir Muhammad, *Muslims in America* (Beltsville, Md.: Amana Publications, 2001).

9. Herbert Berg, "Mythmaking in the African American Muslim Context: The Moorish Science Temple, the Nation of Islam, and the American Society of Muslims," *Journal of the American Academy of Religion* 73 (2005): 685–703.

10. Ibid.

11. Hirsham Aidi, "Jihadis in the Hood: Race, Urban Islam and the War on Terror," *Middle East Report* 224 (2002): 36–43.

12. M. F. Lee, *The Nation of Islam: An American Millenarian Movement* (Syracuse, N.Y.: Syracuse University Press, 1996).

13. Muhammad, *Muslims in America.*

14. Berg, "Mythmaking in the African Muslim American Context."

15. Manning Marable, *Malcolm X: A Life of Reinvention* (New York: Viking, 2011).

16. Karl Evanzz, *The Rise and Fall of Elijah Muhammad* (New York: Pantheon, 1999).

17. Aidi, "Jihadis in the Hood."

18. Muhammad, *Muslims in America.*

19. Excerpt from *The Autobiography of Malcolm X* by Alex Haley and Malcolm X, in J. E. Trupin (ed.), *In Prison: Writings and Poems about the Prison Experience* (New York: New American Library, 1975), pp. 168, 171.

20. Marable, *Malcolm X.*

21. Ibid., p. 94.

22. Robert Dannin, *Black Pilgrimage to Islam* (New York: Oxford University Press, 2002).

23. Berg, "Mythmaking in the African American Muslim Context."

24. Asma Gull Hasan, *American Muslims: The New Generation* (New York: Continuum, 2000).

25. Marable, *Malcolm X.*

26. Gottschalk, *Prison and the Gallows.*

27. Cummins, *Rise and Fall of California's Radical Prison Movement.*

28. Quoted in Taylor Branch, *At Canaan's Edge: America in the King Years 1965–68* (New York: Simon & Schuster, 2006), p. 295.

29. Ibid., p. 374.

30. Excerpt from *Soul on Ice* by Eldridge Cleaver, in J. E. Trupin (ed.), *Writings and Poems about the Prison Experience* (New York: New American Library, 1975), p. 179.

31. Ibid., p. 182.

32. Eldridge Cleaver, *Soul on Ice* (New York: McGraw-Hill, 1968), p. 44.

33. Quoted in Cummins, *Rise and Fall of California's Radical Prison Movement*, p. 70.

34. See James B. Jacobs, *Stateville: The Penitentiary in Mass Society* (Chicago: University of Chicago Press, 1977).

35. Dannin, *Black Pilgrimage to Islam.*

36. Aidi, "Jihadis in the Hood."

37. Gottschalk, *Prison and the Gallows*; James B. Jacobs, "The Prisoners' Rights Movement and Its Impact, 1960–1980," *Crime and Justice* 2 (1980): 429–470.

38. John Irwin, *Prisons in Turmoil* (Boston: Little, Brown, 1980), p. 14.

39. James A. Aho, *The Politics of Righteousness: Idaho Christian Patriotism* (Seattle: University of Washington Press, 1990).

40. Tom Wicker, *A Time to Die* (New York: Quadrangle/NY Times Books, 1975).

41. "Headline: Attica State Prison," CBS Evening News, September 15, 1971, Television News Archive, Vanderbilt University.

42. "Headline: Senate Muskie/Attica Prison Riot," NBC Evening News, September 15, 1971, Television News Archive, Vanderbilt University.

43. Berger, *Outlaws of America*, pp. 182–183.

44. Sam Roberts, "Rockefeller on the Attica Raid, From Boastful to Subdued," *New York Times*, September 12, 2011.

45. Fred Graham, "Crime and Justice," *New York Times*, October 3, 1971.

46. Irwin, *Prisons in Turmoil*.

47. John Hagedorn, "Gangs as Social Actors," in Stuart Henry and Mark M. Lanier (eds.), *The Essential Criminology Reader* (Boulder, Colo.: Westview Press, 2006), pp. 141–152.

48. Loïc Wacquant, *Deadly Symbiosis: Race and the Rise of the Penal State* (Cambridge, U.K.: Polity Press, 2010).

49. Eldridge Cleaver, *Soul on Fire* (Waco, Tex.: Word Books, 1978), p. 80.

50. Bobby Seale, *Seize the Time: The Story of the Black Panther Party and Huey P. Newton* (New York: Random House, 1970; reprint, Baltimore, Md.: Black Classic, 1991), p. 132.

51. Cummins, *Rise and Fall of California's Radical Prison Movement*, p.119.

52. Quoted in Goran Olsson, *The Black Power Mix Tape: 1967–1975* (Louverture Films, 2011).

53. Cleaver quote in Rick Perlstein, *Nixonland: The Rise of a President and the Fracturing of America* (New York: Scribner, 2008), p. 221.

54. Some accounts say that the Grateful Dead also performed, but this is incorrect. They were in Los Angeles that day.

55. Seale, *Seize the Time*, p. 182.

56. Ishmael Reed, preface to Cleaver, *Soul on Ice* (1992 edition), p. xx.

57. Cleaver, *Soul on Ice*, p. 61.

58. Kathleen Rout, *Eldridge Cleaver* (Boston: Twayne, 1991).

59. Cummins, *Rise and Fall of California's Radical Prison Movement*, p. 109.

60. Ibid., p. 112.

61. "Interview: Eldridge Cleaver," *PBS Frontline*, 1997, accessed at http://www.pbs.org/wgbh/pages/frontline/shows/race/interviews/ecleaver.html.

62. Rout, *Eldridge Cleaver*, p. 49.

63. This may be part of Cleaver's mythmaking. Official reports indicate that the Oakland gun battle lasted thirty minutes, not ninety. See Hugh Pearson, *The Shadow of the Panther: Huey Newton and the Price of Black Power in America* (Cambridge, Mass.: Helix, 1996).

64. Perlstein, *Nixonland*, p. 339.

65. "An Eldridge Cleaver Bio-Chronology," *Chicken Bones: A Journal for Literary and Artistic African-American Themes*, accessed at http://www.nathanielturner.com/cleaverbio.htm.

66. Cummins, *Rise and Fall of California's Radical Prison Movement*, p. 144.

67. Rout, *Eldridge Cleaver*.

68. Jerry Rubin, *DO IT! Scenarios of the Revolution* (New York: Simon & Schuster, 1970).

69. Philip S. Foner, ed., *The Black Panthers Speak* (New York: Da Capo, 1995).

70. Quoted in Rout, *Eldridge Cleaver*, p. 92.

71. Cummins, *Rise and Fall of California's Radical Prison Movement*, p. 126.

72. Aho, *Politics of Righteousness*.

73. Pearson, *Shadow of the Panther*.

74. Quoted in Cummins, *Rise and Fall of California's Radical Prison Movement*, p. 159.

75. Excerpt from *Soledad Brother*, quoted in Howard Zinn, *A People's History of the United States: 1497-Present* (New York: HarperCollins, 1980), p. 519.

76. Aho, *Politics of Righteousness*, pp. 60–61.

77. Cummins, *Rise and Fall of California's Radical Prison Movement*, p. 179.

78. Corey Weinstein and Eric Cummins, "The Crime of Punishment: Pelican Bay Maximum-Security Prison," in Elihu Rosenblatt (ed.), *Criminal Injustice: Confronting the Prison Crisis* (Boston: South End Press, 1996), pp. 72–83.

79. Olsson, *Black Power Mix Tape.*

80. Appeal of Herbert Marcuse in Angela Y. Davis, *If They Come in the Morning* (New York: Signet, 1971), p. 271. Davis was later acquitted of conspiracy, kidnapping, and murder.

81. New York State Special Commission on Attica, *The Official Report of the New York Special Commission on Attica* (n.d.); Wicker, *A Time to Die.*

82. Zinn, *People's History of the United States*, p. 520.

83. Perlstein, *Nixonland*, p. 733.

84. Prentice Earl Sanders and Bennett Cohen, *Zebra Murders: A Season of Killing, Racial Madness, and Civil Rights* (New York: Arcade, 2006).

85. Excerpt from *Soledad Brother* in Davis, *If They Come in the Morning*, pp. 164–165.

86. Anti-Defamation League, *Extremism Targets the Prisons* (New York: ADL, 1986), p. 13.

87. Irwin, *Prisons in Turmoil*, p. 88.

88. Jock Young, *The Criminological Imagination* (Cambridge, U.K.: Polity, 2011), p. 223.

89. See Jeffrey Ian Ross, "A Model of the Psychological Causes of Oppositional Terrorism," *Peace and Conflict: Journal of Peace Psychology* 2 (1996): 129–141.

90. Jackson in Trupin's *In Prison*, pp. 185 and 188, emphases in original.

NOTES TO CHAPTER 3

1. Dannie M. Martin and Peter Y. Sussman, *Committing Journalism* (New York: W. W. Norton, 1993).

2. With perhaps one exception: an American convict named Mumia Abu-Jamal, whose life sentence for the 1981 murder of a Philadelphia police officer became an international cause célèbre.

3. U.S. Department of Justice, *A Review of the Federal Bureau of Prisons' Selection of Muslim Religious Service Providers* (Washington, D.C.: Office of the Inspector General, 2004), p. 6.

4. John S. Pistole, Assistant Director, Counterterrorism Division, Federal Bureau of Investigation, testimony before the U.S. Senate Committee on the Judiciary, October 14, 2003.

5. *United States of America v. Zacarias Moussaoui*, United States District Court, Eastern District of Virginia, December 2001.

6. James A. Beckford, Joly Daniels, and Farhad Khosrokhavar, *Muslims in Prison: Challenges and Change in Britain and France* (Basingstoke, Hampshire, U.K.: Palgrave, 2005); Basia Spalek and David Wilson, "Racism and Religious Discrimination in Prison: The Marginalization of Imams in Their Work with Prisoners," in Basia Spalek (ed.), *Islam and Criminal Justice* (Portland, Ore.: Willan, 2002), pp. 96–112; Rachael Zoll, "American Prisons Become Political, Religious Battleground over Islam," Associated Press, June 4, 2005.

7. Farhad Khosrokhavar, *L'Islam dans les prisons* (Paris: Balland, 2004).

8. Nawal H. Ammar, Robert R. Weaver, and Sam Saxon, "Muslims in Prison: A Case Study from Ohio Prisons," *International Journal of Offender Therapy and Comparative Criminology* 48 (2004): 414–428.

9. Felicia Dix-Richardson, "Resistance to Conversion to Islam among African-American Women Inmates," *Journal of Offender Rehabilitation* 35 (2002): 109–126; Michael Waller, "Terrorist Recruitment and Infiltration in the United States; Prisons and Military as an

Operational Base," testimony before the U.S. Senate Committee on the Judiciary, October 14, 2003.

10. Roger Ebert, film review of *Malcolm X, Chicago Sun-Times*, November 18, 1992.

11. Marable, *Malcolm X*, p. 486.

12. See Farhad Khosrokhavar, *Inside Jihadism: Understanding Jihadi Movements Worldwide* (Boulder, Colo.: Paradigm, 2009).

13. Richard Rosenfeld, "Institutional Analysis in Criminology: An Overview of the Current Volume," in Rosenfeld et al., *Contemporary Issues in Criminological Theory and Research*, p. 4.

14. Scott Atran, *Talking to the Enemy: Faith, Brotherhood, and the (Un)making of Terrorists* (New York: Ecco, 2010), p. 289.

15. Ibid., p. 279.

16. Frank Cilluffo and Gregory Saathoff, *Out of the Shadows: Getting ahead of Prisoner Radicalization* (George Washington University/University of Virginia, Critical Incident Analysis Group, 2006), p. i, emphasis added.

17. RAND, *Radicalization or Rehabilitation: Understanding the Challenge of Extremist and Radicalized Prisoners* (Washington, D.C.: RAND Corporation, 2008), p. 49.

18. Michael Kenney, *How Terrorists Learn* (Washington, D.C.: National Institute of Justice, 2008), p. 73.

19. Ian Cuthbertson, "Prisons and the Education of Terrorists," *World Policy Journal* 21 (2004): 15–22.

20. Ryan J. Reilley, "Rand Paul Opposed Synthetic Drug Prohibition to Protect You from Radical Islam," *TPM Muckraker*, February 21, 2012.

21. Quoted in "Jails Are the Jihadist Jack-in-the-Box," PoliceOne.com, 2010, accessed at http://www.policeone.com/corrections/articles/2473312-Jails-are-the-Jihadist-jack-in-the-box/.

22. Philip Jenkins, "Islam in America," Foreign Policy Research Institute, 2003, p. 5.

23. James Austin and John Irwin, *Who Goes to Prison?* (San Francisco: National Council on Crime and Delinquency, 1990).

24. Felecia Dix-Richardson and Billy Close, "Intersections of Race, Religion, and Inmate Culture: The Historical Development of Islam in American Corrections," *Journal of Offender Rehabilitation* 35 (2002): 87.

25. Ammar et al., "Muslims in Prison."

26. Dix-Richardson, "Resistance to Conversion to Islam."

27. Basia Spalek and Salah El-Hassan, "Muslim Converts in Prison," *Howard Journal of Criminal Justice* 46 (2007): 99–114.

28. Zoll, "American Prisons Become Political."

29. Bert Useem and Obie Clayton, "Radicalization of U.S. Prisoners," *Criminology and Public Policy* 8 (2009): 561–592.

30. Jerome P. Bjelopera and Mark A. Randol, *American Jihadist Terrorism: Combatting a Complex Threat*, Congressional Research Service, December 7, 2010.

31. Daveed Gartenstein-Ross and Laura Grossman, *Homegrown Terrorists in the U.S. and U.K.: An Empirical Examination of the Radicalization Process*, Foundation for Defense of Democracies, Center for Terrorism Research, Washington, D.C., April 2009.

32. Quoted in Ron Scherer and Alexandra Marks, "Gangs, Prison: Al Qaeda Breeding Ground?" *Christian Science Monitor*, June 14, 2002.

33. Paul Rogers, Terrorism: Radical Islamic Influence of Chaplaincy of the U.S. Military and Prisons, testimony before the United States Senate Committee on the Judiciary, October 4, 2003.

34. Mark S. Hamm, *Terrorist Recruitment in American Correctional Institutions: An Exploratory Study of Non-Traditional Faith Groups* (Washington, D.C.: National Institute of Justice Final Report, 2007), p. 66.
35. Useem and Clayton, "Radicalization of U.S. Prisoners," p. 564, emphasis in original.
36. Garsteen-Ross and Grossman, *Homegrown Terrorism in the U.S. and U.K*, p. 59.
37. Andrew Silke et al., *Literature Review and Current Research on Violent Extremism and Potential Interventions* (London: Home Office, 2008).
38. A rare exception is Khosrokhavar, *Inside Jihadism.*
39. Harley G. Lappin, Director of Federal Bureau of Prisons, testimony before the U.S. Senate Committee on Terrorism, Technology, and Homeland Security, October 23, 2003.
40. Donald Van Duyn, Deputy Assistant Director, Counterterrorism Division, Federal Bureau of Investigation, testimony before the Senate Committee on Homeland Security and Governmental Affairs, September 19, 2006.
41. Craig Trout, "The Correctional Intelligence Initiative (CII): Preventing Prison Radicalization," presentation at the American Correctional Association 137th Annual Congress of Corrections, Kansas City, August 14, 2007.
42. George W. Knox, "Melanics: A Gang Profile Analysis," *Journal of Gang Research* 9 (2002): 1–76.
43. Cilluffo and Saathoff, *Out of the Shadows.*
44. Richard Warnes and Greg Hannah, "Meeting the Challenge of Extremist and Radicalized Prisoners: The Experiences of the United Kingdom and Spain," *Policing* (2008): 402–410.
45. Cited in Chris Allen, "(Muslim) Boys-N-the-Hood," *ISIM Review* (2006), Autumn: 40–41.
46. Greg Box, "Exclusive: The Jail Run by Al-Qaeda," *Mirror* (2006), online version, January 30.
47. James Brandon, *Unlocking Al-Qaeda: Islamist Extremism in British Prisons* (London: Quilliam, 2009), p. 3.
48. Alison Liebling, *An Exploration of Staff-Prisoner Relationships at HMP Whitemoor: Twelve Years On* (London: Home Office, 2011), p. 143.
49. Mark S. Hamm, "Prison Islam in the Age of Sacred Terror," *British Journal of Criminology* 49 (2009): 667–685.
50. Ibid., p. 674.
51. Officials estimate that 10 percent of the U.S. prison population is involved in white supremacy gangs. In California prisons, the Aryan Brotherhood alone has some fifteen thousand members. See Randy Blazak, "The Prison Hate Machine," *Criminology and Public Policy* 8 (2009): 633–640.

NOTES TO CHAPTER 4

1. U.S. Department of Justice, *A Review of the Federal Bureau of Prisons' Selection*, p. 6.
2. James Austin, "Prisons and Fear of Terrorism," *Criminology and Public Policy* 8 (2009): 641–646.
3. This differs from *incidence*, which is used by criminologists in reference to the number of crime events occurring during a specific period of time in a specified population. An *incident* is different. It is a definite, distinct occurrence or an event that occurs anywhere and at any point in time.
4. John H. Laub and Robert J. Sampson, "Turning Points in the Life Course: Why Change Matters to the Study of Crime," *Criminology* 31 (1993): 301–325.

5. This definition was accessed at http://www.fbi.gov/stats-services/publications/terrorism-2002-2005/.

6. The database does not address the separate but equally important issue of prisoners who are already in custody on terrorism charges. That issue is addressed in chapter 9.

7. Available mental-health records revealed that two of the terrorists suffered from severe psychological problems.

8. Brandon, *Unlocking Al-Qaeda*.

9. Years in which there were no attacks (e.g., 1975–1982) are omitted from the table.

10. Marc Sageman, *Leaderless Jihad: Terror Networks in the Twenty-First Century* (Philadelphia: University of Pennsylvania Press, 2008).

11. Brian Michael Jenkins, *Would-Be Warriors: Incidents of Jihadist Terrorist Radicalization in the United States since September 11, 2001* (Santa Monica, Calif.: RAND, 2010).

12. Brent L. Smith, *Terrorism in America: Pipe Bombs and Pipe Dreams* (Albany: State University of New York Press, 1994).

13. Marc Sageman, *Understanding Terror Networks* (Philadelphia: University of Pennsylvania Press, 2004). Only one of Sageman's four hundred subjects had a prior criminal record.

14. Robert A. Pape, *Dying to Win: The Strategic Logic of Suicide Terrorism* (New York: Random House, 2005).

15. See Aho, *Politics of Righteousness*; Michael Barkun, *Religion and the Racist Right: The Origins of Christian Identity* (Chapel Hill: University of North Carolina Press, 1997); Jeffrey Kaplan, *Radical Religion in America: Millenarian Movements from the Far Right to the Children of Noah* (Syracuse: Syracuse University Press, 1997).

16. Southern Poverty Law Center, "Pagans and Prison," *Intelligence Report*, Spring 2000.

17. Jenkins, *Would-Be Warriors*.

18. Alan B. Krueger, "What Makes a Homegrown Terrorist? Human Capital and Participation in Domestic Islamic Terrorist Groups in the U.S.A.," *Economics Letters* 101 (2008): 293–296.

19. Margaret A. Zahn, "Conversion, Radicalization, and the Life Course: Future Research Questions," in Rosenfeld et al., *Contemporary Issues in Criminological Theory*, pp. 209–211. I thank Professor Zahn for this critique.

20. Again, not all Salafists are violent. Many Salafis throughout the world are doctrinally rigid but peaceful.

21. Homeland Security Advisory Council, *Report of the Future of Terrorism Task Force* (Washington, D.C.: Department of Homeland Security, 2007).

22. Jenkins, *Would-Be Warriors*.

23. Sageman, *Understanding Terror Networks*, p. 1.

24. Bruce Lawrence (ed.), *Messages to the World: The Statements of Osama bin Laden* (London: Verso, 2005), p. 87.

25. Fawaz A. Gerges, *Journey of the Jihadist: Inside Muslim Militancy* (Orlando, Fla.: Harcourt, 2006), p. 3.

26. U.S. Department of Justice, *A Review of the Federal Bureau of Prisons' Selection*.

27. Quintan Wiktorowicz, *The Management of Islamic Activism: Salafis, the Muslim Brotherhood, and State Power in Jordan* (Albany: State University of New York Press, 2001).

28. Sageman, *Understanding Terrorist Networks*.

29. Rohan Gunaratna, "Combatting al Jama'ah al Islamiyyah in Southeast Asia," in Ann Aldis and Graeme P. Herd (eds.), *The Ideological War on Terror: Worldwide Strategies for Counter-Terrorism* (New York: Routledge, 2007), pp. 113–127.

30. Fuad Ajami, "Osama bin Laden, Weak Horse," *Wall Street Journal*, May 3, 2011.

31. "DHS: Attempted Attacks on U.S. at All-Time High," CBS News, May 27, 2010.

32. Lawrence Wright, "The Man behind Bin Laden," *The New Yorker*, September 16, 2002.

33. Lawrence Wright, *The Looming Tower: Al-Qaeda and the Road to 9/11* (New York: Knopf, 2007), p. 55.

34. Ibid.; Brandon, *Unlocking Al-Qaeda*.

35. Lawrence Wright, interview in *My Trip to Al-Qaeda*, a film produced by Alex Gibney and Lawrence Wright, HBO Entertainment, 2010.

36. Anthony Summers and Robbyn Swan, *The Eleventh Day: The Full Story of 9/11 and Osama Bin Laden* (New York: Ballantine, 2011).

37. Anonymous, *Through Our Enemies' Eyes: Osama bin Laden, Radical Islam, and the Future of America* (Washington, D.C.: Brassey's, 2002).

38. Hassan M. Fattah, "Militant Uprising at Jordanian Prison Is Quelled," *New York Times*, April 14, 2006.

39. See Mark Juergensmeyer, *Terror in the Mind of God: The Global Rise of Religious Violence* (Berkeley: University of California Press, 2000).

40. Ariel Merari, "The Readiness to Kill and Die: Suicidal Terrorism in the Middle East," in Walter Reich (ed.), *Origins of Terrorism: Psychologies, Ideologies, Theologies, States of Mind* (Washington, D.C.: Woodrow Wilson Center Press, 1990), pp. 192–207.

41. Sageman, *Leaderless Jihad*.

42. Edwin Bakker, *Jihadi Terrorists in Europe: Their Characteristics and the Circumstances in Which They Joined the Jihad: An Exploratory Study* (The Hague: Clingendael Institute, 2007).

43. Quoted in Michael B. Farrell, "Are America's Prisons Incubating Radical Islamists?" *Christian Science Monitor*, October 18, 2009.

44. See Khosrokhavar, *Inside Jihadism*.

45. Arthur D. Nock, *Conversion* (New York: Oxford University Press, 1933).

46. Jean-Charles Brisard, *Zarqawi: The New Face of Al-Qaeda* (New York: Other Press, 2005), p. 43.

47. Ibid., p. 40.

48. Khosrokhavar, *Inside Jihadism*.

49. Peter L. Bergen, *The Longest War: The Enduring Conflict between American and al-Qaeda* (New York: Free Press, 2011), p. 161.

50. Michael Scheuer, *Marching toward Hell: America and Islam after Iraq* (New York: Free Press, 2008).

51. James Risen, *State of War: The Secret History of the CIA and the Bush Administration* (New York: Free Press, 2006), p. 136, emphasis in original.

52. Unless otherwise noted, claims made about the cases are based on information found in the database column marked Sources which are listed in appendix 2.

53. Paul Kelso, "Boys Behind Bars," *The Guardian*, November 22, 2000.

54. My interviews with current and former staff at the institution indicate that Feltham also has the highest suicide rate of any correctional facility in Britain.

55. John Geoghegan, "Kenya Bomb Charge Briton: 'Was Normal Schoolboy,' " BBC News, January 9, 2012.

56. Atran, *Talking to the Enemy*, p. 206.

57. Ibid., p. 196.

58. Sageman, *Leaderless Jihad*, p. 159.

59. Sageman questions Lamari's leadership role in the plot but not his radicalization in prison. Of Lamari, Sageman notes: "He probably was picked up [recruited into the plot] because he happened to know some bad guys, got pissed off in jail, and came out ready to kill someone." Quoted in Atran, *Talking to the Enemy*, p. 504 (note 3).

60. Mark S. Hamm, *Hate Crime: International Perspectives on Causes and Control* (Cincinnati, Ohio: Anderson, 1994).

61. See Blazak, "The Prison Hate Machine."

62. Dina Temple-Raston, *A Death in Texas: A Story of Race, Murder, and a Small Town's Struggle for Redemption* (New York: Henry Holt, 2002), p. 81.

63. This conclusion remains controversial years after the Jasper murder. While prosecutors did make the case that King was intent on starting a race war, King's defense team argued that the claim was more a legal strategy designed to win a conviction than an accurate description of motive. The truth, perhaps, is known only to King, who awaits execution on death row.

64. See also the case of Abdullah Salih al-Ajmi in Bergen, *Longest War*, p. 307.

65. According to Justice Department memos released in 2009, the intelligence derived from CIA detainees during the war on terrorism resulted in more than six thousand reports, and half of the intelligence gathered on al-Qaeda. The intelligence was collected through enhanced interrogation primarily at CIA "black sites." Little of it, if any, came from Guantanamo. See notes 66–70 and "The 9/11 Decade," *Washington Post*, September 10–11, 2011.

66. Mayer, *Dark Side*; Andy Worthington, *The Guantanamo Files: The Stories of the 774 Detainees in America's Illegal Prison* (London: Pluto Press, 2007).

67. Somini Sengupta and Salman Masood, "Guantanamo Comes to Define U.S. to Muslims," *New York Times*, May 21, 2005.

68. Seymour M. Hersh, *Chain of Command: The Road from 9/11 to Abu Ghraib* (New York: Harper, 2005), p. 14.

69. Erik Saar and Viveca Novak, *Inside the Wire: A Military Intelligence Soldier's Eyewitness Account of Life at Guantanamo* (New York: Penguin Press, 2005), p. 71.

70. Scott Shane and Benjamin Weiser, "Judging Detainees' Risk, Often with Flawed Evidence," *New York Times*, April 25, 2011.

71. Kohlmann, "The Eleven."

72. Steven Erlanger, "Yemen's Chaos Aids Evolution of Qaeda Cell," *New York Times*, January 3, 2010. Saudi sources maintain that Shihri was killed in a U.S. bombing attack on AQAP in Yemen sometime between 2010 and 2011. Confidential interview.

73. The White House, a news conference by the president, December 22, 2010, accessed at http://www.whitehouse.gov/the-press-office/2010/12/22/news-conference-president.

74. Hersh, *Chain of Command*, p. 3.

75. Homeland Security News Wire, "Gitmo Repeat Offender Rate Rises Sharply."

76. Bruce Hoffman, "The Myth of Grass-Roots Terrorism," *Foreign Affairs* (2008), May/June, accessed at http://www.foreignaffairs.com/print/63408; Marc Sageman and Bruce Hoffman, "Does Osama Still Call the Shots? Debating the Containment of al-Qaeda's Leadership," *Foreign Affairs* (July/August 2008), accessed at http://www.foreignaffairs.com/articles/64460/marc-sageman-and-bruce-hoffman/does-osama-still-call-the-shots.

77. Elaine Sciolino and Eric Schmitt, "A Not So Very Private Feud over Terrorism," *New York Times*, June 8, 2008.

78. Sageman and Hoffman, "Does Osama Still Call the Shots?"
79. *New York Times*, May 7, 2011.
80. Hoffman, "The Myth of Grass-Roots Terrorism."
81. Interview with a bin Laden bodyguard, Abu Jandal, in *The Oath*, a film by Laura Poitras (Praxis Films, 2011).
82. Brisard, *Zarqawi*.
83. Dan Bilefsky and Maia de la Baume, "France Suspect Seen as a Home-Grown Militant," *New York Times*, March 22, 2012.
84. Steven Erlanger, "Crisis in Toulouse Alters Campaign's Tone in Sarkozy's Favor," *New York Times*, March 22, 2012.
85. Vincent J. Webb, "Searching for a Needle in the Haystack: A Look at Hypotheses and Explanations for the Low Prevalence of Radicalization in American Prisons," in Natasha A. Frost et al., (eds.), *Contemporary Issues in Criminal Justice Policy* (Belmont, Calif.: Wadsworth, 2010), p. 368.
86. Austin, "Prisons and Fear of Terrorism," p. 645, emphasis added.
87. This does not include the American Carlos Bledsoe (case 49), who was radicalized in a Yemen prison.
88. Pearson, *Shadow of the Panther*.
89. Rout, *Eldridge Cleaver*.
90. Patricia Campbell Hearst with Alvin Moscow, *Every Secret Thing* (New York: Doubleday, 1982).
91. Aho, *Politics of Righteousness*, p. 66.
92. Andrew Gumbel and Roger Charles, *Oklahoma City: What the Investigation Missed and Why It Still Matters* (New York: William Marrow, 2012); Mark S. Hamm, *In Bad Company: America's Terrorist Underground* (Boston: Northeastern University Press, 2002); Stuart A. Wright, *Patriots, Politics, and the Oklahoma City Bombing* (New York: Cambridge University Press, 2007).
93. For further discussion of Felton's crime as an act of domestic terrorism, see Jack Levin, *Social Snapshot 5: Seeing Social Structure and Change in Everyday Life* (Los Angeles: Pine Forge Press, 2008).

NOTES TO CHAPTER 5

1. Quoted in Sciolino and Schmitt, "A Not Very Private Feud over Terrorism."
2. Southern Poverty Law Center, *SPLC Report* (Summer 2011): 1.
3. Barton Gellman, "How the G-Man Got His Groove Back: Inside Bob Mueller's 10-Year Campaign to Fix the FBI," *Newsweek*, May 9, 2011.
4. Andrew Blejwas, Anthony Griggs, and Mark Potok, "Terror from the Right," *Intelligence Report* (Southern Poverty Law Center) (Summer 2005): 33–46.
5. Jenkins, *Would-Be Warriors*.
6. Howard S. Becker, "The Epistemology of Qualitative Research," in Charles C. Ragin and Howard S. Becker (eds.), *What Is a Case? Exploring the Foundations of Social Inquiry* (New York: Cambridge University Press, 1995), p. 208.
7. Jenkins, *Would-Be Warriors*, p. 6.
8. Letter from Amir Abdul Muhaimeen (Ruben Shumpert) to U.S. District Judge Marsha J. Pechman, June 5, 2006.
9. Ibid.
10. *USA v. Ruben Luis Leon Shumpert*, CR04-494MJP.

11. Paul Shukovsky, "14 Arrested in Raids by Terror Task Force," *Seattle Post Intelligencer*, November 19, 2004, accessed at http://www.seattlepi.com/news/article/14-arrested-in-raids-by-terror-task-force-1159972.php.

12. *USA v. Shumpert.*

13. Al-Shabaab, "Stories from the Muhajireen: Ruben Shumpert," accessed at http://revolution.thabaat.net/?p=741; Mark S. Hamm, *Terrorism as Crime: From Oklahoma City to Al-Qaeda and Beyond* (New York: New York University Press, 2007).

14. Paul Shukovsky, "Sheik Depicted as a Danger," *Seattle Post-Intelligencer*, February 10, 2006.

15. Letter to Judge Pechman.

16. Ibid.

17. Ibid.

18. *USA v. Shumpert.*

19. Shukovsky, "Sheik Depicted as Dangerous."

20. Al-Shabaab, "Stories from the Muhajireen."

21. Ibid.

22. "Seattle Case Raises Question about War on Terror," CNN.com, December 18, 2006.

23. Al-Shabaab, "Stories from Muhajireen."

24. Edmund Sanders, "Conditions May Be Ripe for Al Qaeda to Gain in Somalia," *Los Angeles Times*, August 25, 2008.

25. John Lee Anderson, "The Most Failed State: Letter from Mogadishu," *New Yorker*, December 14, 2009.

26. Andrea Elliott, "A Call to Jihad, Answered in America," *New York Times*, July 12, 2009.

27. Bruce Loudon, "Islamists Plotted to Kill Clinton in Nairobi Hotel," *The Australian*, September 8, 2009.

28. Berger, *Jihad Joe.*

29. FBI Director Robert S. Mueller III, speech before the Council on Foreign Relations, Washington, D.C., January 23, 2009.

30. The pipeline is thought to have run from Minneapolis to Mexico to Mogadishu. See Laura Yuen, "Family IDs Minn. Man Allegedly behind Somali Suicide Bombing," Minnesota Public Radio, June 7, 2011.

31. *USA v. Ruben Luis Leon Shumpert*, Magistrate's Docket No. 06-631 M.

32. Al-Shabaab, "Stories from the Muhajireen."

33. Spencer S. Hsu and Carrie Johnson, "Somali Americans Recruited by Extremists," *Washington Post*, March 11, 2009.

34. Quoted in Eric Vogt, "Terrorists in Prison: The Challenges Facing Corrections," *Inside Homeland Security*, no date, accessed at http://www.icpa.ca/tools/download/622/Terrorists_in_Prison.pdf.

35. Russ Buettner, "Manhattan Man Indicted in Pipe Bomb Case," *New York Times*, February 29, 2012.

36. Letter to the author from Marc Ramsey, September 15, 2010.

37. Ibid.

38. Ibid., emphasis in original.

39. Associated Press, "Officials: Threat to McCain Colorado Office," press release, August 22, 2008.

40. Letter to author from Marc Ramsey.

41. CBS News, "Inmate Charged for McCain Office Threat," August 22, 2008.

42. Ibid.

43. Letter to author from Marc Ramsey.

44. Howard Pankratz, "Inmate Sentenced for White Powder McCain Threat," *Denver Post*, March 3, 2009.

45. My attempts to correspond with Adolf were unsuccessful.

46. U.S. Department of Justice, *Outlaw Motorcycle Gangs in the United States* (Washington, D.C.: n.d.).

47. Quoted in David Holthouse, "Killer Kindred," *Intelligence Report*, Southern Poverty Law Center 137 (2010): p. 27.

48. This overall narrative is a composite based on various news articles in the *Greeley Tribune*.

49. John Piazza, "Feds: Trio of Would-Be Obama Assassins Not Much of 'Threat,' " *New York Daily News*, August 27, 2008.

50. David Johnston and Eric Schmitt, "Denver Police Brace for Convention," *New York Times*, August 5, 2008; *Convention*, a documentary by AJ Schnack (Sundance Films, 2009).

51. *Convention*.

52. Mark Hosenball, "A Racial Plot?" *Newsweek*, August 27, 2008.

53. Frank Cardona, "Obama-Plot Figure Sentenced," *Denver Post*, January 30, 2009.

54. *USA v. Shawn Robert Adolf.*

55. Hamm, *In Bad Company.*

56. Ibid.

57. Andrew Gumbel, "Seeds of Terror in Norway," *Los Angeles Times*, July 28, 2011.

58. Aho, *Politics of Righteousness*, p. 66.

59. Mark S. Hamm, "Apocalyptic Violence: The Seduction of Terrorist Subcultures," *Theoretical Criminology* 8 (2004): 329.

60. Barack Obama, *Empowering Local Partners to Prevent Violent Extremism in the United States*, the White House, August 2011, p. 1.

61. Albert K. Cohen, "Prison Violence: A Sociological Perspective," in Albert K. Cohen, George F. Cole, and Robert G. Bailey (eds.), *Prison Violence* (Lexington, Mass.: D. C. Heath, 1976), p. 8.

62. Robert J. Sampson and John H. Laub, "A Life-Course Theory of Cumulative Disadvantage and the Stability of Delinquency," in Alex Piquero and Paul Mazerolle (eds.), *Life-Course Criminology: Contemporary and Classic Readings* (Belmont, Calif.: Wadsworth, 2001), p. 159.

63. Sageman, *Understanding Terror Networks*, p. 82.

64. Pew Research Center, *Muslim Americans: Middle Class and Mostly Mainstream* (Washington, D.C.: Pew Research Center, 2007).

65. Berger, *Jihad Joe*, p. 209.

66. Robert J. Sampson and John R. Laub, "Socioeconomic Achievement in the Life Course of Disadvantaged Men: Military Service as a Turning Point," *American Sociological Review* 61 (1996): 347, emphasis added.

67. Cited in Bergen, *Longest War.*

68. Clark McCauley and Sophia Moskalenko, "Mechanisms of Political Radicalization: Pathways toward Terrorism," *Terrorism and Political Violence* 20 (2008): 415–433.

69. Sageman, *Understanding Terror Networks.*

70. Bergen, *Longest War*; *New York Times*, June 22, 2011.

71. Myriam Benraad, "Prisons in Iraq: A New Generation of Jihadists?" *CTC Sentinel* (December 2009): 16–18.

72. Ray Rivera, "Afghan Jails Are Accused of Torture," *New York Times*, September 9, 2011.

73. Alissa J. Rubin, "Afghan Jails Again Get Detainees from NATO," *New York Times*, February 16, 2012.

74. "Taliban Fighters Escape in Mass Afghan Prison Break," *The Telegraph*, April 25, 2011.

75. Interview with confidential sources, 2011.

76. Ayub Khan, "Interview with Hamid Mir: Bin Laden Biographer," Islamonline.net, October 23, 2001, accessed at http://www.islamonline.net/servlet/Satellite?c=Article_C&pagename=Zone-English-Muslim_Affairs/MAELayout&cid=1156077760398.

77. Ramon Spaaij, "The Enigma of Lone Wolf Terrorism: An Assessment," *Studies in Conflict and Terrorism* 33 (2010): 854–870.

78. "Obama: 'Lone Wolf' Terror Attack Biggest Concern," *Time*, August 16, 2011.

79. The following composite is drawn from Competency Evaluation for Abdulhakim Mujahid Muhammad, Arkansas Department of Human Services, Arkansas State Hospital, Forensic Report, July 20, 2010; Kristina Goetz, "When Carlos Bledsoe Became Abdulhakim Mujahid Muhammad," *Memphis Commercial Appeal*, November 14, 2010.

80. Bergen, *Longest War*.

81. Goetz, "When Carlos Bledsoe Became Abdulhakim Mujahid Muhammad."

82. Mark S. Hamm, "Lone Wolves on the Rise: The New Threat of Lone Terrorists, from the Unabomber to the Standalone Jihadist," International Centre for Counter-Terrorism—The Hague (2010), http://www.icct.nl/events_past_vervolg.php?id=14; Jenkins, *Would-Be Warriors*.

83. Because the case has not yet gone to trial, relevant investigative documents remain sealed.

84. Aho, *Politics of Righteousness*.

NOTES TO CHAPTER 6

1. Michael Streissguth, *Johnny Cash at Folsom Prison: The Making of a Masterpiece* (Cambridge, Mass.: Da Capo, 2004), p. 44.

2. Kenneth E. Hartman, *Mother California: A Story of Redemption behind Bars* (New York: Atlas, 2009), p. 34.

3. Folsom Prison Museum, *History of Folsom Prison*.

4. Mikal Gilmore, *Stories Done: Writings on the 1960s and Its Discontent* (New York: Simon & Schuster, 2008), p. 197.

5. Streissguth, *Johnny Cash at Folsom Prison*, p. 163.

6. Ruth Wilson Gilmore, *Golden Gulag: Prisons, Surplus, Crisis and Opposition in Globalizing California* (Berkeley: University of California Press, 2007).

7. Laura Sullivan, "Folsom Embodies California's Prison Blues," National Public Radio, August 13, 2009.

8. Davis, *If They Come in the Morning*.

9. Larry Linderman, "Penthouse Interview: Johnny Cash," in Michael Streissguth (ed.), *Ring of Fire: The Johnny Cash Reader* (Cambridge, Mass.: Da Capo, 1975/2002), p. 157.

10. Shane Goldmacher, "California Prison Population Falls for Third Straight Year," *Los Angeles Times*, March 17, 2010.

11. Craig Haney, "The Wages of Prison Overcrowding: Harmful Psychological Consequences and Dysfunctional Corrective Reactions," *Washington University Journal of Law and Policy* 22 (2006): 265–293.

12. Hartman, *Mother California*, p. 71.

13. Sullivan, "Folsom Embodies California's Prison Blues."

14. Haney, "Wages of Prison Overcrowding."

15. Tony Platt, "Crime and Punishment—California's Conundrum," SFgate. com, December 31, 2006, accessed at http://articles.sfgate.com/2006-12-31/ books/17326857_1_prison-system-nation-s-largest-prison-prison-construction.

16. Sullivan, "Folsom Embodies California's Prison Blues."

17. Roughly 70 percent of U.S. state prisoners report regular pre-incarceration intravenous drug use. See Lisa Leone, "Inmates Are Often High-Risk for Hepatitis C," *Congress Daily* 21 (2007): 2–4.

18. Eugene Alexander Dey, "The Real Hep C Crisis," *Metroactive*, May 24–30, 2006, accessed at http://www.metroactive.com/metro/05.24.06/hepatitis-c-0621.html.

19. Carol J. Williams, "Who Should Control California's Prison Budget?" *Los Angeles Times*, June 12, 2010.

20. Adam Liptak, "Supreme Court Hears Arguments on California Prison Crowding," *New York Times*, November 30, 2010.

21. Jennifer Medina, "Prison Personifies Supreme Court Ruling," *New York Times*, May 25, 2011.

22. Jennifer Steinhauer, "Bulging, Troubled Prisons Push California Officials to Seek a New Approach," *New York Times*, December 11, 2006.

23. John Irwin, *The Warehouse Prison: Disposal of the New Dangerous Class* (New York: Oxford University Press, 2007).

24. Debra J. Saunders, "Supreme Court's Scary Ruling on State's Prisons," *San Francisco Chronicle*, May 24, 2011.

25. Sasha Abramsky, "Prison Breakdown," *In These Times*, October 22, 2007; Robert Weisberg and Joan Petersilia, "The Dangers of Pyrrhic Victories against Mass Incarceration," *Daedalus: Journal of the American Academy of Arts and Sciences* 139 (2010): 124–133.

26. United States Bureau of Justice Statistics, *Correctional Populations in the United States 2011* (Washington, D.C.: U.S. Bureau of Justice Statistics).

27. Commission on Safety and Abuse in America's Prisons, *Confronting Confinement* (New York: Vera Institute of Justice, 2006).

28. Hamm, *Terrorist Recruitment in American Correctional Institutions*.

29. Since 1992, New Folsom has also been called the California State Prison-Sacramento.

30. This is consistent with the work of Quintan Wiktorowicz. See his *The Management of Islamic Activism*.

31. Marc Sageman, "Data-Based Predictions of Terrorism," address before the Prediction of Terrorist Attacks International Experts Meeting, Max Planck Institute, Freiburg, Germany, March 21, 2009.

32. Jackson in Trupin's *In Prison*, p. 184. Alpentice "Bunchy" Carter was a black gang member from Los Angeles who converted to the Nation of Islam at Soledad in the early 1960s while serving time for armed robbery. Upon his release, Carter returned to Southern California and became a founding member of the L.A. faction of the Black Panthers. He was killed in a shootout with Panther rivals at UCLA on January 17, 1969.

33. Rob Harris, "Kevin James and the JIS Conspiracy," *The Enemy Within, Frontline,* October 10, 2006.

34. Quintan Wiktorowicz, *Radical Islam Rising: Muslim Extremism in the West* (Lanham, Md.: Rowman and Littlefield, 2005).

35. Miles Corwin, "High-Tech Facility Ushers in New Era of State Prisons," *Los Angeles Times*, May 1, 1990.

36. John Lofland and Rodney Stark, "Becoming a World-Saver," *American Sociological Review* 30 (1965): 868.

37. James T. Richardson and Mary Stewart, "Conversion Process Models and the Jesus Movement," *American Behavioral Scientist* 20 (1977): 819–838.

38. Lofland and Stark, "Becoming a World-Saver."

39. David A. Snow and Richard Machalek, "The Sociology of Conversion," *Annual Review of Sociology* 10 (1984): 170.

40. Shadd Maruna, Louise Wilson, and Kathryn Curran, "Why God Is Often Found behind Bars: Prison Conversions and the Crisis of Self-Narrative," *Research in Human Development* 3 (2006): 161–184; Jim Thomas and Barbara J. Zaitzow, "Conning or Conversion? The Role of Religion in Prison Coping," *The Prison Journal* 86 (2004): 242–259.

41. Dina Temple-Raston, "New Terrorism Advisor Takes a 'Broad Tent' Approach," National Public Radio, January 24, 2011.

42. Ken Mercer, "Terror behind the Walls," presentation at the American Correctional Association 137th Annual Conference, Kansas City, Missouri, August 12, 2007.

43. Ibid.

44. Divulging inmate names is prohibited by Institutional Review Board policies covering this section of the research. Pseudonyms are used instead.

45. In the interest of full disclosure, I may have played a role here. Gus was an enthusiastic participant in the study. He was the first to sign up for an interview at New Folsom, and he appeared at the interview with another skinhead. Both indicated that they had been influenced by my 1993 book, *American Skinheads*, and they asked for autographs.

46. Howard S. Becker, *Outsiders: Studies in the Sociology of Deviance* (New York: Free Press, 1963).

47. Rebecca Trammell, "Values, Rules and Keeping the Peace: How Men Describe Order and the Inmate Code in California Prisons," *Deviant Behavior* 30 (2009): 746–771.

48. Jack Katz, *Seductions of Crime* (New York: Basic Books, 1988).

49. Bo Lozoff, *We're All Doing Time* (Chapel Hill, N.C.: Human Kindness Foundation, 1985).

50. Hartman, *Mother California*, p. 101.

51. Elinor Ostrom, "Beyond Markets and States: Polycentric Governance of Economic Systems," Nobel Prize lecture, Stockholm University, June 22, 2009.

NOTES TO CHAPTER 7

1. Wacquant, *Deadly Symbiosis*.

2. Loïc Wacquant, "Class, Race and Hyperincarceration in Revanchist America," *Daedalus* 139 (Summer 2010): 81.

3. Irwin, *Prisons in Turmoil*, p. 192.

4. John Irwin, *The Felon* (Berkeley: University of California Press, 1987), p. 4.

5. Peter R. Neumann, *Prisons and Terrorism: Radicalization and De-Radicalization in 15 Countries* (King's College, London: International Centre for the Study of Radicalization and Political Violence, 2010).

6. Farhad Khosrokhavar, cited in Neumann, *Prisons and Terrorism*.

7. Neumann, *Prisons and Terrorism*, pp. 26–27.

8. Eric Longabardi interview with Kevin James, Santa Ana (California) City Jail, April 2009.

9. Ibid.

10. Ibid.

11. Andy Farillo, "Pressures Building in State's 32 Prisons," *Sacramento Bee*, January 19, 1997.

12. Longabardi interview.

13. "Kevin James and the JIS Conspiracy," *Frontline*, October 10, 2006.

14. Bernard Lewis, *The Crisis of Islam: Holy War and Unholy Terror* (New York: Random House, 2003).

15. *USA v. Kevin James*. All references to the "JIS Protocol" and other writings by James are contained within this legal document.

16. Hamm, *Terrorist Recruitment in American Correctional Institutions*, pp. 100–101.

17. "Kevin James in the JIS Conspiracy."

18. Michael Stackman, "Fashion and Faith Meet, On Foreheads of Pious," *New York Times*, December 18, 2007.

19. *The al-Qaeda Documents, Vol. 1* (Alexandria, Va.: Tempest, 2002), unpaginated.

20. "Experts Say Indigenous Terror Threat Real," Associated Press, September 4, 2005.

21. "Kevin James and the JIS Conspiracy."

22. "Four Indicted in Los Angeles Terror Probe," *Los Angeles Times*, September 1, 2005.

23. Ibid.

24. "Officials Checking Whether Alleged L.A. Plot Linked to Prison Gang," Associated Press, August 18, 2005.

25. Atran, *Talking to the Enemy*; Louise Richardson, *What Terrorists Want: Understanding the Enemy, Containing the Threat* (New York: Random House, 2006).

26. Atran, *Talking to the Enemy*; Bergen, *Longest War*; "Kevin James and the JIS Conspiracy."

27. Dana Milbank and Claudia Dean, "Poll Finds Dimmer View of Iraq War, 52% Say U.S. Has Not Become Safer," *Washington Post*, June 8, 2005.

28. Allison Scahill, "Church Leaders Call on U.S. to Change Iraq Policy, End War," United Methodist Church, July 1, 2005.

29. "Bush Evokes 9/11 to Bolster Iraq War," *Guardian*, June 29, 2005.

30. "Cheney: Iraq Will Be 'Enormous Success Story,' " CNN, June 24, 2005.

31. Worthington, *Guantanamo Files*, p. 273.

32. *U.S. v. Samana* (D.D.C.A.), No. 05-16662M.

33. "Terror Plot Hatched in California Prison," ABC News, August 16, 2005.

34. *U.S. v. Samana.*

35. Hamm, *Terrorism as Crime.*

36. *U.S. v. Samana.*

37. Ibid.

38. "Authorities Investigate Radical Prison Gang," *Los Angeles Times*, September 4, 2005.

39. Erving Goffman, *Stigma: Notes on the Management of Spoiled Identities* (Englewood Cliffs, N.J.: Prentice-Hall, 1963).

40. Hamm, *Terrorist Recruitment in American Correctional Institutions*, p. 101.

41. Sageman, *Leaderless Jihad.*

42. John Irwin and Donald Cressey, "Thieves, Convicts and the Inmate Culture," *Social Problems* (Fall 1962): 142–155.

43. Hamm, *Terrorism as Crime.*

44. Adam Dolnik, *Understanding Terrorist Innovation* (London: Routledge, 2007).

45. In 2010, guards discovered nearly nine thousand cellphones in California's prisons, including one found in the possession of Charles Manson. Kim Severson and Robbie Brown, "Outlawed Cellphones Are Thriving in Prisons," *New York Times*, January 3, 2011.

46. Trout, "Correctional Intelligence Initiative (CII)."

47. See chapter 3 for figures on yearly prison conversions to Islam since the attacks.

48. Mark S. Hamm, "Prisoner Radicalization: Assessing the Threat in U.S. Correctional Institutions," *NIJ Journal* 261 (2008): 14–19.

49. United States Attorney's Office, Central District of California, press release, December 14, 2007.

NOTES TO CHAPTER 8

1. Ronald L. Akers, "Type of Leadership in Prison: A Structured Approach to Testing the Functional and Importation Models," *The Sociological Quarterly* 18 (1977): 378–383.

2. Donald Clemmer, *The Prison Community* (New York: Holt, Rinehart and Winston, 1958), p. 299.

3. Victor Hassine, *Life without Parole: Living in Prison Today* (New York: Oxford University Press, 2008), p. 52.

4. Gresham M. Sykes and Sheldon Messinger, "The Inmate Social System," in Richard Cloward et al., eds., *Theoretical Studies in the Social Organization of the Prison* (New York: Social Science Research Council, 1960).

5. Clemmer, *Prison Community*.

6. Bernard B. Berk, "Organizational Goals and Inmate Organization," *American Journal of Sociology* 71 (1966): 522–534.

7. See generally Irwin's *Prisons in Turmoil*.

8. James B. Jacobs, "Street Gangs behind Bars," *Social Problems* 21 (1974): 395–409.

9. All quotes from interviews (unless noted otherwise) are from Hamm, *Terrorist Recruitment in American Correctional Institutions*.

10. Though ideology can vary, in the United States Black Hebrew Israelite groups are composed of African Americans who believe that they are the authentic descendants of the ancient Israelites, not Jews.

11. The book is considered the primary text for some Black Hebrew groups. Yahweh Ben Yahweh (1935–2007) served time in prison for conspiracy to commit more than a dozen murders in Florida during the early 1990s. See Sydney P. Freedberg, *Brother Love: Murder, Money, and a Messiah* (New York: Pantheon, 1994).

12. Excerpt from *The Autobiography of Malcolm X* in Trupin's *In Prison*, p. 170, emphasis in original.

13. John Irwin, *Lifers: Seeking Redemption in Prison* (New York: Routledge, 2009), p. 1.

14. Ibid., p. 2.

15. Ibid., p. 68.

16. The following history is based on Tamim Barghouti, "Al Mugiddima Explains Why States Fail," accessed at www.leanonwire.com/0311/03112902DS.asp; Faud Baali, *Society, State, and Urbanism: Ibn Khaldun's Sociological Thought* (Albany: State University of New York Press, 1988); Charles Issawi and Oliver Leaman, "Ibn Khaldun, 'Abd al-Rahman (1332–1406)," accessed at www.muslimphilosophy.com/ip/rep/H204.htm; Arnold Toynbee, *A Study of History (Vol. 3): The Growth of Civilizations* (New York: Oxford University Press, 1962).

17. Toynbee, *Growth of Civilizations*, p. 322.

18. Quoted in al-Barghouti, "Al Muguididima Explains Why States Fail."

19. Quoted in Ernest Gellner, *Plough, Sword and Book: The Structure of Human History* (Chicago: University of Chicago Press, 1988), p. 239.

20. Toynbee, *Growth of Civilizations*, p. 328.

21. Quoted in Simon Sebag Montefiore, *Jerusalem: The Biography* (New York: Knopf, 2011), p. xxii.

22. Toynbee, *Growth of Civilizations*, p. 322.

23. Quoted in Montefiore, *Jerusalem*, p. 195.

24. Max Weber, *Protestant Ethics and the Spirit of Capitalism*, translated by Talcott Parsons (New York: Scribner, 1958).

25. Robin Wright, *Rock the Casbah: Rage and Rebellion across the Islamic World* (New York: Simon & Schuster, 2011).

26. Arie W. Kruglanski, Michele Gelfand, and Rohan Gunaratna, "Detainee De-radicalization: A Challenge for Psychological Science," *APS Observer* (January 2010).

NOTES TO CHAPTER 9

1. Remarks of Denis McDonough, Deputy National Security Advisor to the president, Office of the Press Secretary, the White House, March 6, 2011.

2. Opening Statement of Representative Peter King, "The Threat of Muslim Radicalization in U.S. Prisons," House Homeland Security Committee, June 15, 2011.

3. Ibid.

4. Van Duyn testimony.

5. Patrick Dunleavy, "The Threat of Muslim American Radicalization in U.S. Prisons," testimony before the House Committee on Homeland Security, June 15, 2011.

6. U.S. Department of Justice, *A Review of the Federal Bureau of Prisons' Selection*, pp. 7–8, emphasis added.

7. Used interchangeably with Salafism, Wahhabism is the narrow, strict, puritanical form of Sunni Islam upon which al-Qaeda is based.

8. Quoted in "The Right Ear," *Human Events* 59 (2003): 21.

9. Waller, "Terrorist Recruitment and Infiltration in the United States."

10. Zeyno Baran, "Combatting al-Qaeda and the Militant Islamic Threat," testimony before the U.S. House of Representatives, Committee on Armed Services, Subcommittee on Terrorism, Unconventional Threats and Capabilities, February 16, 2005.

11. Daveed Garstein-Ross, "Wahhabi Prison Fellowship: The Teaching of Jihad in American Penitentiaries," *Weekly Standard*, September 26, 2005.

12. Quoted in Frank Gaffney, "The Enemy Within," *FrontPageMagazine*.com, August 19, 2005.

13. Mark Silverberg, "The Silent War: Wahhabism and the American Penal System," *New Media Journal*, May 6, 2006.

14. Ibid.

15. Van Duyn testimony.

16. Abraham Miller, book reviews, *Terrorism and Political Violence* 1 (1989): 391–392.

17. Testimony of Bert Useem, Committee on Homeland Security, U.S. House of Representatives, Hearing on the threat of Muslim-American radicalization in U.S. prisons, June 15, 2011.

18. Aviezer Tucker, *Our Knowledge of the Past: A Philosophy of Historiography* (New York: Cambridge University Press, 2004).

19. Pistole testimony.

20. Kruglanski et al., "Detainee De-radicalization."

21. Hamm, *Terrorism as Crime*.

22. Scott Shane, "Beyond Guantanamo, a Web of Prisons for Terrorist Inmates," *New York Times*, December 11, 2011.

23. They are Khalid Sheikh Mohammed, charged with overall organization of the attacks; Walid Muhammad Salih bin Attash, accused of running an al-Qaeda training camp in

Afghanistan and researching flight simulators; Ramzi bin al-Shibh, who allegedly helped find flight schools for the hijackers; Ali Abdul-Aziz Ali, accused of helping nine of the hijackers travel to the United States and sending them money for flight training; and Mustafa Ahmad al-Hawsawi, accused of helping the hijackers obtain money, clothing, travelers' checks, and credit cards (*New York Times*, June 1, 2011).

24. U.S. Department of Justice, "The Federal Bureau of Prisons' Monitoring of Mail for High-Risk Inmates" (Washington, D.C.: Office of the Inspector General, Evaluation and Inspections Division, Report Number I-2006-009, 2006), p. 49.

25. Ibid., p. ii.

26. Carrie Johnson and Margot Williams, " 'Guantanamo North': Inside Secretive U.S. Prisons," NPR News, March 3, 2011.

27. Shane, "Beyond Guantanamo."

28. Office of the Israel Prison Service, *Security Inmates in the Israel Prison Service*, 2007.

29. Ariel Merari, *Driven to Death: Psychological and Social Aspects of Suicide Terrorism* (New York: Oxford University Press, 2010).

30. Anat Berko, Edna Erez, and Julie L. Globokar, "Gender, Crime and Terrorism: The Case of Arab/Palestinian Women in Israel," *British Journal of Criminology* 50 (2010): 670–689.

31. Quoted in Debra Rubin, "Documentary Offers Window on Israeli Prisons," *New Jersey Jewish News*, February 17, 2009.

32. Jimmy Carter, *Palestinian Peace Not Apartheid* (New York: Simon & Schuster, 2006), pp. 198, 214.

33. See Angela Browne, Alissa Cambier, and Suzanne Agha, "Prisons within Prisons: The Use of Segregation in the United States," *Federal Sentencing Reporter* 24 (2011): 46–49.

34. Her Majesty's Prison Service, *Extremism and Radicalization*, n.d.

35. Robert S. Mueller III, statement before the Senate Select Committee on Intelligence, January 11, 2007.

36. Ministry of Justice, *Extremism: A Digest of Learning* (London: National Offender Management Service, 2011).

37. Quoted in Steve Coll, *The Bin Ladens: An Arabian Family in the American Century* (New York: Penguin, 2008), p. 503.

38. Warnes and Hannah, "Meeting the Challenge of Extremist and Radicalized Prisoners."

39. Richard English, "The IRA's Attempted Murder of Prime Minister Margaret Thatcher," paper presented at the Innovation in Terrorism Conference, U.S. Naval Postgraduate School, Monterey, California, August 5–6, 2010.

40. Raffaello Pantucci, "Britain's Prison Dilemma: Issues and Concerns in Islamic Radicalization," *Terrorism Monitor*, March 24, 2008.

41. Ministry of Justice, *Extremism*.

42. Warnes and Hannah, "Meeting the Challenges of Extremist and Radicalized Prisoners."

43. David Leppard, "Terrorists Smuggle Fatwas Out of Secure Prisons," *Times* (of London), November 15, 2009.

44. Ibid.

45. Pantucci, "Britain's Prison Dilemma."

46. RAND, *Radicalization or Rehabilitation*.

47. Liebling, *Exploration of Staff-Prisoner Relationships*.

48. Leppard, "Terrorists Smuggle Fatwas Out of Secure Prisons."

49. Ibid., p. 70.

50. Ibid., p. 80.

51. HM Chief Inspector of Prisons, *Report on Unannounced Full Follow-Up Inspection of HMP Whitemoor* (London: HM's Inspectorate of Prisons, 2008), p. 43.

52. Quoted in Leppard, "Terrorists Smuggle Fatwas Out of Secure Prisons."

53. Malcolm M. Feeley and Jonathan Simon, "The New Penology: Notes on the Emerging Strategy of Corrections and Its Implications," *Criminology* 30 (1992): 449–474.

54. Liebling, *Exploration of Staff-Prisoner Relationships*, p. 147.

55. "Jail craft" is a term also used in relation to prison staff.

56. *The al-Qaeda Documents, Vol. 1.*

57. Sengupta and Masood, "Guantanamo Comes to Define U.S. to Muslims." A 2007 BBC poll found that seven out of ten Europeans disapproved of the treatment of Guantanamo detainees, while half thought the United States played mostly a negative role in the world. Cited in Bergen, *Longest War*, p. 120.

58. Comments made by Sri Lankan and Saudi experts at the Conference on Rehabilitation and Reintegration of Violent Extremist Offenders: Good Practices and Lessons Learned, International Centre for Counter-Terrorism, The Hague, December 8–9, 2011.

59. Jonathan Simon and Malcolm M. Feeley, "The Forms and Limits of the New Penology," in Thomas G. Blomberg and Stanley Cohen (eds.), *Punishment and Social Control* (New Brunswick, N.J.: Transaction, 2011), p. 78.

60. Carl Ungerer, *Jihadist in Jail: Radicalization and the Indonesian Prison Experience* (Sydney: Australian Strategic Policy Institute, 2011).

61. Francis T. Cullen and Paul Gendreau, "From Nothing Works to What Works: Changing Professional Ideology in the 21st Century," *Crime and Delinquency* 81 (2001): 313–338.

62. Hamid Reza Kusha, *Islam in American Prisons: Black Muslims' Challenge to American Penology* (Surrey, U.K.: Ashgate, 2009).

63. Kruglanski et al., "Detainee De-radicalization."

64. Hamed El Said, "De-Radicalizing Islamists: Programs and Their Impact in Muslim Majority States," International Centre for the Study of Radicalization, 2012.

65. Max Taylor, "Countering Violent Extremist Narratives," panel discussion at Ten Years after 9/11: Evaluating a Decade of Intensified Counter-Terrorism Conference, International Centre for Counter-Terrorism—The Hague, December 12–13, 2010.

66. George W. Knox, *The Problem of Gangs and Security Threat Groups in American Prisons Today: Recent Research, Findings from the 2004 Prison Gang Survey* (Chicago: National Gang Research Center, 2005).

67. U.S. Department of Justice, *A Review of the Federal Bureau of Prisons' Selection*. The practice varies, however. Some inmates have been locked up in the CMUs for taking leadership positions in prison religious communities. See Johnson and Williams, "'Guantanamo North.'"

68. Neumann, *Prisons and Terrorism*.

69. Atran, *Talking to the Enemy*, p. 291.

70. John Horgan, *Walking Away from Terrorism: Accounts of Disengagement from Radical and Extremist Movements* (Abingdon, U.K.: Routledge, 2009); Michael Jacobsen, *Terrorist Drop-Outs: Learning from Those Who Have Left. Policy Focus* (Washington, D.C.: Institute for Near East Policy, 2010).

71. McDonough remarks.

72. Quintan Wiktorowicz, "Joining the Cause: Al-Muhajiroun and Radical Islam," paper presented at the Roots of Islamic Radicalism Conference, Yale University, May 8–9, 2004.

73. Irwin, *Lifers*, p. 6.

ACKNOWLEDGMENTS

This research benefited from the support of many, and I am pleased to thank them. In California, access to the Folsom Prisons would have not been possible without the backing of Dan Johnson, Rick Rimmer, Grant Parker, Ira Book, Dennis Merino, and Scott Lines. My understanding of innovations in terrorism was enhanced by a distinguished group of scholars at the Center for Contemporary Conflict in Monterrey: Gary Ackerman, Peter Bergen, Lindsay Clutterbuck, Martha Crenshaw, Adam Dolnik, Mohammed Hafez, José Olmeda, Maria Rasmussen, and Stuart Wright. My appreciation of guns and the gangs of Los Angeles was similarly enriched by Andrew Gumbel and Kathryn Del Vecchio.

At a meeting of the American Correctional Association in Kansas City, Jim Thomas and Barbara Zaitzow helped me understand religious conversions in maximum-security prisons.

Studying the religious lives of prisoners in Florida was not easy, and for helping me work through it all I offer my sincerest thanks to John Hope, Alex Taylor, William Smith, Douglas Gingerich, and Dwight White.

At the University of Illinois at Chicago, Edna Erez and Aaron Weisburd introduced me to trends in terrorist recruitment via the Internet. At the Prisoner Radicalization Working Group of the Anti-Terrorism Advisory Council in Springfield, Illinois, I was familiarized with current investigative techniques by Dan Bacon and Chris Bolinger. I'm obliged to them all.

For their collegiality, at Indiana State University I thank Samory Rashid, Frank Wilson, Jennifer Grimes, Chuck Norman, and Dave Polizzi. Devere Woods and Brenda Starkey of the ISU Institute of Criminology supported much of my travel and for that I am grateful, as I am to the convict criminologist John Frana and to Heather Litchford for their research assistance. To my best friends, Lou Hamm and Marla Sandys, thanks for your love and sanity.

In Washington, D.C., I thank Thomas Feucht and Jennifer Hanley at the National Institute of Justice (NIJ) and Jay Albanese, the former NIJ director, who recognized early on the need for research in this area. Thanks also to Carrie Johnson of National Public Radio for her coverage of the prisoner radicalization hearings and the Communication Management Units.

In New York, one could not ask for more encouragement than I received at the Center on Terrorism at the John Jay College of Criminal Justice— thanks to Charles Strozier, Andrea Fatica, and the late Michael Flynn, along with the sociologists David Brotherton, Carla Barrett, Barry Spunt, and the inimitable Jock Young. I offer a special note of thanks to Ilene Kalish at New York University Press for bringing this work into print; to Paul Leighton for his helpful comments on an earlier draft; and to Christine Dahlin for some excellent editing.

At the Institute of Crime Science in London, my thanks go out to Noemi Bouhana, Elliot Humphrey, and Stewart Govrick. I greatly appreciate the support of Chris Greer at the City University of London and several anonymous officials at Scotland Yard. Keith Hayward and Phil Carny were gracious hosts at the University of Kent. At Cambridge University, I thank Alison Liebling, Kate Painter, and especially Paddy Baldry for his generosity. Thanks as well to Zainab Al-Altar at Manchester Prison. Late in the research I attended an extremely helpful roundtable discussion on violent extremism in prisons hosted by the Foreign Commonwealth Office at Wilton Park. Many thanks to Julia Purcell, the program director, and to several participants who provided international perspectives on prisoner radicalization: Peter Atherton, Hassan Syed, Victoria Blakeman, Richard Pickering, Ann Snow, Claire Cooper, Andrew Coyle, Abdul Aziz Mohamed, Monica Floyd, Carl Ungerer, Elaine O'Connor, Michael Jacobson, and Phil Wragg.

At the Max Planck Institute in Freiburg, Germany, my conceptualization of this study benefited from discussions with Marc Sageman, Ariel Merari, Dipak Gupta, Peter van Kuijk, and Andrew Silke.

I learned much about international trends in terrorism from the European Expert Network on Terrorism in Brussels, Belgium, where Gert Vercauteren and Uwe Kemmesies directed my attention to the threat of lone-wolf terrorism, more than a year before the Norway massacre.

At the International Centre for Counter-Terrorism, The Hague in the Netherlands, concern about lone wolves was taken to an even greater depth by Peter Knoope and Edwin Bakker. Thanks also to Leena Malkki and Beatrice de Graaf.

Even though right-wing terrorism had long been a focus of my research I had no idea that programs existed for the de-radicalization of neo-Nazi youth until I visited those working in the EXIT program in Stockholm, Sweden. I am indebted to Camila Salazar Atias and Robert Orell, as well as Judy Korn of the Violence Prevention Network in Berlin and Lise Wacker of the

British Council. For their insights on effective Islamic de-radicalization programs, I am equally indebted to Hamed El Said and Tinka Veldhuis at the United Nations Interregional Crime and Justice Research Institute.

The transparency of officials at the Israeli Prison Service was remarkable. I thank General Orit Adato and Rohan Gunaratna of the International Centre for Political Violence and Terrorism Research at Nanyang Technological University, Singapore, for sharing information on de-radicalizing al-Qaeda prisoners.

Thanks to Jeff Ferrell and Ken Tunnell for helping me explain the legacy of Johnny Cash in prison; mainly, I thank them for their spirit.

Finally, it is my honor to dedicate this book to the memory of John Irwin. At the same time that Irwin was conducting his ethnography of lifers at San Quentin, I was independently doing the same thing at Folsom. I am grateful that these two works have reached a common shore. Irwin was a role model for my generation of penologists. He was a towering figure in the field, a scholar capable of great generosity yet tough enough to cut through the obstacles, contradictions, and general bullshit of prison life. Anyone with a passing understanding of prison can hurl stones at the machinations of bureaucrats, technocrats, and bad government. But few could hear the convict's discontent like John. His like may never pass this way again.

INDEX

Mark S. Hamm is a former prison warden from Arizona and is currently a professor of criminology at Indiana State University and a Senior Research Fellow at the Terrorism Center, John Jay College of Criminal Justice, the City University of New York. His books include *Terrorism as Crime: From Oklahoma City to Al-Qaeda and Beyond* (NYU Press); *In Bad Company: America's Terrorist Underground*; *Apocalypse in Oklahoma: Waco and Ruby Ridge Revenged*; and *American Skinheads: The Criminology and Control of Hate Crime.*